Advance Praise for
Forest Time: Footnotes to an Outdoor Education

"Jeremy Lloyd's immensely reflective exploration into a professional life in the wilds of the Smoky Mountains bridges a chasm often present in naturalist literature and connects us all as humans to the treasures, challenges, and, most importantly, surprises our natural world can provide just when we need them most. With an ear for irony and human folly, Lloyd acts as a trail guide for readers who may have no experience in our national parks while able at the same time to provoke wonder and intrigue in even the most seasoned wilderness explorer."

—ANNETTE SAUNOOKE CLAPSADDLE,
author of *Even As We Breathe*

"Jeremy Lloyd's epic curiosity and powers of ebullient reflection make *Forest Time* the most enjoyable book of its kind I've yet read. Lloyd's ability to share nature's beauties and subtleties is balanced by his awareness of Earth's many grave wounds, but since his students in the forests are often young school children, he takes care that his enthusiasm matches the students' own. To quote Lloyd himself, 'I figured out early on that with the forest as my classroom… bombing was virtually impossible. Also, that teaching didn't always mean direct instruction and sometimes didn't require instruction at all. Much of the time my role was simply to act as an intermediary, and the trick was in knowing when to get out of the way and let the forest do the teaching.' I will add, as a forest-loving writer myself, that Jeremy Lloyd's writing is as deft and light of touch as his teaching. Happy reading!"

– DAVID JAMES DUNCAN,
author of *The River Why, The Brothers K,* and *Sun House*

Forest Time

Forest Time

Footnotes to an Outdoor Education

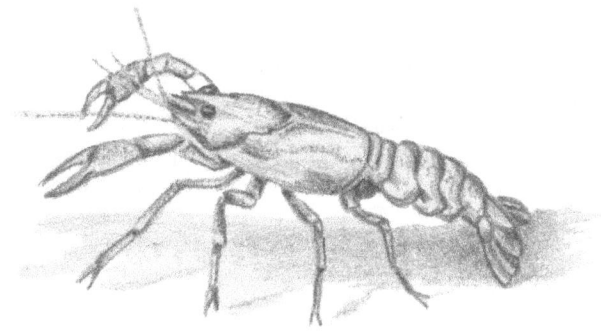

JEREMY LLOYD

Illustrations by Kelly Lecko

The University of Tennessee Press
Knoxville

Copyright © 2026 by The University of Tennessee Press / Knoxville.
All Rights Reserved.
FIRST EDITION.

Library of Congress Cataloging-in-Publication Data
Names: Lloyd, Jeremy author
Title: Forest time : footnotes to an outdoor education / Jeremy Lloyd.
Description: First edition. | Knoxville : The University of Tennessee Press, 2026. |
Summary: "In his twenties, broke, brokenhearted, and fearful about the future, Jeremy Lloyd stumbled into a job that would change his life. More than two decades later, still an educator at Tremont in Great Smoky Mountains National Park, Lloyd recounts his journey as a teacher and student of the great outdoors in Forest Time: Footnotes to an Outdoor Education. Blending natural history, daring-and sometimes foolish-adventure, and spiritual balm for a world suffering from widespread disconnection from nature, Forest Time is equal parts personal, educational, and existential"—Provided by publisher.
Identifiers: LCCN 2025045076 (print) | LCCN 2025045077 (ebook) |
ISBN 9798895270912 paperback | ISBN 9798895270929 epub
Subjects: LCSH: Lloyd, Jeremy | Great Smoky Mountains Institute at Tremont | Outdoor life—Great Smoky Mountains (N.C. and Tenn.) | Outdoor education—Great Smoky Mountains National Park (N.C. and Tenn.) | Outdoorsmen—Great Smoky Mountains (N.C. and Tenn.)—Biography | LCGFT: Autobiographies
Classification: LCC GV191.42.G73 L56 2026 (print) | LCC GV191.42.G73 (ebook)
LC record available at https://lccn.loc.gov/2025045076
LC ebook record available at https://lccn.loc.gov/2025045077

*For my mother and father
and for Élan*

CONTENTS

Prologue
1

Part One: Sapling

Initiation
17

Class Begins
25

Cabin in the Woods
39

Naming the World
49

Meeting the Neighbors
61

Part Two: Heartwood

Winter Light
79

Border Crossings
85

Skunked
99

In the Flow
107

Stepping Out
119

Interlude: Making Tracks
133

Part Three: Second Growth

Beethoven's Lowliest Disciples
145

Balancing Acts
157

End of the Road
169

Out of the Woods
181

Secret Spot
189

Part Four: Succession

To Be Alone
199

Deer Stand
215

Off Trail
225

Staying in Character: A Travelogue
235

Nightwalking
253

Coda: Exit Music
265

Acknowledgments
273

Prologue

AS A CHILD I inherited a shoebox full of postcards from my grandmother. Instead of going into the trash when she downsized and moved into a smaller house, dozens of four-by-six-inch cardboard images she had purchased over the years on her travels came to me. Colorful images portraying natural wonders and exotic cityscapes leaped out. One postcard bore an image of a log cabin, neat and tidy, its roof matted with grass. The caption said a poet had once lived there. I immediately fantasized about one day living in a cabin in the woods, someplace trouble couldn't reach and where the earth spun more slowly on its axis. That would be the life, I thought, if the world was still around then.

Years later I got my wish when I moved into a cabin in the largest untamed forest east of the Mississippi River. My motivation had nothing to do with fulfilling a boyhood dream induced by my grandmother's postcards, much less living out high-minded principles like those of Henry David Thoreau. The real reason was that I was desperate.

I had managed not long before this to become broke and brokenhearted all at once and had fallen into a miserable state of mind. Following college, I'd taught English overseas, worked for a magazine in Washington, DC, and assisted an off-campus college program in Oregon while cleaning horse stables to earn my keep—and met a girl along the way. After running out of money,

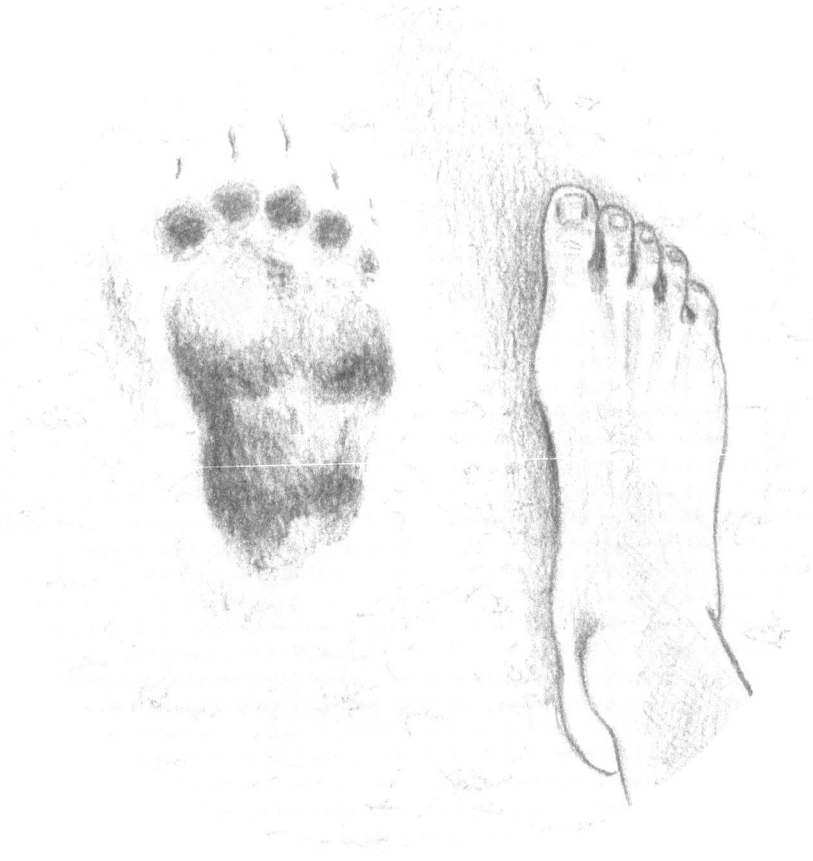

I moved back into my parents' home in Pennsylvania, where news arrived from my girlfriend announcing our breakup. Naively believing a bold act was what this situation called for, I relocated to the city in Michigan where she was living. The heartfelt speech I'd memorized was sure to change her mind and send her running back into my arms. Within weeks of my arrival, however, she bolted town, leaving me stranded working in a mill that made industrial door frames, the only steady employment I could find. The assembly line was tolerable at first and even gratifying in that it felt like just punishment for my rash decision-making. But as each ten-hour shift crawled by in the windowless finishing room, where tar clogged my pores and paint fumes stung my throat, the romance of blue-collar work wore off, and I longed for escape.

A phone call from a friend could not have come at a better time. Greg worked in the Great Smoky Mountains in Tennessee and invited me for a visit. Another incentive for making the long drive became apparent when I learned that a position had opened at his workplace. Though landing the job seemed like a long shot, applying and hoping for an interview would at least help get my mind off things for a while.

Greg was employed by a small nonprofit organization named Great Smoky Mountains Institute at Tremont, located inside a national park that called itself an environmental learning center and outdoor school. A nature center, in other words, though of a distinctive variety, as I would learn. I had visited a few nature centers before and was ambivalent about the prospect of working for one. Heavy on learning and short on entertainment, each one had seemed to serve up a heaping of broccoli when my appetite at the time ran more along the lines of a Big Mac. Always situated among pretty scenery, they provided windows into parts of the world that were fascinating yet that I didn't inhabit on a daily basis, and the tiny signs many used to announce the names of plants I would never remember only reinforced how ignorant I felt about the particulars of the natural world. Picturing myself as an employee of one was certainly a stretch.

At first glance Greg's workplace appeared to offer even less than other nature centers I'd visited. Altogether missing were any interpretive signs, live animals on display, a ropes course—even a concession stand. There wasn't much to look at other than a handful of aging buildings and woodsy meeting spots with benches and campfire circles. On the plus side, surrounding the campus were densely forested mountains stretching for miles in every direction, broken only by streams and a vast trail network.

I understood next to nothing about the work Tremont carried out, and I barely cared. Anything sounded better than serving more time as an inmate in a factory where the foreman blasted Mötley Crüe through loudspeakers at full volume at six o'clock each morning. It also suited me to imagine leaving the past behind by escaping to the woods. I had once imagined just such a life for myself back when I wondered if the world was going to end.

Within hours of my arrival, I discovered there was a lot more going on than I first realized. Rather than breezing through like many visitors to the national park, guests stayed for days at a time. They ate meals family style and slept in close quarters in large bunkrooms. They spent mornings and afternoons taking field classes under the open sky and gathered around a campfire at day's end. A peculiar kind of school-away-from-school where all the classes were held outdoors, the place was inseparable from its surroundings, as wild as any I'd seen.

Weeks after submitting my application, I was surprised to learn I'd been granted an interview—out of courtesy to Greg, I was sure. With no holidays in sight or vacation days to take time off work, I quit my job at the factory and made the long drive, this time keenly aware I was making what might turn out to be yet another regrettable decision. When the appointed hour arrived, I took my seat in the office of the executive director whose beard, fleece vest, and hiking boots gave him an appearance unlike that of any head honcho I'd ever met. Following several easy-to-answer questions, he asked me a confounding one: "What is your vision for environmental education?"

The interview, going so well up to this point, ground to a halt. I had no vision for environmental education whatsoever, having learned only weeks before that such a field existed. I sat in embarrassing silence for a long moment before babbling something about trees and butterflies and how nature was like, you know, important. An aunt and uncle of mine ran a nature center in Alaska that I'd once visited, though I never fully grasped what their work entailed. I had even spent a week in elementary school at a learning center just like this one, yet I failed in my nervous state of mind to draw any connection between then and now. All I knew was that spending my days in the woods instead of surrounded by cinderblock walls was so appealing it sounded too good to be true.

Which, in fact, turned out to be the case. The interview wrapped up quickly, and days later, back in Michigan, I learned I'd been turned down for the job.

I began working in a bookstore where I was put in charge of a section no one else seemed to want and about which I knew nothing: medicine. Mercifully, few customers ever browsed the aisle filled with tomes on pathology, neurology, and the like, and for the most part I was left alone.

A week went by, and then the phone rang. It was the nature center's executive director, Ken, calling with unexpected news. The job was mine if I still wanted it, but only for ninety days, after which time I would be offered a full-time position or let go. Shipped back to the bookstore or factory, as it were, if I didn't prove myself. Mutual desperation was apparently the order of the day. The top applicant for the position, who had scored high on his interview, had listed bad references on his résumé. Ken's other prospects had accepted other job offers. I was the last person on the list.

"You start in two weeks," he said.
"I'll be there," I said and hung up.
I started packing that afternoon.

Long before I ever dreamed of living in a cabin in the woods, and longer still before the Great Smoky Mountains became my home and workplace wrapped into one, a forest—a small wilderness behind my house in the foothills of the Allegheny Mountains in western Pennsylvania—had shaped my childhood. Its emissaries beckoned even before I could answer the call, as on the morning my father found me in my bedroom, standing at attention and pointing a finger into the air. Having no word yet for "bird," neither was I tall enough to peer over the windowsill and locate the source of the song reaching my ears. In time I discovered that learning words for things could summon them into being, and I began reporting to my mother the giraffes, elephants, and lions I spotted in our backyard. Once old enough to roam outdoors on my own, I battled imaginary foes with sticks I fashioned into spears and laser blasters. I encountered every stage of life in the woods. A raccoon climbed into the oak tree that shaded me and my sister on sun-drenched afternoons and died; body parts floated to the earth for days afterward, each one a strange message borne by wind and gravity.

Though unpredictable and filled with mystery, the forest was a comforting and inviting presence. Neither the terrifying place depicted in movies nor the one filled with the cold indifference permeating the rest of the nonhuman world described in books I read in school, but rather a part of home. Years would pass before I recognized it for the gift it was—one that many people I would eventually shepherd into the forest lived without or did not feel welcome to enter. I would come to understand, too, that I had been living a close approximation of my childhood dream all along.

Around the time I reached an age when I began paying attention to the news, a gnawing sense of dread crept into my consciousness. Suddenly there were reasons to fear the world—and fear for it. Mushroom clouds were predicted to swallow nearby cities whole, regardless of which atomic power pushed the button first, in a scenario fittingly called MAD, or mutually assured destruction. At school we practiced the tornado drill, which doubled as a bomb drill in disguise, sheltering in the hallway with our hands folded over our heads. Though a single feeling or state of mind hardly sums up my youth, dread became a recurring theme and imminent doom a truth I lived by many days during my teenage years. In my mind I pictured everything I loved—my family, friends, home, the pair of maple trees outside my bedroom window, the rolling hills of northern Appalachia—burned up and cast into nothingness. On the bookshelf sat a paperback copy of Hal Lindsey's best-selling *The Late Great Planet Earth*, filled with prophecies of tribulation and bloodshed. After reading several pages, I was too afraid ever to pick it up again.

So much of adult society seemed hell-bent on annihilation for someone, somewhere, sometime. I complied by getting ready for it, storing canned goods at home in a crawlspace beneath the basement stairs in case of attack. Possessing no notion yet of what I wanted to do with my life and figuring I might never get the chance, I at least knew how to prepare for the end of the world.

Though the end did not come—or not yet—predictions of its demise foreshadowed by wars, earthquakes, and terrorist attacks seeded my imagination with any number of possible disastrous outcomes. Apocalypse awaited me many mornings like a shirt to be put on. "Try smiling," girls at school would tell me, the mirror their words held up serving as a reminder of how difficult it was to bear secret knowledge of the world's futurelessness along with my own.

Amid my fears, however, there remained moments of forest time. Cast like a spell over me whenever I escaped to the woods, anywhere, anytime I could, they provided a chance to exhale and glimpse a future that lay beyond my opaque self. Each time I went, it was in search of something I could not name. But eventually I could see that the woods offered more than a mere refuge from the world, for it was really an entryway back into it. Inside my bedroom I managed to find some measure of catharsis through music. But outside it were places redolent of spice and leaf decay and a history longer than my own, where trees unconcerned with the news cycle turned green each spring and I could touch living things and they touched me back.

The apocalypse, it turned out, was real after all, at least for me, and at least according to the original Greek definition: a revelation, an unveiling. The truth of it came slowly, arriving in fits and starts throughout high school and college. My sense of foreboding and an expectation of the world coming undone never fully went away. To be a Cold War kid would always mean carrying the weight of dire possibilities on a cosmic scale and having my psyche forever marked by the worst imaginable scenarios. But borrowing trouble had its limits, especially when there were more immediate losses to attend to: leaving home for a college campus located five hundred miles away, the death of a close friend my age during my first semester, falling grades, breakups. My instinct many times was to steal away to the woods, any I could find. And there, in what for me was the center of Creation, a seed took root. It was the realization that while the end might come someday, the world was to be loved in the meantime, however hard that sometimes was. What other choice was there, really? For no matter how many ordeals and troubles awaited the cosmos and me—for surely there were more to come—the world kept turning. It had a future, and so it appeared did I.

Glimpsed from any vantage point atop one of its tree-smothered peaks, the Great Smoky Mountains are deceiving. What looks like folds in the landscape resulting from the collision of tectonic plates are in fact due to millions of years of weathering and erosion. Most of what once comprised the mountains was carried away long ago by water, and so profuse is the vegetation covering what bedrock remains that a good deal of imagination becomes necessary to picture the mountains, among the oldest on earth, once standing as tall as the Himalayas, now nearly five times higher.

The countless ridgelines undulating toward the horizon today resemble giant green waves arrested in time. Their beauty disguises an unpredictable character, however, for here is where the land twists in maddening ways and reaches confounding heights and depths, leading to fifty plane crashes over the last century and causing hikers unaccustomed to a forest so immense to take shortcuts that last for days.

Here in North America's most astonishingly biodiverse landscape, visitors of all ages also spend time at a learning center founded by local educators in the 1960s, a decade marked by a widespread concern for environmental stewardship and conservation. The pocket-sized campus is located up a narrow river valley along a dead-end road where trees obscure it from view much of the year.

"What exactly is this place?" ask curious tourists who stumble upon the tiny welcome center. "Are you closed?" sometimes, too, since the place appears deserted while guests are off in the woods or exploring the river. Older people get the point right away. "Oughta bring my grandkid out here to you folks. Brain's rotting from staring at gizmos. Forgets what fresh air smells like."

Perhaps no pair of words sounds a less inspiring note in an era of human history so captivated by speed and innovation than *nature center*. It's partly because their purpose for existing is so often misunderstood that many nature centers of an overnight, live-in variety have struggled to explain their mission in an easily digestible manner. Another challenge is describing the peculiar form of education they carry out: what in academic circles is called informal, experiential, or place-based education, which is often viewed as inessential or only for kids. A hunger for what such places have to offer persists across a wide swath of the public nevertheless: not just a break from the satisfactions consumer and technological culture promise to deliver, but a reminder of what it means to be human.

Overnight nature centers within national parks trace their origin to the National Environmental Education Development program created in the 1960s to cultivate ecologically literate citizens and increase environmental awareness in on-site "outdoor laboratories." Nature centers of all types have come to serve an additional societal function by offering an alternative to conventional notions about what constitutes a classroom. For all the gains made by modern educational institutions during the twentieth century, a least one crucial shortcoming was a trend toward institutionalization itself. Generations of students and teachers whose ancestors left the countryside for the cities spent school days ensconced indoors away from other living things; many came to believe education occurred solely within an edifice during predetermined hours. One result was the segregation of learning from living and the life of the mind from the senses and emotions. The body was regarded as an inconvenience, repeatedly interrupting the important task of stuffing knowledge into the brain's memory banks. The job of education was to make human beings conform to a one-size-fits-all model of learning that resembled a factory. Teachers and students alike were made to conform to large systems with administrative structures answerable to no one in particular, and students disillusioned by irrelevant and impersonal coursework suffered through their school years like prisoners biding their time until the hour of their release.

A mediocre student myself, I liked school okay whenever I wasn't battling feelings of inferiority. I kept quiet, didn't protest (didn't know how), and did my best to disappear in a sea of faces to avoid being called upon by a teacher. Excelling in school, so far as I could tell, meant figuring out the secret to impressing teachers and regurgitating a sufficient supply of correct answers on exams, a mystery that lay beyond me most days.

My happiest moments as a student took place not in any building but at McKeever Environmental Learning Center, where every willing sixth grader in the school district got a weeklong outdoor education, thanks to a school system that recognized the value of such programs. Two hours away from home, I found myself set loose in the more-than-human world where dirt replaced linoleum underfoot, and a ceiling of trees towered overhead. I spent time each day in my assigned "magic spot," sitting cross-legged on the ground as I observed the play of shadows and sunlight on fallen leaves, watched ants crawl along the ground, and scribbled in my journal. My body was otherwise in constant motion, and at night I fell into my bunk filled with firsthand knowledge of the forested world and its wild inhabitants. I began to see that there was more to life than school and more to school than just sitting at a desk.

Over the course of that week, I got something of a visceral, hands-on "environmental education" in humankind's first classroom. Though nothing of the sort would reoccur throughout the rest of my formal school years, it was an experience that would slowly germinate into the understanding that school was not life. School was nearly all I'd ever known. But while staring out the window one day during class a year following my week at McKeever, watching woodsmoke rise above the rooftops of houses and feeling utterly disconnected from whatever I was supposed to be learning, I sensed that something else might be available to me someday. It was an inkling that education wasn't reducible to whatever subject matter had been deemed most important and wasn't limited to the hours set aside for learning it. Education was something far more. For someone who had believed high marks were the sole measure of intelligence and harbored secret fears about the future of the world, along with questions about the meaning of existence few teachers wished to entertain, this would turn out to be good news indeed. Though, of course, it meant there was more work to do, work that would take a lifetime or maybe longer to carry out.

Now that I was moving to the mountains, I was about to walk in shoes similar to those worn by my instructors at McKeever—or boots rather, the soles of which would soon kiss more dirt and cover more miles than I'd ever be able to tally. Like the pair of college-aged women McKeever hired to lead activities in the woods for me and my classmates, I would turn a forest into a classroom for countless students, both young and old, and learn alongside them.

One difference was that as an underqualified candidate who'd bombed his job interview, I understood less than the average rookie did about what I was getting myself into. On-the-job training was about to take on a whole new meaning. Another difference was how much culture had changed since my youth. Screen time had eclipsed other childhood pastimes, as an increasing number of kids surfed the web or toggled their way through imaginary worlds rather than playing outdoors. Parental fears, too—real or imagined—contributed to a sharp decline in the time children spent in direct contact with nature. There were also fewer places to go exploring compared to previous generations as suburbs expanded and open spaces were paved over, contributing to what lepidopterist Robert Michael Pyle has called the "extinction of experience" for many American youths. I could relate somewhat, having witnessed scrublands I'd once tromped around in with friends in my hometown get bulldozed for a shopping center and highway overpass.

The younger generation, meanwhile, had as many reasons to worry over the fate of the world as I did at their age, perhaps more: terrorism, wars, gun violence, warming temperatures, rising sea levels, an accelerating extinction rate, political tribalism, nuclear catastrophe, and unabated consumption of the natural world. And closer to home: economic instability, poverty, family breakdown, addiction, racial inequities, and prejudice. If storylines in a growing number of popular dystopian books and films were to be believed, long-term prospects for the survival of both human and nonhuman communities alike looked dismal indeed.

Chances of the world coming to an end, from falling bombs to ecological collapse to the slow unraveling of civilization, remained ever present in the back of my mind. Chief among my concerns for the time being, however, was surviving the next three months in my new place of employment, where I would teach not just youths but also college students, working adults, and retirees. What the work ahead would involve did not remotely resemble any other job I knew of. I would need to

- wear many hats, including that of teacher, naturalist, wilderness guide, living history character, storyteller, musician, firewood splitter, custodian, and more;
- obtain a working fluency in local natural history through field study of forest communities, plants, birds, insects, amphibians, landforms, etc.;
- practice basic pioneering and tracking skills, and learn the region's cultural history;
- count on getting dirty, cold, sunbaked, river-soaked, and blindsided by changing plans;
- get comfortable with speaking in front of large groups (frequently), long hours (often), weather extremes (sometimes), and close encounters with wildlife (any time); and finally,

- expect to be mistaken for a camp counselor, tour guide, and government employee—sometimes all at once.

I would learn that working for a nature center was a lifestyle as much as it was a vocation. With coworkers for housemates and both my place of residence and workplace located inside the national park, a merging of work hours and home life would occur so that each would become virtually indistinguishable much of the time. And with no two days exactly alike, I'd find out as well that monotony and boredom weren't ever going to number among my concerns. As for living in a cabin in the woods, I would have to revise my notions about living a quiet existence far from the fray of modern life because both the center and the park promised a future far busier than any I'd imagined.

Central to the myriad tasks my colleagues and I would carry out would be introducing people to the natural world. Once I began doing so, I understood that whatever else was meant by "environmental education"—a fuzzy term that begged the question of *which* environment one was talking about—conservation in the traditional sense was just the beginning. The field had grown out of a recognition that industrial civilization had resulted in people becoming disconnected from the farms, forests, and bodies of water that sustained them and believing that such things were limitless. The solution in part was introducing people to nature so they would gain firsthand knowledge of landscapes they would fall in love with and seek to conserve for future generations.

Yet what would be good for the natural world would be equally good for people. As Florence Williams demonstrates in *The Nature Fix*, spending time there improves health, stimulates creativity, and nourishes relationships, which is no small thing. College students I'd teach were obsessed with grades and terrified of failure, their education in many cases having served no other purpose than to prepare them for the job market. High school students felt uninspired by what they'd come to expect from school after sitting for seven hours each day, year after year, fatigue and stress long since having smothered their sense of wonder and anticipation of discovery. More than a few of the working adults I would meet admitted regret over their career choice and a longing for a deeper grounding in the natural world. Most schoolkids I would work with were conditioned to the same factory model of education I'd experienced and were largely detached from the concrete reality their education purportedly was about. Many teachers who loved their jobs nonetheless suffered from low morale as they struggled under the pressures of checking boxes and teaching to the test even as their budgets dwindled.

Coming to the woods would provide a balm for each one of them. An antidote to distraction and disconnection amid a complex and fast-changing period of human history, the forest is a place to recenter one's attention and to experience the restorative influence of a landscape left to its own devices. A more creaturely and soulful existence awaited a person there through participation in the boundless life of nature, along with an opportunity to step into a fullness of being that modern life so often withheld. With any luck, whatever a person discovered through direct experience would contribute by degrees to what education was intended for: better humans, stronger communities, a healthier world.

It would sound to me in my early days on the job as if saving the world was the ultimate goal. Sure, why not, I'd tell myself. Having once believed the world would end in my lifetime, it seemed like a fitting job description for the likes of me, even if something more selfish was what would get me out of bed each morning: the chance to live out a childhood dream.

In reality the goal would be far more modest. The work would come about in a single, finite place on earth. A handful of educators, myself among them, would each accompany only a dozen or so people into the woods at a time. Each person would stay for a week or less, and I would often wonder afterward how long their experience stayed with them. The number of people who came to the nature center every year would amount to the population of a small town. Though hardly a model for success in a society that reveres bigger/better/more, it was perhaps the only authentic way forward, something more local and personal replacing the modern urge to fix every large-scale problem with a large-scale solution. The work would chiefly involve middle school students, many from impoverished communities and families who relied on financial aid, largely made possible through the organization's fundraising efforts. For young people without the means to venture beyond their city block or county's borders, such an experience would serve a vital role in widening their understanding of the world and opening new possibilities for how to lead their lives. It would begin not with trying to change minds but with awakening the senses; it would start with us educators ourselves.

All of this lay ahead of me for the time being. For now, I was simply hungry for a change and whatever would come after the long drive ahead.

PROLOGUE

A teacher is first and foremost a student, and among all the students I would meet, the one whose story I know best is my own. My continuing "environmental education," though it doesn't look precisely like anyone else's, has unfolded like that of many others before me on the ancestral homeland of the Cherokee and on lands once inhabited by descendants of European immigrants. Time's long reach has, from the start, been inseparable from the time I've spent there myself.

"Who can express the ecstasy of the woods!" Ludwig van Beethoven penned in a letter two centuries ago. Though a statement and not a question, it is a good question nevertheless. While I don't presume that I am capable of providing a satisfactory answer, I haven't refrained from making an attempt even in an era defined more by agonizing over the natural world than celebrating it.

Entering forest time means adjusting to a different sort of clock or sometimes no clock at all. I've found it can put one out of step with the times. Though adapting to a pace and rhythm different from those of contemporary culture comes with certain challenges, one reward is getting to claim citizenship in a community larger than the sum of its parts. Neither did I plan to follow a career path that involved moving to the mountains—much less one in the outdoor teaching profession—nor did I imagine staying for so long. It was hard to keep away once I claimed a place in the woods for myself and realized my education wasn't finished and never would be. Many years have elapsed since Ken offered me a job, and though I'm not quite the same young man I was back then, I carry him in my thoughts in much the same way I carry on my back all the essential items—water bottle, first aid kit, and raincoat—I still rely on today.

A path leads into the woods. Where does it go? In the Western Hemisphere, near the thirty-fifth parallel, in the company of a vertical landscape cloaked by a deciduous forest and carved by a river racing off the spine of the Appalachian chain—during what might be considered a mere second in the span of deep forest time—I was about to find out.

PART I

Sapling

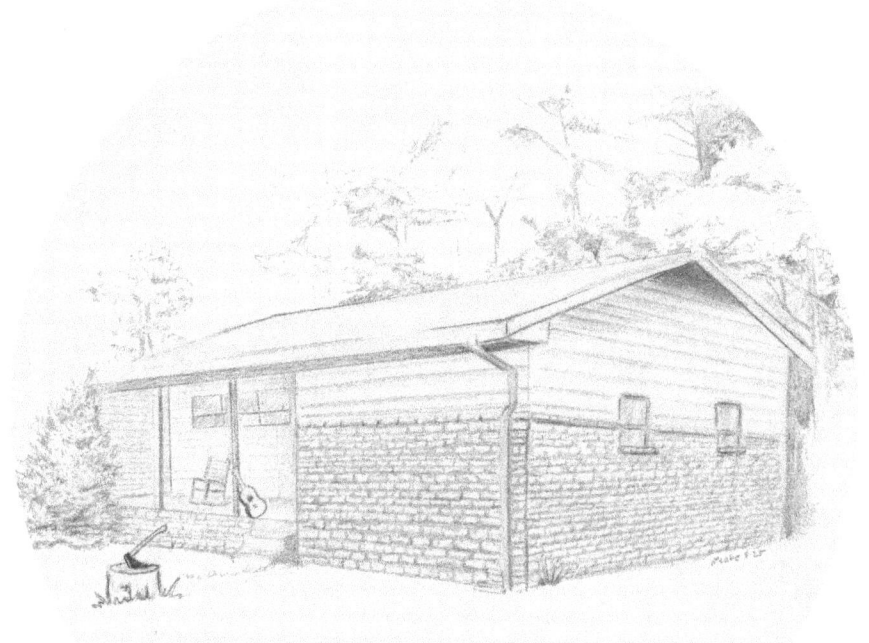

Initiation

MOVING DAY ARRIVED. I packed my car, headed south, and arrived within sight of Great Smoky Mountains National Park five hundred miles later. The hardest part of the journey was yet to come.

A region of superlatives, the Smokies boast the greatest variety of vascular plants in North America, more native tree species than Europe, and nearly as many kinds of mammals as dwell in all of North Carolina, at one-fiftieth the size. More types of salamanders live within the park than in any other place on earth of similar size, and where biodiversity soars, so do the number of human visitors. Between eleven and fourteen million annually—more than Yellowstone and the Grand Canyon combined—make the Smokies the most visited national park in the nation, a fact that became readily apparent when I departed the interstate and joined the bottleneck of motorists trying to reach the mountains.

Anxious to arrive at my new place of residence yet figuring I ought to get to know the region I would now call home a little better, I'd made my approach by way of the busy tourist hub of Pigeon Forge rather than taking the same route I had for my job interview.

My mistake.

The sprawling gateway to the Smokies was where, like other travelers eager to lay eyes on an unspoiled landscape, I instead found myself bumper-to-bumper in ten lanes of traffic while crawling past mile after mile of outlet malls, souvenir shops, Western-wear emporiums, go-cart tracks, miniature golf courses, dinner theaters, all-you-can-eat restaurants, wedding chapels, and entertainment venues galore. If the number of automobiles filling parking spaces was any indication, many visitors appeared all too happy to have become stranded on the shoals of commerce instead of reaching the mountains. Others like myself, despairing over the fact that the distant ridgelines suddenly weren't getting any closer, perhaps gritted their teeth while waiting for the light to change, and the next, and the next.

I pressed on, inch by inch, and faced my next hurdle in bustling downtown Gatlinburg. Along the pedestrian-packed main street jammed with souvenir and T-shirt shops, a mechanical life-sized *Tyrannosaurus rex* snapped its jaws at passersby. A man in ghoulish makeup, his ribcage and spine implausibly visible, grinned from inside a box with a three-way mirror. "Haunted Adventure," said the sign above another business. Specialty shops were seemingly endless in number and variety. If I wanted to buy a sword—and maybe I did—there was a store for that.

Breakneck economic growth is just one of several factors that explains the proximity of such an outsized human footprint to the national park. Whatever the reason, the result for visitors such as myself was to have entered a liminal space where one experiences a kind of geographical whiplash. For all my efforts to reach the mountains, I had somehow ended up in Myrtle Beach.

But at the far edge of town, just past the final streetlight, an altogether different world awaited. The human-made environment abruptly ended and a leafy fortress took over. Dark shadows replaced sun-bleached streets and exhaust fumes gave way to the scent of a lush deciduous forest. Fertility abounded everywhere, producing a feeling of being swallowed whole by green, growing things. The shade was so deep, even in midday, that it was as if I'd entered the Outer Dark. Far from perdition, however, it was instead an earthly paradise with an entrance sign welcoming me and other weary pilgrims, at long last, to Great Smoky Mountains National Park.

At this juncture in my travels, I had the comfort of knowing my final destination. Situated forty minutes away was the house where I would lay my head for that night and many nights to come. To be precise: a bedroom recently vacated by my friend and now colleague Greg (who had gotten married the previous week and moved with his bride Rebecca into an efficiency apartment on the learning center campus up the road). For many travelers, however, a sense of arrival can prove elusive. Overlook the welcome sign despite its large size, and it's possible not to know where precisely on earth you are. I would soon learn that my aunt and uncle had done this very thing countless times over the years on their trips to the region. While visiting the area several weeks after my arrival, they asked about my new place of employment over dinner. Looks of incredulity spread across their faces when I told them I worked in the national park, which, though it was located less than a block from our restaurant, they seemed to have never heard of.

"Oh, you mean the *mountain*," said my uncle, referring to what was for him a nameless geographical barrier dividing Gatlinburg from Cherokee, North Carolina, another popular tourist destination thirty-six miles away. After all these years, he and my aunt finally knew its name.

One source of such confusion is that the Smokies have no entrance fee, a circumstance resulting from a distinctive arrangement forged between the states and the federal government when the land was acquired from private landowners for the park in the 1930s. Virtually unheard of in the national park system, it's also why there are no entrance booths staffed by park rangers welcoming each carload of tourists. As I would learn firsthand, chances of seeing a federally endangered peregrine falcon were often better than spotting someone in a National Park Service uniform. The staff shortage is largely due to chronic budget shortfalls, which stem from the fact that the most crowded national park in North America receives nothing in entrance fees from the throngs of motorists passing through its borders every year.

The overabundance of motorized vehicles is one reason the park has earned a reputation as a drive-through wilderness in which many visitors acquire little more than a "windshield experience." As I was also to learn, many who do so were liable to be labeled "tourons" by locals fed up with heavy traffic, bad manners, and out-of-state drivers puttering along at fifteen miles per hour in hopes of glimpsing a black bear. Like many national parks, the Smokies function as a laboratory for the striking ways in which people alienated from the natural world behave when coming face-to-face with it. On rare occasions, visitors have been known to naively inquire about what time the bears are let out and when the waterfalls are turned off. More extreme behavior also occurs, such as when a man was observed "rescuing" a fawn by pummeling with rocks the yearling black bear that was lunching on it and then rushing the fawn to the nearest ranger station, where it died. Transplants to the region likewise sometimes exhibit attitudes at odds with the place they've become smitten by and chosen to live. A county extension agent I would meet received a phone call from a woman who complained about the gray squirrels populating her backyard.

"They're everywhere," she moaned. "Why do they have to live here?"

"Squirrels have to live somewhere, ma'am," he replied. "And they were there first."

One more newcomer to the area sheltered in automotive comfort, I took my place in a long string of cars winding through a gorge hung with rock walls and at least a dozen shades of green. Like other travelers, I was tempted to pump my brakes and gawk as I coasted through a tableau of picturesque beauty. But most of all, I was ready for the long drive to be over. I reached my destination in less than an hour, arriving at the residence where my new housemates and colleagues were gathered in the backyard as they waited to help unload my belongings and welcome me to my new home.

Right away, I realized how much of an alien to the natural world I'd become over the preceding months. Working in a factory had meant bidding farewell each morning to fresh air and daylight and then stumbling out into what felt like another planet at shift's end. So rare was contact with the outdoors during work hours that when the wind blew cottonwood blossoms through a garage bay one afternoon, on the sole occasion I ever saw the door open, I mistook them for snowflakes, forgetting it was July.

My cobwebbed senses needed dusting off and airing out, and the remedy turned out to be a rather unorthodox one. The time for it came unexpectedly one afternoon during an impromptu excursion with Greg and our mutual friend Mark who was visiting. Also accompanying us was Greg's former co-worker Andy, who like Greg possessed a sense of mischief that lurked beneath his quiet exterior. Though Mark wasn't as clueless as I was, neither of us knew what was coming as we ventured along the riverbank further up the valley. It was there we played a game I cannot in good conscience recommend to the reader but which I found oddly liberating at the time. The rules, so far as I could tell, because they were not explained in advance, were as follows:

1. Pick up a rock or stick.
2. Hurl one at your companions as close as you dare but without trying to hit anyone.
3. Try not to flinch when an object is thrown your way. However, if you are about to get hit, for heaven's sake, move out of the way.

The game was aptly called Primitive Man by Greg and Andy, though it might just as well have been called Getting in Touch with Your Inner Redneck. It began while Mark and I were standing in a dry channel of the riverbed some twenty yards away from the others. Suddenly, a log the size of my leg landed on a nearby boulder and splintered into smaller fragments.

I looked up to see Greg sporting a devilish grin.

"What was that for?" I yelled.

"We're playing Primitive Man," he hollered back. "Consider this your initiation ceremony."

Andy, bearded and muscular, had good aim. He lobbed a grapefruit-sized rock that landed several feet away and shattered, peppering Mark and me with shards of sandstone. Greg heaved another log that split in half upon impact.

"Your turn," said Andy.

Mark and I each picked up rocks and returned volley half-heartedly, not wanting to injure the two people standing opposite us, whose faces said this was all just good fun.

Clearly, we needed to approach the game with more seriousness. The next series of salvos launched in our direction, this time with greater accuracy, reinforced this point. Determining which way each barrage of rocks might ricochet was key—and yet pretty much impossible. It dawned on me now that there were no points in this game and no winning, either. Just surviving.

"Enjoying yourselves yet?" Greg shouted.

Sure, serving as a target for a couple of Neanderthals is a real hoot, I thought. I wondered if my other colleagues, whom I'd barely met, were this rash. The conspicuous absence of women provided a clue. This was a pastime concocted solely in the imaginations of males who'd once resided in the Oasis, the nickname of the house where I now lived.

Greg and Andy both seemed like reasonably intelligent people. They taught *children* for a living after all. So this was free play then, similar, I supposed, to the kind they encouraged among young people under their charge. Though of a very different stripe of course: horseplay for those with a high level of tolerance for calculated risk, and with "safety first" tossed by the wayside. Was I going to protest by telling them we were being reckless and juvenile, which they already knew, and which was the point of the game?

I picked up another rock and flung it harder than before.

Several volleys later, a golf ball-sized rock skipped off a boulder and made a beeline for Mark, who arched his back as it shot toward him, missing his torso by inches. It was a deft move, and I pictured the broken ribs or cracked vertebrae that might have resulted had his reaction time been slower. It seemed to all of us a good time to take a break; to my great relief, my first game of Primitive Man was over.

The relief I experienced that afternoon was also for an altogether different reason. For the first time in months, the distance between my headspace and the physical world had magically collapsed. Equal parts fear and excitement had brought to the surface a visceral awareness of my surroundings, pushing aside every other concern and connecting my mind to my body and both my mind and body to the place where I stood. What might otherwise have taken days or weeks to achieve instead transpired in about twenty minutes, providing the fresh start I hadn't realized I needed. The word *primitive* means crude or unrefined, but also first or prime. Playing the game had managed to meet both definitions at once. Though safer alternatives were available in nearby tourist hotspots, what counted there as "fun for the entire family" often amounted to manufactured experiences and soulless commercial entertainment—the factory model at work once more. And besides, other than a few demolished logs, playing Primitive Man—idiotic though it was—came free of charge.

In the days that followed, I realized playing the game had demolished something else. It was a posture I'd unwittingly embraced while cooped up indoors, one in which I'd become overly protective of nature by being cut off from it, echoing rules ingrained in me at a young age. Do not touch. Do not disturb. Do not step off the path. Do not, do not, do not. A well-functioning society depends on individuals respecting the rules and doing no harm. But we need contact too, and misbehaving has its virtues. Barbaric acts I sometimes inflicted on the natural world as a boy—scorching ants with a magnifying glass or watching crayfish perish in a bucket after catching them—had the paradoxical effect of inducing feelings of empathy in me. Caveman-like behavior did something similar by waking me up to the world around me, in which the only living things liable to suffer were those of us engaged in the game. It turned my thoughts to the job ahead, which would involve getting people to step outside their comfort zone, and made me wonder just how willing I was to step outside mine.

Playing Primitive Man, however, was only the first step I took toward shedding my alien skin that afternoon. When the game ended, I went exploring downstream on my own. The rocks were as slippery as greased melons, and I slipped more than once, landing hard on my side. These were baby steps I was taking toward learning how to walk upright in my new environment. I would need a lot more practice.

I came to a plunge pool ringed by giant blocks of bedrock wallpapered with moss, a spot that looked as if it had been concocted in the imagination of someone with no use for level surfaces. I'd brought my camera along and figured the best angle from which to take a photograph was the opposite side of the river. Getting to the river's edge required navigating over more slippery rocks, and as I inched down the slanted face of a boulder, my feet suddenly came out from under me. The next instant, I found myself sliding like a bag of laundry down a chute until I was ushered into the deepest part of the pool.

Once the initial shock passed, I kicked with my feet and struggled to tread water while holding my camera above my head, a gesture that surely also meant surrender. My soaked boots and clothes would take days to dry out in the humid summer heat. A journey by automobile had delivered me to the place I would now call home. But I'd been mistaken about the moment of my arrival and when it occurred in full, body and soul.

I'd arrived, at last.

Class Begins

MY FIRST DAY on the job did not get off to a good start. Scrambling out of bed in a state of panic when I realized I'd overslept, I threw on my clothes, gulped down a bowl of cereal, and dashed out the door. No time to pause and admire the view from the front porch of my new home. A van was idling and its driver honking the horn. I was conspicuously the last to board.

"You're late," said Ken, sitting behind the wheel.

Muttering apologies, I squeezed down the narrow aisle past my new coworkers and took the last available seat in the way back. What little I understood about the outing at the start of staff training was that we were heading to Cades Cove, a historic district in the park where a farming community thrived in the nineteenth and early twentieth centuries. Not wanting to draw any more attention to myself, I kept quiet as chatter filled the van. When I realized I'd forgotten to bring water for the long day ahead, I leaned my head against the window and shut my eyes, quietly scolding myself.

Twenty minutes later we were there. Rousing myself from a restless half sleep, I peered out the window and watched one meadow after another pass by as the van crawled along a narrow one-way road in heavy tourist traffic. We entered the woods, braking in fits and starts before coming to a complete stop. While we waited for the line of cars to get moving again, I noticed a round dark object near the forest's edge. It looked like a weirdly shaped tree stump until it began to move.

"Bear," I said to the backs of heads, all four rows of them, in front of me. But nobody paid the new guy any mind.

"Hey, there's a bear," I said again, louder. "Three o'clock."

Heads turned, bodies leaned toward starboard, and hands wiped the steamed-up windows to catch sight of the yearling cub. Though it would seem hard to miss at a distance of only twenty feet, it did a remarkable job of blending into its surroundings when it kept still. We all watched as the cub pawed at a rotten log in search of grubs until it grew bored and wandered off.

The rest of the day was a blur, as were the next three months. When my trial period ended and I was hired on full time, I felt the same relief as I did that morning in the van upon spotting the bear, when Ken provided verbal confirmation that my first hours on the job weren't a total failure: "Good eye," he said. "Maybe we'll keep you after all."

Monday mornings begin with a mop bucket. Several hours before a fresh batch of students and their teachers are scheduled to arrive, I meet my co-workers in the dining hall, where we gather cleaning supplies. Doubling as teaching faculty and custodial crew, we get straight to work on our list of chores. After mopping floors, we vacuum carpets, sweep lobbies, wipe windows, scrub tables, empty garbage canisters, and then review the week's schedule. We'll teach classes on forest ecology this afternoon and more tomorrow on salamanders and map and compass. A field trip to Cades Cove takes place the following day and a wilderness hike on the next. Altogether the week will resemble a play in five acts with a full schedule that includes more programs each evening—night walks, campfires, folk dancing, birds of prey, astronomy—plus a living history exercise before the cohort departs on Friday. All that's left to do once our meeting ends is to pore over lesson plans while waiting for the rest of the cast to show up.

Now's the quiet before the rush, as it must be at hundreds of other centers like ours around the country. Our calendar will remain full through spring and summer before August delivers a brief intermission, after which the curtains will rise once more and stay up till the holidays. By year's end, close to six thousand people will have darkened our door.

This week's guests are seventh graders from a public school in urban Nashville. The forecast calls for rain and the brooding sky looks like it just might storm. Rains, however, aren't likely to dampen spirits. Though today's a school day, at no time this week will anyone be sitting behind a desk.

Among the twenty or so people on staff, the distinction for longest-serving member belongs to Ken, who lives on campus with his wife and three children and whose beard closely resembles that of Will Walker, who, in the nineteenth century, settled what would become known as Walker Valley. As Ken tells it, he got hooked on nature study as a teenager while volunteering at a natural history museum in Dayton, Ohio, which led to him choosing a future in environmental education. The sign a prankster posted above his always-open office door announces, *Warning: Recent Bear Activity in This Area Increases Your Danger of an Encounter*, and it's true you had better come prepared with a solid argument if you think you've dreamed up some brilliant idea. Ken almost single-handedly resurrected the center from the dust after it sat shuttered for several years for renovations, and he seems to have grown accustomed to adversity and to enjoy testing limits. Some days he can be spotted stealing into his natural habitat outdoors, binoculars in hand, whereupon he'll return with a lizard or snake to show others at their desks—a moment that would cause a stir in other work settings but which here is just business as usual.

Keeping an overnight learning center in operation year after year, especially one located inside a national park, comes with a unique set of challenges. Besides keeping the lights on with a shoestring budget in lean financial times, one must contend with the public's misconception that we survive thanks to the largesse of the federal budget, when in fact every dollar we spend we earn through tuition fees or raise through donations. Another is making the best use we can of structures originally erected during Lyndon Johnson's administration as part of a Job Corps center. A building where construction supplies were once stored and vocational training took place now houses bunk beds for more than a hundred guests. In another, students eat meals where trainees once shot hoops, the original gymnasium floor still visible underfoot. Mother Nature interrupts the usual flow of activities from time to time. In Ken's early days at the center, a wildfire came within a couple of miles of campus and burned more than a thousand acres of forest. One winter he had to contend with a blizzard that stranded students inside the park for four days and knocked out power for ten. A flood destroyed parts of the road the following year, preventing the public from entering Walker Valley for two years but not a school bus filled with students that arrived the following week.

Through all this, there are meals to cook, bills to pay, phones and emails to answer, aging structures to maintain, and a small team of people besides us teaching faculty to do it. Visiting teachers also play a heroic role by giving up evenings at home in exchange for zero overtime pay while sleeping in bunk rooms next to farting, flashlight-waving kids. Just such a kid myself once, when my class spent a week at McKeever Environmental Learning Center, my teacher Mr. Johnson lulled us boys to sleep by reciting "The Cremation of Sam McGhee" by Robert W. Service. By poem's end, we dug into our sleeping bags and dreamed of the day we'd just spent in the Pennsylvania woods while Sam sat in his furnace in the Yukon, warm for the first time since leaving Tennessee.

The sound of engines rumbling through the valley reaches our ears inside the office. Moments later a pair of buses pulls across the bridge. Everyone springs into action, grabbing backpacks and class materials before heading outdoors. It's showtime.

I'd have protested had someone told me in college that I would one day make my living as a teacher, much less one whose classroom would be outdoors. Born into a family of educators, I didn't hold anything against the profession. My grandmother began her career teaching in a one-room schoolhouse, and my mother, father, and sister have spent part or all of their working lives as teachers of various stripes. I knew only that I wanted to break the mold, figuring something more glamorous lay in store for me, even though I had no idea what I wanted to do instead. Besides, I rarely felt comfortable standing before large groups of people despite ample experience doing it—all those solemn faces staring through me while acting in school plays or singing in choir. Children, too, had a way of setting me on edge, even in casual settings, and their apparent indifference to my presence whenever I tried to relate to them only heightened my self-doubt.

Out of a process of elimination, I became an English major in college. Of all the subjects I studied, it was the one that made me feel the least incompetent and lost. Over time I discovered that I was drawn to the big questions literature asked. Halfway through my final year, however, I still lacked any sense of what I would do next and clung to the hope that the girl I was dating would rescue me from my doubts and lack of ambition. My first serious relationship, it was also the only thing that tethered me to concrete reality during a year I largely spent inside my head. Drowning in unread reading assignments and unwritten papers, I whiled away evenings alone in my room while doing existential gymnastics, wondering how modern civilization had produced the most violent and destructive century in human history—witness to two world wars, the Holocaust, nuclear devastation in Hiroshima and Nagasaki, the Gulag, the Chinese Cultural Revolution, the killing fields of Cambodia, genocide in Rwanda and Bosnia—and had seen the best scientific minds and most sophisticated technological advances put to the task of inventing weapons that could destroy the planet many times over. What good were institutions, education, science, literature, and the arts if they'd led to this? What possibility was there for living a happy life when there was so much suffering in the world and so little justice? When human action so often seemed inadequate, and even small solutions were so difficult to achieve? What exactly was the point of being alive? The most influential thinkers of the age—Marx, Freud, and Darwin among them—had contributed to the body of human knowledge and offered theories for describing the world as they saw it, yet offered little that was satisfying about life's ultimate purpose and meaning.

As is the case with many young people questioning the world and their place in it, my days were marked by self-absorption and self-pity. As the ambivalence and doubts swirling around my mind grew louder, however, the drive-by shootings that occurred on a weekly basis in my neighborhood served as a reminder that my questions weren't merely theoretical. Other than the time I spent with my girlfriend, daily existence began to feel intolerable. Unable to laugh at myself, I'd turned into a joyless black cloud. And on top of all my other questions, another kept hounding me: of what value was my own seemingly purposeless and undreamt life? "Not much," came the easy answer, though I knew ending it was an equally easy answer and therefore out of the question.

And yet in the days ahead and all the years of my life to come, rising each morning to trudge to some meaningless job, going through the motions in the absence of any authentic source of hope and joy, probably in an office cubicle, what was there to look forward to? What exactly was the point of it all?

For the moment, The End had returned. Unlike the ending I'd faced as a teenager, however, I didn't know how to prepare for this one, which loomed over me just when I was about to embark on the grand journey of adulthood.

My girlfriend figured out long before I did that I was not ready for a real relationship, and in January, she broke up with me—just like my next girlfriend would a few years later when I was working in the doorframe factory. In time I would see that there was no future for us in the absence of a vision for my own future, and I would come to regard our parting as a blessing in disguise. But this realization was still months away, and, for the time being, winter's darkness turned darker still. I withdrew from social circles and all but a few close friendships. Getting dumped confirmed that on top of all my other reasons for basking in despair, chief among them that the world was inhospitable and therefore unlovable, there was another, which was that I, too, was unworthy of love.

Throughout that long winter, I waited for deliverance, an epiphany, a sign—some proverbial as well as literal parting of the clouds—and began searching for some way to get as far away from my present circumstances as possible. Halfway around the world sounded appealing. I spotted an advertisement calling for volunteers to teach English in Mongolia during the coming summer. I filled out an application and landed a spot, even though it would mean doing the very thing I'd already ruled out: teaching. With summer still months away, however, it was too soon to breathe a sigh of relief over my impending escape.

What finally helped loosen my white-knuckled grip on life came as something of a surprise. During one social gathering I decided not to blow off, I wandered into the host's kitchen, where a new mother was holding her newborn. A circle of people had gathered around to admire the baby, and not wanting to be rude, I joined in.

"Want to hold her?" asked the mother, and before I could mouth a response, she slipped her daughter into my arms.

Coached by the mother, I did my best to execute the finer points of baby-holding: cradle the warm bundle of flesh in the crook of my arm, support the head, bounce a little, and for heaven's sake, don't let go. I had held a baby once or twice in the long-ago past, though never with so much relief or out of such need. Solution for despairing young men questioning the point for existence and their place in the world: give them babies to hold. Yes, of course, I wanted to hold her. With her eyes squinched tight and tongue probing the air, she looked like a hairless pink kitten. But did the baby want to be held by me? Miraculously, it seemed so.

"She likes you," said the mother.

"The feeling is reciprocated," I said awkwardly.

I found myself in the presence of children on several other occasions that spring and was surprised to discover that I enjoyed their company. Having been one of these little persons once, I recognized their vulnerability in myself. Their neediness was partly what had made me nervous to be around them, sensing but not able to name, until now, the awkwardness I often felt living in my own skin. My despondency began to evaporate while in their presence, and later when it returned, when I was once more in the solitude of my mind, the weight did not feel so heavy as before.

In time it would occur to me that children offered by their very existence at least a partial answer to my most pressing questions and doubts. After night, morning. After darkness, light. In spite of wars and catastrophes and uncertainties about the future, Creation kept happening all the time. Children continued to be born, more of them every day, providing a sobering reminder of the care and forethought the rest of us owed to those who were on the way.

"Not my job" is a phrase I would never hear uttered at the nature center, the tasks too numerous and the hands too few for such an excuse. Improv artists of a sort by trade, each of us often took on other roles behind the scenes in accordance with the part of the job description that falls under "and other duties as needed." Cleaning up vomit and plunging clogged toilets were skills I honed early on, so often did such opportunities arise. When the kitchen staff was stretched thin, there were dishes to wash, and when snowstorms prevented them from driving to work, there were meals to cook. A black bear attracted by the scent of fried chicken wafting out of the dining hall had to be chased back into the woods. Rattlesnakes and copperheads that had holed up near buildings and walkways needed to be relocated to a safer distance. If high water washed out a footbridge spanning a side channel of the river, I spent the day with Ken and other coworkers coaxing a new one into place with a pry bar and come-along. If I wasn't teaching, constructing steps out of stone or logs on a rugged section of trail made for an afternoon's project. When windstorms knocked down trees across a footpath, I hoofed up the mountain with a chainsaw and Pulaski to clear them out of the way. Depending on the time of year and the needs of ongoing research, there was data to collect on salamanders and birds and mushrooms, or park biologists might need an extra pair of eyes while searching for a rare fern species. A park ranger might ask for my assistance baiting a bear that had been harassing backpackers at a backcountry campsite. Or a hiker would take a bad fall and I would join a search-and-rescue team on a carryout. Lost hikers sometimes stumbled onto campus looking for help at the oddest hours, which was how I once missed my own birthday party, giving a ride to three teenagers who'd taken a wrong turn while my coworkers enjoyed pints of beer in town in my absence.

Always there were logs to chop and stack for firewood, tables to set, floors to mop, and new guests to greet. But at the heart of my job were the classes I taught and the lessons I learned through teaching them.

Like many novice educators, I held the reins too tightly during my first season and treated foals as if they were bucking broncos. My students were easier to communicate with compared with those to whom I had taught English in Mongolia. And yet they were always different: middle schoolers this week, college students or working adults the next. Teaching, I assumed at first, was about me telling them what they needed to know. It took time to figure out what Freeman Tilden, a journalist who created his Six Principles of Interpretation after visiting national parks in the 1970s, meant when he wrote, "Information does not equal interpretation," and to follow the advice of Joseph Cornell in his book *Sharing Nature with Children*: "A sense of joy should permeate the experience." Joy would come eventually, but for now, there was a pile of books to read and veteran coworkers to observe when I wasn't simply learning how to teach the old-fashioned way: by doing.

No matter the class, there were numerous dos and don'ts to keep in mind. Don't stand with your back to the sun, making everyone else stare into it. Don't give a tour: you are not a docent, and students are not empty receptacles. Don't put people to sleep by droning on and on or acting like a know-it-all. Resist the urge to strangle boys (almost always boys) who refuse to follow instructions. Ask questions students can answer for themselves through hands-on investigation. When asked a question you don't know the answer to, rely on the mantra beloved by honest naturalists: "I don't know, let's figure it out." Untrain behaviors drilled into students from a young age by encouraging them to touch this, hug that, and dig in the dirt. Improvise as necessary, embrace some level of chaos, keep everyone safe within reason, and above all, patience, patience. Crucially, always return to campus with the same number of people you left with.

Worry filled my mind the first few times I led students into the woods when I pictured one of them tumbling off a steep section of trail or being struck by a falling limb. Asking myself if it would be better to stick closer to campus helped set my mind at ease, knowing it wasn't and that my students didn't think so either. One more calculated risk, like riding in an automobile, teaching in the woods relies on not conquering but managing fear.

I figured out early on that with the forest as my classroom and students who were grateful to be unchained from their desks, bombing was virtually impossible. Also, that teaching didn't always mean direct instruction and sometimes didn't require instruction at all. Much of the time, my role was simply to act as an intermediary, and the trick was in knowing when to get out of the way and let the forest do the teaching. One reason was that unforeseen circumstances could arise at any moment, or my lesson plan would become upstaged by a surprise guest.

"Mr. Jeremy, we saw a bear," announced a breathless girl in the middle of class during my first season.

Students were spending the afternoon searching the woods for landmarks using maps and compasses, an activity whose success depended on mutual trust since we were out of sight of one another much of the time. My instructions were for them to explore in pairs before returning to our meeting spot. Now that there was a bear in the area—Matilda probably—I called everyone back with a whistle blast.

White oak acorns, I'd learned, are beloved by black bears for the lower amounts of bitter-tasting tannins they contain compared with other oak species. Matilda, a bear I encountered on numerous occasions that fall, had likely discovered the stand of white oak trees nearby and was fattening herself before the coming winter. Counting heads as students gathered around, I deliberated over the wisdom of showing them a wild bear with only empty defenseless space between us and the nearest hospital miles away. Scenarios that would get me fired or land me in jail began running through my mind. But so too did the message I would send the students and their classroom teacher if I chose not to introduce them to the bear—that nature is scary and best studied indoors. Worse, I'd reinforce the modern myth that children ought to be shielded from every conceivable risk, thus robbing them of the opportunity to acquire the same fear-management skills I was learning to depend on as an outdoor educator.

With my decision made and blessed by the teacher, I went over several safety points before starting up the hillside in search of Matilda, a dozen eleven-year-olds in tow. Guided by the sound of her loud mandibles working on acorns, we at last caught sight of her and crept to within a hundred feet and knelt in the leaves. Matilda chomped. We watched and listened in utter silence, less out of reverential awe than simple curiosity. A creature has needs and the forest's bounty satisfies them. Food falls from the trees, and a bear—this one right in front of us—eats it hungrily. Matilda largely remained a question mark to us: how big was her territory and where did she sleep? But for several moments we got to share space with her and glimpse the mystery and gift that was her life, and by the time we departed, it was clear that a class that had begun with students practicing skills in navigating a landscape under their own powers had turned into something far more.

The length of each class period—three hours or an entire day—was a luxury compared with the hour-long classes first instituted in the nineteenth century by reformers inspired by the Industrial Revolution. Teachers who had never accompanied their students outside their school buildings warmed right away to this interruption-free rhythm as one subject flowed seamlessly into another and another, the next mealtime the only time constraint.

We relied on these same teachers to conduct classes during their stay, a feature unique to our center, the purpose of which was to give educators experience teaching outside the familiar comfort of their classrooms and to provide them with skills for continuing to do so once they returned home. Many first attended weekend workshops to acclimate to their new teaching environment and review lesson materials. Learning alongside their students—minus any pressure to prepare them for exams—perhaps also made them feel young again and helped them reclaim whatever enthusiasm for teaching might have been drained out of them by the system under which they labored.

Once in a while, unleashing visiting teachers into the wild could lead to unintended consequences. When Wendy, a visiting classroom teacher, and her students failed to show up at lunchtime, I headed up the trail where they were last seen, filled with some urgency because Wendy was five months pregnant. "No sign of them," I reported over a two-way radio twenty minutes later. Neither had they been spotted on the rest of the loop they ought to have completed an hour earlier. I headed down a draw off trail that resembled a path, albeit a rather overgrown one, and which in fact had been an old road in pre-park days. Eventually it led to a hollow called the Spicewoods. Still no Wendy or students—and now I was out of radio range. Using my best tracking skills (which were pretty meager at this stage in my development as a naturalist), I searched the valley floor for footprints, scuff marks, anything. Overturned leaves on a sidehill by a creek indicated the group was heading even farther away from the established trail and campus, where lunchtime had concluded by now. (Retracing one's steps, I was finding out firsthand, was something most people were reluctant to do when lost.) Dashing back up the draw until I was once more in radio range, I delivered the news that Wendy and her students were bushwhacking down the creek. Not an altogether bad plan, as it turned out, since they would eventually reach a road, at which point a park ranger spotted them and shuttled them back to campus, where Wendy's colleagues and the rest of the kids' classmates were sitting on a bus awaiting their journey homeward.

The incident marked the last time we ever sent teachers that way by themselves.

Far more often, however, rewards far outweighed the risks involved with taking students out of a controlled environment and into a less predictable one outdoors. Before teaching any new subject, I would first watch a more experienced coworker teach a class, as I did one afternoon during a geology hike. The rugged mile-long trail we were following eventually brought us to a waterfall. At the sight of it, one boy spontaneously belted out the opening stanza to "The Star-Spangled Banner."

As the students splashed in the creek, I noticed a boy standing off by himself and facing away from the others. The wet spot on the front of Theo's trousers told me why: he was so excited he'd peed himself.

"My mom would never let me do this if she were here," he whispered when I asked if he was okay.

Theo's body shook and his eyes bulged as he gazed spellbound at the wall of falling water. The hike itself and the freedom he had been given to explore were too much for him—and yet just right.

"Well, she's not here," I said, tying his jacket around his waist to obscure the pee stain from view of his classmates. "But I bet she'd be proud of you."

I hiked at the end of the line on the return trip to campus, watching as Theo's clumsy feet tripped over easily avoidable objects. He glanced around each time in search of the culprit rock or root, the astonished expression on his face speaking for him: "What in the world was that?" As thunderheads roiled across the sky, down in the leaf shade of a temperate rainforest, a boy was making first contact with the earth. I felt lucky to be witnessing it.

More ordinary moments were the norm. The entire production depended on numerous support staff, including bus drivers, school administrators, parents, cooks, and maintenance and office workers who wouldn't get to take a direct part in the experience themselves. Meanwhile what might have passed for the ordinary counted as extraordinary out in the woods. Folds in bedrock told the story of moving mountains. A tree trunk with rows of horizontal holes hinted at a drama involving a yellow-bellied sapsucker. Crusty leaf-like matter growing on a boulder revealed a symbiotic relationship between "Alice Algae" and "Freddy Fungus," who "took a lichen" to each other.

A sense of wonder, native to the country of childhood, was the easy part. Slowing down took a little more effort and hinged on resisting the urge to hurry so that another mystery could be encountered and unpacked. Whenever a situation called for it, I would adopt the persona of a "sage on the stage," a teaching style (overused by some educators) that relies on charisma and expert knowledge to impress students and hold their attention. It didn't take me long to realize that another guise, called a "guide from the side," suited both my needs and those of my students far better. Expert knowledge would be a long time coming anyway, and I was more than content to end up a footnote in their learning rather than an exclamation mark.

A good jolting provided by a sage on the stage served a purpose nonetheless—both in my teaching and in my life. Whenever I thought back on my final college semester during a winter I thought would never end, I was reminded that such a lesson could sometimes arrive at the unlikeliest times and through the unlikeliest teachers.

One afternoon during that long winter I stepped outside to smoke a cigarette. Still lost in a mental quagmire and smarting from my recent breakup, I hadn't yet attended the party where the newborn would permanently jar something loose inside me. It was a warm day, so I crawled through the second-story window of the house where I was living to sit on the porch roof and lick my wounds out in the fresh air for once. On the roof, however, my internal weather pattern remained unchanged: dark and overcast with a likelihood of despair.

The neighborhood where I lived was rough, and drive-by shootings were just one symptom of desperation among many that redlining and White flight had set in motion decades earlier. One of my housemates had his car stolen weeks earlier, and another had been followed home by police who suspected him of entering our block to buy drugs; they drew their weapons on him in our driveway. So I had reason to be leery when a stranger spotted me from the sidewalk and strode up to the house uninvited.

"Hey, brother. Up there on the roof," he said.

"That's me," I replied.

The man peered up at me, beaming a curious smile. Perhaps ten years older than me, his shabby clothes made me wonder if he'd spent time in prison or was looking to score drugs. I offered him a cigarette hoping he would then go away.

"Naw, man," he said. "I just saw you sitting there, thought I'd say hello. What a day! I'm just glad to be out in it. You feel me?"

"I guess."

The cheery stranger bounced as he spoke. Maybe he was high. Or maybe just happy. For my part, I must have appeared to him like I was thinking of jumping and wished it were from a height higher than a single story.

"Whatever's troubling you, it'll be all right," said the man. "Things will get better. You'll see." And with that, he turned and walked back down the driveway, holding his head high as he bellowed skyward, "What a day!"

Ah, there it was—now I could see it. Not the end of unhappiness just yet, but a glimpse of the radiant world beyond my knotted-up self. A gift from a stranger who, despite my best efforts to the contrary, had gotten me to look and take in the view.

The view was even better years later as I was coming to terms with my role as both teacher and student of the woods. With plenty still to learn and knowing I would have to think on my feet every step of the way, I had a solid foundation to build on. One thing seemed certain: I was going to love this job.

Our Nashville guests exit their buses excited as kittens, their faces every shade of color. Wide-eyed as they take in their new surroundings, they haul their luggage into the lodge and claim bunks. For some of them, the experience of eating three meals a day and getting a full night's sleep will be as novel as walking in the woods.

We eat lunch in the dining hall family style, waiting our turn as we pass platters of food. Afterward we gather in a circular outdoor structure modeled after a Cherokee council house. Introductions are made and rules explained, and then it's time to break into small groups. Mine's the Otters. Luckily, they have all come prepared with ponchos, a good thing now that it has begun to rain.

Over the next several hours, during a forest investigation class, the Otters and I will play a game of tag that illustrates the food chain. We'll portray the life of a tree from birth to death through bodily movements and gestures. Blindfolded, we'll use our sense of touch and smell to study trees and then sketch them. We'll identify half a dozen species using dichotomous keys and investigate the forest community by searching for its parts: restaurants (fruiting trees), plumbing (creeks), garbage collectors (decomposers), and factories (tree leaves photosynthesizing). Climate change, extinction, and other urgent matters will come up with a light touch if they come up at all. For now, it will be enough to unmuzzle the students' senses and let them fall in love with the world.

Humankind's relationship with nature "vibrates in the dark and remains below language," according to Martin Buber. If words fail to completely capture what a week in the woods means to a child, they might at least come up with something like this: "I wasn't sure places like this one actually existed in the world until now. I didn't know such sights, smells, and sounds were even possible. I never knew I could feel this way—feel at home in nature—and now that I know, everything is different." I recall sensing the same thing as a sixth grader during my week at McKeever when I peered up each day at a bright blue sky against which I have measured every autumn sky I've seen since. I felt *placed* at McKeever and came to understand something about belonging in the world—at least to this one part of it—I hadn't known before. So much so that when I returned home and gazed at the woods behind my house that I thought I knew so well, it was as if I was seeing them for the first time.

Another memory from that week has stayed with me through the years. At week's end I climbed into the car that would take me home and looked through the rear window at the two women who'd taught my classes and were seeing us off. As the car pulled away, I watched, mystified, as one of them smiled through the tears rolling down her cheeks as we waved goodbye to one another. Growing older, I learned to avoid such open displays of raw emotion and the innocence and vulnerability from which they spring, just as I learned to distrust sentimental descriptions of nature's beauty amid a world beset by violence and destruction. But when else than childhood to become open to beauty, without any hint of irony, and to the intense feelings that accompany moments spent forging deep bonds with a place and with the people alongside whom one has forged them? And where better than in the company of children to find reasons for hope and to experience such intensities all over again?

The Otters are all staring at me while awaiting instructions from their leader. That's me, I realize, still relatively new to all of this. It's raining full on now, rivulets running down our legs and soaking our socks. The afternoon has barely begun and already we're a sloppy mess. No one complains as we step onto the trail and head into the woods.

Cabin in the Woods

FRIDAY NIGHT AND ALL IS CALM in the forest, relatively speaking. The school buses filled with students have gone away, and the tourists with them now that darkness has fallen. My rare pleasure tonight is having the Oasis, the former ranger living quarters I share with my coworkers Jeff and Steve, all to myself. With both of them away for the weekend, I'm the sole remaining inhabitant of this corner of the park. Besides the river's ceaseless murmur, the only sound reaching my ears is the sporadic trilling of a toad looking for a mate out in the dark.

Before he moved back to Moscow to finish school several months after I moved in, my housemate Kostya wasted no time taking advantage of moments like these. Nights I worked late, I'd come home to find him sitting in the dark, eyes closed and head swaying as the windows rattled and the stereo speakers blasted Tchaikovsky at full volume. I'm content tonight to leave the stereo off and light the room with a table lamp, the only source of light visible for a mile or more in any direction. Slouching deeper into the cushions of what many house visitors claim is the world's most comfortable sofa (I'm inclined to agree), I inhale the fecund scent of the woods drifting through the window screen. Without moving a muscle, I savor the room's stillness, basking in what might amount to torment for someone in need of more sensory stimulation, but which is heaven for me.

When I dreamed as a boy of someday living in a cabin in the woods, one with vinyl siding wasn't what I'd pictured, though you'll hear no complaints from me. The immensity of the surrounding forest more than makes up for the less-than-postcard-perfect appearance of the Oasis. Like many children, I once defined size according to my environment and used *big* to describe almost everything, beginning with the modest no-name "mountain" behind the house where I grew up. My sister and I drew a map indicating landmarks important to us, naming the red oak with four trunks the Big Tree. The boulder we were convinced lightning had split in two we called the Big Rock, and the mysterious crater tucked a short distance uphill the Big Hole. The place encompassing it all, which to us seemed larger than the sum of its parts, was the Big Woods. We hid the map in the basement between the springs of a foldout couch, which years later was hauled to the Salvation Army. For all I know, someone today is sitting on the secrets of our then-universe.

Back then, it was as if the world was a place I would eventually grow into, like a suit of clothes several sizes too large. I still define size much as I did in my youth, but now that the world feels smaller, I'm no longer confident about finding the right sense of proportion. Viewed from an airplane, much of what once formed large unbroken stretches of forest throughout the eastern United States has been reduced to islands crosscut by roads and girdled by subdivisions and other forms of development. Had I glimpsed it from above, I would have understood the Big Woods was an in-between place too inconvenient for bulldozers to reach and occupying only a couple of hundred acres.

At eight hundred square miles, the Smokies are a Very Big Woods and the super-sized fulfillment of a dream I'd had in microcosm. For whatever reason, once I'd settled in, I began to feel an exclusive sense of ownership over the place. This despite daily reminders that it also belonged to three hundred million of my fellow citizens, more than a few of whom likely harbored dreams similar to mine. And yet the more I grew attached, the clearer it became that my tenure here, like that of every park visitor, was only temporary. No matter how long I might live here, I couldn't stay forever.

Equally impossible to ignore was the fact that many others had come before me, including the ancestors of the Cherokee people who were living throughout the region at least seventeen thousand years ago. It didn't take a stretch of the imagination to picture hunters making use of the spot where the Oasis sits as a temporary camp on forays deeper into the valley. Though arrowheads are rare finds in the mountains, students spot them from time to time. One discovered a projectile point during a class led by one of my colleagues; an archaeologist later determined it was among the oldest such specimens in the park's collection. The forebears of Cherokees who today reside in the Qualla Boundary typically made their homes along wider floodplains and likely deemed the valley too narrow for permanent habitation—another reminder that my presence here is a historical anomaly in the vast scheme of things.

Still others made the valley their lifelong home, including Will and Nancy Walker, who arrived as a young married couple in 1859. While Nancy never once left the valley after moving there, her husband was a tad more mobile. A Union sympathizer who prevented raiding parties from entering the valley during the Civil War, he took another woman as his wife once the strife ended and then another a few decades later, building a cabin for each and fathering twenty-seven children in all. Nancy, by all accounts, accepted the unusual situation, deciding her childbearing years were over after losing three of her seven children in childbirth and acting as midwife to the other women.

Erroneous newspaper reports at the time claimed upward of fifty-four children and alleged that the large family was Mormon. On the contrary, they were Baptists who similarly took inspiration from Old Testament patriarchs. At the turn of the twentieth century, Will petitioned for a schoolteacher to educate the community's growing numbers and built a teacherage as a summer residence. A foundation stone located in a now-overgrown clearing near the only cemetery in the valley provides one of the few pieces of evidence from those days.

After Will, Nancy, and Mary Ann (wife number two) died in old age and Moll (wife number three) moved away, the remaining children sold the land to a lumber company. A town sprang up virtually overnight farther upriver, numbering more than a thousand residents and lasting only as long as the timber did. Loggers were said to have wept out of sadness over the loss of their jobs and way of life on the day the final load of logs was hauled away—an image that looms large in my imagination because the spot where those logs were stored before they were shipped to the mill is where the Oasis now resides. To the end of his days, Will Walker had refused to sell his vast acreage to the company. So it was easy to picture him weeping too, had he known what would become of his forest, though for different reasons entirely.

The ground for shedding tears among those who razed the forest for their livelihood would eventually become a source of joy for others. The twentieth century witnessed the destruction of forests on a global scale never before seen in human history. Yet thanks to the establishment of the national park and a burgeoning conservation movement, so was it a period of recovery and rewilding as devastated ecosystems, including the Smokies, flourished once more.

Within a few short months, I'd gained a greater depth of knowledge about the people who once resided in the valley where I now lived than I ever had about the former inhabitants of the region where I'd spent the first eighteen years of my life. One reason for digesting local history was that there was no better motivation for tackling a subject than knowing I would have to teach it. Another was that the stories I learned were about people who had once walked and dreamed and labored on the same ground I now did. The past was alive and still had a voice, and I listened from the porch of the Oasis, where I had a front-row view of the Smokies' second act.

The house where I live acquired its nickname from former occupants inspired in part by Garth Brooks's hit song "Friends in Low Places." The protagonist in the song confesses an aversion to "social graces" and escapes to a watering hole called the Oasis. But it's the lowliness referenced in the song title that is most fitting given the geographical depths at which the house resides, not to mention the depths some of its residents went to in dreaming up a game such as Primitive Man.

Further inspiration for the name is on account of the haven the Oasis provides for a tiny slice of civilization in the middle of nowhere—civilization, in this case, being a questionable term. The house has no central air and heating, only a woodstove and cranky baseboard heating units. On frigid winter mornings when indoor temperatures dipped into the high forties, my Ukrainian housemate Kostya called it Little Siberia.

Far more mice than humans reside in the Oasis. One winter we trapped seventeen in a matter of weeks (though, admittedly, this pales in comparison to the thirty-five water snakes Ken and Greg removed from an old trailer on campus). Copperheads, five in all, found the garage an ideal habitat one summer. Adjacent to a ranger substation and the place backboards, inflatable rafts, and other emergency equipment are stored, the garage is not ours to use. Fine by me. The rangers can have it. Except that snakes do not recognize arbitrary human boundaries, as evidenced by the snakeskin discovered beneath the stove burners inside the Oasis—possibly a prank played by Steve or Jeff, neither of whom has ever confessed, but also a reasonably cozy spot to incubate eggs before giving birth if you are a snake.

The most rapacious organism inhabiting the house by far, however, is mold. So determined is it to return the Oasis to the wild, overtaking it inch by inch, there is hardly any object in the house it hasn't touched. The sign that was posted for a time on the front door—"House Protected Three Nights a Week by Man with Shotgun: You Guess the Night"—accomplishes nothing when it comes to mold. Eternal vigilance is the sole line of defense. Steve lived in a teepee out West one summer, where he discovered mushrooms sprouting from the curled pages of a paperback. Though fruiting bodies have yet to appear inside the Oasis, I've found mold growing in several unwelcome places:

Utensil drawer
Sinks
Toilets
Bathtub
Desk drawers
Footwear
Bedsheets
Various cupboards, doors, windows, floor mats, walls, etc.
Books
My skin

The dark spots I discovered on my abdomen one day—and which lingered for months—I learned were caused by a type of fungus afflicting people who live in very humid conditions. Clearly, the Oasis was leaving its mark on me. Some three thousand kinds of fungi are known to inhabit the Smokies, and biologists estimate thousands more likely do, making it at least possible that one or more undiscovered species dwells under our roof.

Aiding and abetting this situation is the house's location in the shadow of a north-facing mountainside. Erected at the bottommost point between two ridges, it greets sunrise several hours later and sunset several hours earlier than do dwellings outside the mountains. For weeks at a time in the dead of winter, sunlight never reaches parts of the tiny backyard. So damp are the surrounding woods, summer and winter, even rolling stones seem to gather moss. It is a place ripe for rot. When the living room carpet was peeled away for long-overdue replacement, maggots were discovered squirming in the cesspool that had collected there over the years.

Creepy crawlies, mice, and mold aren't the house's only unwanted guests. The Oasis, for a time, was believed to be haunted. Decades ago, a ranger's daughter spotted a little girl in a white dress through the living room window. In the years since then, several visitors who found themselves alone in the house at night reported independently of one another that they became so frightened without any apparent reason they burst into tears. Because mysterious occurrences beg explanations and each one of these visitors happened to be female, it was concluded that a ghost friendly only to men was the cause. (Elsewhere in the park, a female ghost is rumored to target men, single men especially, rangers included, taking special delight in making off with their car keys.) Perhaps this explains the good fortune of Kostya, who despite a fondness for eating raw bacon strip by strip like a king gorging on grapes, never fell ill. In any case, no one has heard from the ghost in a long time, and men and women alike have come and gone from the house for many years without incident. Given enough time, each human occupant of the Oasis grows accustomed to the high volume of intruders, whatever their kind, even warming to the house spiders spying from the corners of every room. And really, they might as well because they have no other choice.

Nature alone, however, can't be blamed for the Oasis undergoing its own kind of rewilding. Steve once turned the living room into a workshop for making a handmade bow, lathing away with his grandfather's old-fashioned woodworking tools until wood chips gave the room the appearance of an oversized hamster cage. It is Steve's proclivity as well to capture his own meat (outside the park), walk barefoot outdoors, sew his own footwear (for occasions when he must wear them), launder his clothes by hand, start fires without using matches, and bathe without using soap in the Middle Prong, the river that runs through the valley. Of average height and with a ready smile, he does not strike an imposing figure in most ways. Yet his grizzled appearance, replete with long brown hair and a beard reaching to his chest, prompts some visitors to regard him as a curious and somewhat intimidating throwback to a bygone era. More than anyone I know, he embodies the bedrock ideals of thrift and self-reliance. The "middlemen" in his daily economy appear far less often than they do in mine.

For Jeff, the house, such as it is, offers the sort of luxury he hadn't experienced for some time before moving in. Having spent more than a year living in a school bus while traveling the country in an expeditionary graduate program, he'd grown used to sleeping in a different place every few days. Upon moving into the Oasis, he rearranged the living room three times in as many weeks, presumably to replicate the changing scenery he was accustomed to viewing through a bus window and leaving Steve and me to guess where our recently itinerant housemate with his sandy blond hair and sharp wit would move the couch to next. At last, the unfolding of each season seemed to satisfy his craving for change, and the furniture stayed put.

For better or worse, Thoreau's romantic notion of eking out one's existence absent human company fails here. One supposes that the misanthrope, who famously omitted from *Walden* his frequent trips home where he benefited from his mother's cooking and laundry-washing, would not have abided cabinmates, let alone busloads of schoolchildren visiting his pond each week. If solitude and independence are part of the allure of living in a cabin in the woods, as they once were for me, the reality of "simple country living" is more complicated, especially in a national park. And anyway, rugged individualism has its limits. One needs neighbors, and mine happen to live under the same roof I do.

Absent from the Oasis are numerous conveniences that might otherwise keep us in good standing with purveyors of modern fashion and taste, including a television, computers, and telephone. By the time I arrived in the Smokies, too poor to own a computer, internet connectivity was widely available, including on the nature center campus up the road. The surrounding ridges render cell phones useless in the Oasis, however, further limiting the number of potential distractions. It never occurred to me to protest this state of affairs when I moved in. Call it Luddism by osmosis, accepted by all and enforced by no one.

Radio provides our sole means of connection to the outside world, though reception is spotty. We instead spend off-work hours listening to music, reading books, debating ideas, brewing beer, or discussing the probable lifespan, in months, of Steve's rusty pickup truck, the Millennium Falcon. If I am the first to retreat to my bedroom too many evenings in a row to read, Jeff will give me grief about spending so much time in my "Jer-a-torium," as he calls it, and understandably so since our communal life is less robust without each person's participation. On weekends when we're in the mood for a movie or eating out, we'll drive to town thirty minutes away. Such occasions often leave me feeling behind the times, like a country bumpkin come out of the hills. They remind me of what I'm missing while living in the boonies, though I soon find I don't really miss it much. By the time we head home and pass out of reach of town lights, plunging at last back into the comforting blackness of the nighttime forest, I start breathing easier.

Other nights we'll gather around the woodstove with our fellow educators and perhaps put Steve's grandfather's hand drills to use. One night we spent several hours burrowing a hole through the long end of an oak log for a cord to a tottering lamp we had rescued from the dust heap. Though an electric drill would have achieved the same result in ten minutes, efficiency was never the goal. I learned to keep such details to myself since whenever visiting students and adults inquired what we did for fun living in the park, it was enough to suffer their pity for thinking us certifiable for living without a telephone.

What living in the Oasis revealed to me was that absence and not necessity alone kindles invention. Life was fuller when distractions were fewer in number. Absence created space for attentiveness to my immediate surroundings, making it impossible to take the place where I lived for granted. If, or more likely when, technology's presence increased in my life, it would not be a wholly undesirable thing. But for now, I resisted it, preferring the drama I participated in every day over becoming a spectator to whatever was going on elsewhere in the world.

Occasional phone calls made to family and friends on the landline a mile and a half up the road remained a necessity. "I'd go crazy living there," a friend remarked when I described for him what living in the mountains was like. But what looked to him like deprivation I realized was a unique gift, and already I was beginning to think I would go crazy living anywhere else.

Before settling onto the couch tonight in an empty Oasis, I got a craving for a taste of civilization and drove out of the valley for the first time since last weekend. The park border isn't far from the Oasis, but the psychic distance is enormous, as I was reminded again today. Outside the park towering walls of green no longer eclipsed huge chunks of the sky, and the early curfew imposed by mountain shadow and tree shade to which I was accustomed gave way to ubiquitous daylight. Though it was a contrast I'd experienced plenty of times before, I found it startling. Sunsets are wonders never glimpsed from the Oasis's front porch, and when evening colors blossomed across the horizon, all but ignored by the stream of humanity going about its business on the road leading into town, I leaned forward in my seat, spellbound.

When I headed home the forest and river presented themselves as they always do whenever I've been absent, even for only a brief period. Arcing tree limbs formed a tunnel over the road, and the vines hanging from them resembled giant spidery fingers. Rolling down the window, I listened to the river sliding over rocks whose shapes looked as fluid as the current polishing them. Moisture seemed to cling to every air molecule, and everywhere there was the scent the river gives off in springtime, generous in its seductive powers as it filled my nostrils. My senses had more than they could handle and I was still only in my car.

Mountains that get up in your face is how one colleague who had a difficult time adjusting to the Smokies described them. Ansel Adams gave up trying to shoot them after making only three photographs, frustrated by his inability to back away a sufficient distance to gain perspective. The Appalachians are no place for a claustrophobe and might well give a Westerner accustomed to big skies and wide-open spaces the shivers. Yet neither are they the sort of mountains one fears. Instead, though it may be your first visit, you feel as if you've been here before. Hundreds or perhaps thousands of miles away from your point of origin, you feel as if you've come home.

That the ancient Greeks might have gazed upon mountains such as these in horror, as they're said to have done regarding their native ranges, is difficult to imagine once you're thick in the middle of them. Those same people found winter unnerving, according to historians. Ushering in darkness, winter for them portended doom. As for me, winter often passes by too quickly, and I've grown comfortable with the all-encompassing dark once night descends and erases every object from sight, whatever the season. It's springtime I can't quite get a handle on.

Leaf-out marks a pivotal time in the growing season, when buds that have been developing into leaves at last close the canopy overhead, shutting out much direct sunlight. In anticipation of this event, I have been keeping an eye on a maple tree behind the Oasis. The start of this week witnessed what was likely the final frost of the season, followed by several warm days—sure signs I failed to notice and which led me to believe I'd missed it. But I'd forgotten in my impatience how spring works: here but not here yet, here but still on the way. A pair of leaves on one twig had unfolded while another pair remained wrapped tight. The pattern was similar elsewhere on the tree. I was reminded that spring isn't like a baby swooshing into the light of day at a particular point on the calendar. It's more like a weekslong festival whose climax becomes apparent only once it has passed.

Dogwood trees pepper the woods at this time of year with their sparkling white flowers. In another week, their petals will brown and begin dropping off, fooling me into forgetting how very different they once appeared. But tonight is still the festival and tomorrow the white petals will be there.

My toad neighbor at this late hour has finally ceased his amorous melody-making. Perhaps he found what he was looking for. The ensuing silence feels like an invitation to make noise. Eager to make mischief but too comfortable to want to peel myself off the sofa, I feel like a bear on the verge of exiting its den and stretching its muscles. Stalked by whatever force is prowling the dew-heavy air, I make easy prey tonight. A breeze moves up the mountainside toward where the pines grow and bobcats sleep. When I turn off the lamp, the blackness is so deep that opening or closing my eyes makes no difference. Bedtime calls and I obey, entombing myself in perfect and companionable darkness.

Naming the World

NOT WHAT YOU WOULD CALL a morning person, I face a distinct challenge at the start of most workdays. Namely, striking up a conversation with the teacher or parent seated across from me at the breakfast table before either of us has consumed a sufficient amount of coffee. Making guests feel welcome is part of the job, and table talk serves an additional purpose by creating an opportunity for total strangers to connect, however awkwardly. Mountain hospitality has a long and storied history, and I like to think we uphold the practice at Tremont in our own peculiar way.

Students and adults alike dine at separate cafeteria-style tables. Once the meal begins, I search for an opening with Quinn, a father chaperoning his child's school trip, seated opposite me.

"How did the kids do last night?" I ask, trying out my standard opening line, which is code for: "How is your mental well-being after sleeping in a bunkroom with thirty rowdy boys?"

"After fifteen minutes they were out like a light," Quinn says, providing confirmation that if anything can wear out even the most indefatigable soul, it's a long full day in the woods.

And we're off and away. Talk becomes inevitable at some point inside the cramped dining hall where personal space is virtually nonexistent and elbow-bumping and inadvertent games of footsie with one's tablemates impossible to avoid. While perhaps not anyone's top choice for how to begin a day among strangers, it's satisfying nonetheless, this civilized family-style ritual of mutual dependency in which hungry strangers pass platters of biscuits and eggs back and forth, practicing how to be human again.

"So when does your internship end?" I am often asked at such times—a pardonable question given that the person asking it is doing their level best to hold up their end of a conversation at eight o'clock in the morning. They also likely spotted me setting tables before mealtime, unaware of the loose hierarchy at our center compared to other work settings, where performing such a task would out me as an underling. All the same, underlying such a question is an unmistakable assumption held by many adult guests, which is that mine isn't a "real" job. Lacking rigor in a conventional academic sense, the role of an environmental educator at first glance resembles that of a glorified camp counselor. It also looks fun, and real jobs aren't supposed to be fun.

"This happens to be my career choice," Jeff often says in response, adding that he holds a graduate degree in environmental education. When a father who was a NASA scientist once asked me when my "internship" was going to end, I resisted the temptation to tell him that finding life elsewhere in the galaxy sounded easy compared to convincing school administrators and elected officials to allow students to spend more class time outdoors looking for life on earth. "Actually, this is my full-time job," I said instead, as graciously as possible, an answer that produced, as it often does, awkward silence.

Another question I'm asked on occasion concerns my job title, officially "teacher-naturalist," the second part of which sometimes leads to confusion, largely because it is no longer a household term.

"Let me ask you something," another father, David, said to me on arrival day, his voice filled with distrust. "That word 'naturalist.' Now, what exactly do you all mean by that?"

Having cornered me in the lobby as we were departing the dining hall, he was standing in front of his eleven-year-old son as if to shield him from me. As I searched his face for clues about what was bothering him, I didn't think it likely that he'd mistaken us for *philosophical* naturalists, or secular humanists, many of whom subscribe to a creed that everything in existence is governed by purposeless mechanical forces explainable through scientific inquiry. Perhaps his concern was that we were "naturists" of a certain stripe intent on turning his child into a tree-hugging, sun-worshipping hippie. It then occurred to me that by "naturalist," he perhaps thought we meant "nudist." I decided it was better not to ask.

"A naturalist is someone who pays attention to nature and shares what they've learned from and about it with others," I replied, trying to set him at ease. "Your son will be one himself by the end of the week. You will too."

David relaxed and nodded his tentative approval before heading out the door, no longer worried, I hoped, about protecting his son from a bunch of raving naturalists.

A worthy question, of course, is why anyone would *want* to spend time studying nature. That is, why anyone would bother learning local natural history, which takes time and requires slowing down, contributes little toward one's future employment prospects, and seems pointless when information is available at the click of a button.

Until only a few generations ago, natural history was a well-known and respected field, and many people would have aspired to follow in the footsteps of William Bartram, John James Audubon, Florence Merriam Bailey, and many others. Reading the book of nature was considered as vital for understanding the world as reading actual books, and taxonomists were regarded as valuable members of the scientific community. Natural history's decline began around the end of the nineteenth century as people abandoned the countryside for cities. As leisure and consumerism replaced agrarian values, Creation came to be seen as merely the source of raw materials available for exploitation as well as providing a refuge for middle-class and upper-class urbanites. In the meantime, a new generation of scientists dismissed personal knowledge in favor of objective facts discovered solely through the scientific method under the guidance of highly trained specialists. The emotions and the inheritance of wisdom traditions lost their foothold as ways to understand the material world, and naturalists were rebranded by leading scientific thinkers of the day as amateurish nature lovers. Robert Michael Pyle has pointed out that when bomb making rather than taxonomic skills became necessary to win World War II and fight the Cold War, abstract subjects replaced natural history in many universities, sealing its fate. It might be said that a person knowledgeable about the workings of nature was no longer pictured as a net-wielding naturalist chasing butterflies but as a detached technician in a lab coat staring solemnly into a microscope.

I've come to think that modern science's rejection of personal knowledge acquired through the senses explains in part why I tuned out of every science class I was made to suffer through. Science seemed to have little to do with the actual world I inhabited outside the walls of my school, and for many years I believed it was a subject that wasn't in my nature to understand. So abstract were the concepts described in my earth science textbook *Matter, Matter Everywhere* that my study partner and I referred to it as *Splatter,*

Splatter Everywhere. I found the rote memorization required in high school biology so stultifying that I fell asleep during slide shows, including during one embarrassing instance when I was the one the teacher had put in charge of advancing the slides. History and social studies similarly demanded fact acquisition much more than they provided opportunities to wrestle with the material, but they at least offered narratives I could place myself within.

In hindsight, the chief source of my struggles as a student wasn't solely having to sit at a desk hour after hour, which, if nothing else, managed to teach me patience and self-discipline. Rather, I struggled because this was deemed the only authentic kind of educational experience imaginable. In time I would count classical methods of learning, such as lectures and close reading, among the most rewarding aspects of my education. Too often, however, to be a student was to be regarded as an empty container on an assembly line into which knowledge was poured measure by measure, and not even knowledge much of the time but mere information. Whatever was discussed in class, I assumed, was of utmost importance, even as I failed to understand why. And so I believed the inverse also to be true—that whatever was left undiscussed must be unimportant and unnecessary for becoming "successful" in life.

Save for my time at McKeever, the natural world ranked lowest among the "unimportant" subjects in my life as a student and remained an untapped source for discovery and uncorking my imagination, at least during school hours. The pattern took a similar course outside school. Like many others of my generation, I grew up knowing infinitely more about faraway events and the private lives of celebrities than I did the names of the blooms and birds inhabiting my backyard.

All of this changed when I arrived in the Smokies. Suddenly my backyard and workplace were one, and the plants and animals themselves were celebrities of a certain kind. For my students, natural history served as a starting point much of the time, rarely the final destination. It was a means of developing a more conscious way of noticing and peopling the world—with other living things besides just people. If they learned "sweetgum," a common tree on campus, and forgot it five minutes later, this was no loss. Chances were better that they would recall "prickly-seed tree" or whatever imaginative name they dreamed up for it. What mattered most was the personal bond they formed with the place, as well as skills of observation and investigation they acquired that they would carry through life.

The task ahead for me as a fledgling student of the woods, on the other hand, was more daunting. Not knowing the names of organisms that I crossed paths with every day meant not knowing my neighbors and feeling like an alien in my adopted home. Another reason for learning them was because my students included working adults and college students who expected not an expert exactly but someone with sufficient expertise to help guide them toward discovering the forest and its inhabitants on their own terms.

I had a lot of catching up to do, and the learning curve was steep. The science degrees nearly all of my colleagues possessed gave them a leg up in learning the park's flora and fauna, whereas I was starting almost from scratch. Even more intimidating was the fact that the Smokies were home to thirty-one species of salamanders, 130 species of trees, two hundred species of birds, and eighteen hundred species of flowering plants, along with an astounding variety of arachnids, beetles, and lichens. The natural world all of a sudden seemed like a library I'd been visiting all my life, only to discover I'd never gotten past the lobby.

Where to begin? Plants seemed like a good starting point. They were everywhere and didn't scurry off when I got near them.

I was bent over a familiar-looking plant one afternoon when a visiting botanist passed by. "Do you know what plant that is?" she asked. A retired university professor, she had probably posed this question to thousands of students over the years. Her old-school gruffness was refreshing yet set me on edge. I hadn't woken up that morning expecting a test. The plant had three leaves. *Leaves of three, let it be,* I recalled from my boyhood.

"Poison ivy?"

The botanist's eyebrows clenched into a disapproving V. "Over there's poison ivy," she said, pointing. "This one is hog peanut, so named because its tubers are edible. Notice the trailing hairless vine and the smooth margin of the leaf."

"I see what you mean. Thanks for showing me," I said, deciding not to give her further cause for doubting my intelligence by asking if the plant was so named because hogs ate it.

I found hog peanut everywhere after that day, as if it hadn't populated the woods until now. I was only noticing it where it had been living all along, of course, thanks to a new pair of goggles the botanist had given me to help me see it. What I needed were more such goggles so I could discover everything else hidden in plain view.

Before long came group work. I joined my coworkers on a fern walk, during which we searched for every fern species we could find. I didn't know anything about ferns. When someone began describing their parts, I wrote down in my journal, "Frond = leaf, kind of." I started a list by matching names to members of the oldest group of plants in the world, adding ebony spleenwort, maidenhair fern, and *Botrychium*. Some species bore names too elusive to pin down at first meeting. Walking fern, for instance, which never touches the ground, and hay-scented fern, which smelled like every other kind of fern to me. Group work was contagious, as one person, followed by another, spotted a fern and pointed out its attributes until we eventually arrived at a name.

Several people at one point began frantically waving their arms and slapping themselves. "Run!" yelled someone. Fleeing the swarm of yellow jackets whose nest we'd disturbed, we kept running until we reached the trailhead, where we inventoried our wounds. Enough ferns for one day, we all agreed. If learning about plants occurred most often through repetition and paying attention to details, it came about this other way, too, through full-contact nature study that exacted a toll on one's flesh.

I eventually gained enough confidence to join my coworkers in one of their favorite mealtime topics of conversation: who had noticed the first individual of any given species to appear in spring and where and when it had been spotted. A list hanging in the dining hall helped us keep track. Taken all together, it constituted the vital signs of the valley, the pulse of the place.

"Parula warblers are back," Ken would begin. "Heard one by the river this morning." Someone else would report seeing the first firefly of the year and speculate about why fireflies, which aren't flies, were not instead called "flash beetles." Then it was back to the parula warblers again: "Is it pronounced pa-RU-la, or PAIR-ula?" Odd fare for mealtime conversation, I thought at first, as I'm sure visitors overhearing our talk did too. While people elsewhere were discussing world events on their lunch break, we were exchanging news of the most local kind imaginable.

Anyone who knew anything about the natural world became a teacher. As time allowed, I acquired tree basics from Ken, geology fundamentals from Jeanie, tracking skills from Wanda and Steve, and forest ecology essentials from visiting forest ranger Edwin Dale. Like a biblical Adam scratching about my own little corner of paradise, I was slowly learning to attach names to the world around me. If the study of natural history had all but disappeared, save for in museums and a few corners of academia, it was alive and well at our center, where the veil that so often seemed to conceal the natural world in secret knowledge obtainable only by experts was lifted.

Setting out alone on weekends, armed with field guides and a journal, I went on a plant identification frenzy. For each plant that I committed to memory, a dozen more kept my pride in check. Soon enough a new season would usher in a fresh host of blooms, populating the woods and forest edges in various sizes, shapes, and colors. Inseparable from each plant's existence were the peculiarities of the place where I discovered it growing. In contrast to people who moved from one location to another, often heedless of the places where they lived and judging them according to arbitrary and changing standards, a plant's chances of survival were inextricably linked with the place where it took hold. Without the right conditions—soil composition, elevation, and position of the land in relation to the sun—a plant's ability to thrive was slim. Place was everything.

I learned Cherokee names for some plants, such as sochan or green-headed coneflower. Others I learned from students who had grown up in the region, including possum tongue or wood sorrel. Learning a plant's name was just the beginning. Wild plants raised questions about the forest communities they lived in as well as their cultural uses. Bloodroot, for instance, thrived in shade-loving cove forests and has traditionally been used by Cherokees as a dye, which led to further questions about colonization and the Trail of Tears and how, in William Faulkner's well-known phrase, the past is never dead because it isn't even past. The old saw that everything is connected was true. Each life-form was a piece of a giant puzzle that, among other things, exposed the myths of pure self-sufficiency and rugged individualism.

Fundamental to what I was doing was learning the art of observation. One thing became clear as I sharpened my skills, which was that a single lifetime wouldn't be long enough to master the plant life of the southern Appalachians. Yet I could also see that if I kept at it, someday I would reach a tipping point and be able to recognize the most common plants, which would become my familiars in an ever-growing lexicon. I would no longer feel like a newcomer able to speak only a handful of words in a foreign tongue. I would instead become something of a native myself.

All this time, I was acquiring knowledge with far more than just my brain. Each plant was there not just to be seen but also touched, smelled, and, in some cases, nibbled. It felt right in a way that much of my formal schooling never had, and I was confirmed in my suspicion that something had been missing all along from modern forms of education. As a slew of thinkers critical of modernity tell it, Enlightenment thought had overthrown a fuller understanding of what it means to know the world by reducing knowledge to what the mind alone could grasp, disconnected from embodied creatureliness. An inheritor of this centuries-long line of reductionistic thinking, I was now experiencing what it was like to learn with my entire being, senses and all. The old magic, half asleep since my childhood, was waking up and back at work once more.

Other living things besides plants became objects of fascination and sometimes paid the price for my education. While splitting firewood at the Oasis one afternoon, I noticed numerous vertical tunnels of dirt caked onto the vinyl siding of the house. I'd heard about mud daubers, a type of wasp whose temper was not easily aroused and which fashioned its nest in an organ pipe pattern. What I didn't yet know was that mud daubers further the continuation of their species by preying on spiders and injecting them with a neurotoxin that keeps them alive in a state of paralysis until springtime, when wasp larvae hatch and find a military-style MRE waiting for them. Using a stick, I broke one wasp home apart. A pair of yellow larvae and several catatonic spiders spilled out. I recalled what a visiting teacher had uttered to his students in class one day while we were observing one insect eat another: "You're looking at nature at its finest." While staring at the gooey mess, however, I identified more with a student who'd declared, "Nature is gross."

"The Bad Naturalist Strikes Again" provided the heading for the journal entry I made that night. I wasn't bad exactly, just ignorant about many things, and now more aware than before of the difficulty of applying the physician's motto of "first, do no harm" to the natural world while making my observations.

As spring got rolling, I decided I needed a project to advance my training as a naturalist. Following a life-form from birth to death over the course of the growing season seemed like a worthwhile challenge. Rather than choosing a single organism as my subject, I settled on four trees living behind the Oasis. Once a week, at minimum, I would keep watch over a cluster of buds on each tree and study their progress.

With the eagerness of a rookie reporter on his first day on the beat, I made my initial journal entry in early April. The leaves on the sweetgum tree I'd chosen among my foursome were just beginning to open, and those on the chestnut oak appeared toy-like and felt like suede to the touch. The curled-up leaves on the red maple sapling looked like a baby's fingers wrapped around an adult's, while those on the ironwood remained cocooned inside its bud. *Still a fetus by all measures*, I wrote, noting its length and width.

Two days later, I paid another visit. *Little change*, I added, impatient for something to happen.

Plenty else was to happen over the next several weeks, during which I made just one journal entry, already neglecting my duties. Several hard frosts descended over the valley, kicking it temporarily back into winter. A pair of violent thunderstorms slashed at the just-waking forest soon afterward, and then bigger news came: Greg and Rebecca's baby had arrived. Three months early.

The previous fall, just a matter of weeks after tying the knot, the couple was shocked to learn they were expecting. It was a difficult pregnancy, and near the end of her second trimester, Rebecca was admitted to the hospital, where doctors informed her that around-the-clock bedrest would be necessary until the baby came. That same afternoon while nurses evaluated Rebecca upstairs, Ken and I sat with Greg in the hospital dining area, trying to absorb the difficult news. Greg's pager suddenly lit up. A little unbelieving, we rushed upstairs to find nurses wheeling Rebecca into the delivery room. Forget weeks or months of waiting—the birth was happening now. Her premature baby boy, born minutes later and weighing less than two pounds, was rushed into the neonatal intensive care unit. A highly optimistic prognosis put the baby's chances for survival at 50 percent.

"Don't get too attached," a doctor advised the couple. As if that were humanly possible.

Nervous for my friends and feeling powerless to help them, I distracted myself by resuming my leaf study. The ironwood leaf, now doubled in length from base to tip, was thriving. The sweetgum leaf looked malnourished and deformed, and its potential for reaching maturity seemed doubtful. The red maple leaf was no better. As for the oak leaf, a caterpillar had lunched on it, leaving tears and holes where new growth had barely begun. Writing in my journal, I lamented how much I'd missed since my last entry, trying not to draw all too obvious comparisons between the damaged young leaves and the newborn struggling for his life in an incubator twenty miles away.

Greg and Rebecca relocated to Knoxville to live in a Ronald McDonald House closer to the hospital, where they made daily visits to see their son. I busied myself with learning plant names and watching my leaves grow, feeling at times as if I were a doctor making his rounds. By mid-June, caterpillars had devoured the ironwood leaf, and red spots were showing on the sweetgum and maple leaves. The chestnut oak leaf alone seemed no worse off than before, perhaps even a little improved.

In my quest to learn the names of living beings inhabiting the planet, I added one more: baby Jonah, whose parents had yet to hold him in their arms. Visitors were finally permitted entry into the neonatal ward at the University of Tennessee Medical Center, and I got to see him for the first time, peering into the contraption that contained him like a miniature whale in a terrarium. Lacking even an ounce of the fat one expects to find on a newborn, he looked like a wizened, miniature old man.

Soon enough, however, whatever parallel paths existed between my leaves and the baby lying in the preemie unit were about to diverge. Growth was a thing of the past for many of my leaves, while it still remained possible for Jonah. In physical appearance, it was as if he were aging in reverse and needed only time to slip into his newbornness before growing into a child. Many more weeks spent lying in the incubator would be necessary before there was any chance of his coming home. Antibodies needed to be secured in his system, girth added, and warmth conserved. Yet the period of risk and danger was nearing an end, and his prospects for surviving the ordeal were looking better every day.

Relieved at this turn of events and unburdened from incessant worry, I returned to my leaf watch and found my attention span stretched to its limits. Scrounging for fresh observations, I was reminded first of a guitar and then a woman when describing in my journal the undulating shape on the margin of one leaf. Fresh details, including others of a ridiculously cosmetic variety, otherwise seemed to have dried up. A long wait through the summer months lay ahead and promised little action. All there seemed left to do was watch and wonder what would become of each leaf. When I wasn't letting weeks slip by between visits, I found myself regarding each new hole or tear as a threat to the entire tree's well-being. I was a deadbeat dad and an overprotective mother all in one.

Jonah was at last brought home from the hospital at the end of summer, becoming the youngest human inhabitant of the national park. I read up on the life cycle of leaves as fall got underway. Chlorophyll was taking flight everywhere in the forest, replaced by scarlet anthocyanins and yellow-and-orange carotenoids coveted by leaf lookers, who flocked to the mountains to see them. My leaves, too, began turning color.

The red maple leaf fell in mid-October, followed by the sweetgum several weeks later. By the time the chestnut oak leaf dropped to the ground, I realized how lost in the details I'd become, missing not only the forest for the trees but the trees themselves, save for a few of their leaves. I hadn't given a thought to each tree's trunk, crown, and root system. Whatever intricate web of relationships existed between soil, fungi, insects, and neighboring trees were mysteries I hadn't even considered. But I wasn't ready for all of this yet. I first needed to indulge myself in the simplicity of lowly leaf watching, along with a little anthropomorphizing, before I was ready for more.

A single leaf mattered to my trees probably as much as a single strand of hair did to a dog. And yet, for me, a leaf ranked among a tree's most human-like parts, providing it with a voice in the way that it signaled changes going on throughout the growing season. After seven-and-a-half months, all four voices I'd been listening to fell silent, and within weeks the boot prints marking the route I'd made from tree to tree began to fade.

The time I spent studying tree leaves wasn't a thrilling experience by any measure. It did not provide any meaningful data for science or produce insights into the laws of the universe other than to confirm them. What it granted me instead was the opportunity to see something taking place in the world that would have otherwise escaped my notice. An ordinary thing that will be seen again and again for as long as there are trees and people to observe them, and observe themselves while looking, never through the same eyes as anyone else.

As Jonah continued to grow, so did my knowledge of plants, one species at a time. I might have dispensed with memorization since I could have looked them up any time it seemed necessary. And yet adding the name of a fern or flower to my vocabulary was like keeping a light from going out in the world, each one expanding my field of vision and sparking more curiosity about what else there was to discover.

And my observations accomplished something more. Not since I was a boy had I felt so attached and paid such close attention to a place over an extended period of time. As a result, whatever sense of alienation still lingered from the years I'd spent fearing for my future and the fate of the world lost another foothold. I was now more acquainted with a single, small patch of earth than anyone else alive. Having laid claim to it through a habit of tedious and often flawed devotion, I belonged to it now. Like the club mosses and bryophytes I had yet to acquaint myself with, I counted myself a fellow member. We were connected.

To be a naturalist as well as a teacher meant being an active observer of the natural world among a community of fellow teachers and learners. Natural history was an invitation to integrate the knowledge acquired from a wide range of subjects rather than to approach each one as if it were a specialized category disconnected from the rest. Learning a plant often meant entertaining questions reliant on the social sciences and humanities, which helped me assemble a generalist's knowledge base as I continued to piece together reality.

Despite my best efforts, however, I often felt like a fraud when referring to myself as a "naturalist," knowing that my nascent abilities couldn't hold a candle to those of André Michaux or Asa Gray, two eminent naturalists of the eighteenth and nineteenth centuries respectively; nor my aunt Carole, who had mastered the butterflies of coastal Alaska and documented a species of butterfly previously unknown to live in the state; nor even average Victorian-era citizens shuffling about their flower garden. By comparison, calling myself a naturalist felt like claiming the mantle of a college graduate when I was barely out of kindergarten.

Every so often I would confess my lack of confidence to my supervisor Amber, herself a skilled birder and botanist. Halfway through each pity party, she would shake her head and wave a hand, telling me in so many words to shut up, for while I still struggled to commit more than a handful of Latin names to memory, it was the looking that counted.

One Latin term I would have no trouble remembering was *amator*, the root word for amateur, which means "lover." Forget mastery. Forget trying to catch up with my colleagues. There would always be a bloom I didn't know existed and another that was still being born, just as the world, despite rumors of its imminent collapse, was being born. Henceforth every hour of forest time would be amateur hour for lovers only. Ignorance was going to be bliss.

Meeting the Neighbors

LATE ON A SUNDAY NIGHT in August, having finished my monthly phone calls to friends and family members, I step outside the empty office building and realize my mistake. It was daytime when I came to campus hours ago, but nighttime in the mountains is cave-dark and I left my flashlight at home. Further complicating matters is the fact that the Oasis resides a mile and a half away, and my means of transportation tonight is a bicycle.

Calling to ask for a ride isn't an option: the Oasis has no phone. I consider begging for one from coworkers who live in staff quarters several hundred yards away until the thought of stepping on a snake warming itself on the pavement (as they often do this time of year) crosses my mind. So does the old adage "Make do or do without." And so, recalling also that John Wesley Powell paddled the Colorado River with just one arm, I figure navigating the road in the pitch dark can't be that difficult.

Moonlight points the way forward at first, painting the river in silver. As soon as I pedal across the bridge and enter tree cover, however, I can't see a thing. Every inch of the blacktop vibrates up through my handlebars, forcing me to tighten my grip and hope I don't hit a pothole. Despite having bicycled the road countless times, I've found its curves, which nudge frighteningly close to the riverbank in many places, too numerous to commit to memory, and when I picture myself running headlong into a tree or plunging into rocky waters, I brake to a stop. Time for Plan B.

Plan B, though, is no better since it would mean fighting gravity on my way back up the road to campus. Besides, the longer I weigh my options, the stronger my night vision grows. The outlines of trees gradually become visible as their trunks turn a lighter shade of black. The moon, hidden low in the sky, helps further by illuminating more trees farther downstream.

I decide to keep going and cautiously release my brake while straining not to lose my balance. Envying bats and their handy adaptation of using echolocation to avoid bumping into objects, I resort to singing songs to ward off anything lurking in my path. "Happy trails to you," I sing, a bicycling cowboy now, as the forest rushes by. Gaining confidence, I release the brake and coast at a faster pace. The combined darkness and smooth surface of the road before long make me feel as if I'm a bird floating in the air. The sensation is so exhilarating I wonder why I haven't tried this before.

I'm more than halfway home when I come around a bend and make out an object directly in my path. It is only by sheer luck that moonlight angles over the treetops and brightens the blacktop in this spot, thus rendering guesswork unnecessary about what the object is and what I must do. Squeezing my brakes hard, I come to a stop in the middle of the road, narrowly avoiding running smack into the hindquarters of a creature that is furry, round, and at least three times my size.

Outside the Oasis lives a family of five-lined skinks, a species of lizard that sports a sky-blue tail as a juvenile and likes to dart up and down the vinyl siding of the house in warm weather. Owls, tree frogs, and deer, including a young doe Jeff affectionately calls Nora, dwell close by as well. Holed up inside the house are, of course, numerous four- and six- and eight-legged creatures; I have likewise taken to calling these my neighbors, which isn't as bighearted as it may sound. They were here first, after all, and they are everywhere.

The American black bear (*Ursus americanus*) also numbers among the neighbors I meet in Walker Valley. I had been delighted to spot a yearling through the van window on my first day of work; several weeks later I had my first solo encounter with a bear. While hiking over the weekend, I stepped off the trail to explore an appealing stand of large trees and heard the sound of tiny objects tumbling through the leaves overhead. Curious about what was making the sound, I followed it to the base of a tall oak, where I found dozens of broken acorn shells littering the ground. Looking up, I saw a bear balancing on the highest branches of the tree. Just when I raised my camera to my eyes, it spotted me.

Rule number one, say the experts: do not run from a bear under any circumstance. But if you are a new resident of the mountains and see a bear aiming right for you as it shimmies down a tree, tens of feet of the trunk at a time passing through its paws, as if it were a firefighter sliding down a firehouse pole, with nothing but vertical space separating you from it, expert advice is your last concern. And so run is what I did, for dear life, stopping only once I realized the bear wasn't pursuing me but fleeing in the opposite direction. The next moment it dawned on me how badly I'd lost track of time—and here a pattern emerges. For just like on the night a year later when I came close to plowing into a bear on my bicycle, I'd forgotten to bring a flashlight and completed my journey home in the dark while carefully toeing my way down the mountain.

Wondering if I'd only gotten lucky, I began reading up on a suddenly relevant topic: the likelihood of death by a bear or other large predator. According to the best sources I could find, chances were extremely remote. Black bears had killed fewer than seventy people in North America between the start of the twentieth century and 1990, mostly in Alaska and Canada. Cougars had killed fewer than thirty people in the US, all of them out West, while wolves in the lower forty-eight states had killed no one. In stark contrast, domestic dogs killed thirty people each year in the US on average, murders numbered around sixteen thousand, and fatalities from automobile accidents totaled between thirty and forty thousand. Tellingly, at least thirty-seven deaths were from misadventures involving vending machines. Human-caused threats, in other words, far outnumbered any posed by wildlife. Another dark irony was that white-tailed deer contributed to around 130 annual human deaths every year in automobile collisions. Statistically speaking, cleansing landscapes of large predators such as cougars and wolves, which might otherwise have kept deer populations in check, had made people *less* safe.

As time went by and my contact with bears increased in frequency, so did my level of comfort with being in their presence. I would even lend a hand to those in need of assistance, once helping to carry an orphaned bear, tranquilized and lying on a stretcher, to a van that would transport it from a rehabilitation center back to the wild. I would keep watch over a dying bear addled by disease as it lay sprawled on a popular hiking trail until rangers arrived to euthanize it. And I would assist a ranger in hauling a bear out of the river where it had drowned after being struck by a motorist. As for more ordinary encounters with healthy bears, I quickly lost count.

Getting along in bear country required a heightened sense of awareness for keeping both people and bears out of harm's way. "*Our* territory," said a ranger during a meeting I attended for park staff about how to minimize interactions between bears and people. Showing us a map like a field marshal might during truce negotiations, he pointed to a campground and picnic area where tourists risked attracting bears if they left food sitting out. "*Their* territory," he said, sweeping his hand across the green areas representing the vast acreage of woods and fields covering the rest of the map. It struck me while listening to him talk what a generous act the presence of the national park accomplished by ceding dominion and relinquishing sovereignty over space people would have otherwise occupied and perhaps altered beyond recognition. This was no truce, I thought, it was a strategic retreat producing the kinds of benefits that were possible only when human will and the urge toward conquest were restrained. Absent destruction of a landscape that both wildlife and humans depended on, the park was instead a living laboratory in which creatures could flourish and humans could learn from its example.

Living in the middle of the Other's territory rendered meaningless the dubious aphorism "fences make good neighbors." My territory, if it could be called that, was barely contained within four walls and ended the second I stepped outside the Oasis. However long I might live in the park, I would have to give up most privileges private landowners possessed. It certainly meant forgoing extreme measures of the sort exercised by my supervisor Amber's grandmother. As she tells it, her grandmother resorted to firing a shotgun into a tree to silence a mockingbird singing merrily into the wee hours outside her bedroom window night after night. When that failed to quiet the bird, her grandmother cut down the tree.

Grin and bear it, a manual might instead instruct newcomers to the mountains, if one existed. Don't bully or pick fights. Play nice and try to fit in. You're still the alpha predator, and everything else knows it.

Though I would add: not quite everything does.

As I'm straddling my bicycle mere yards away from the largest black bear I had yet laid eyes on, I realize it hasn't yet noticed me. King of the road, his ample posterior awash with moonlight, he just keeps lumbering down the double centerline without a worry in the world. When he finally does register my presence, he quickens his pace and slips into the shadows.

Just what I am supposed to do now isn't at all clear. Resort to Plan C? Which would be what exactly? I try to think of what I would do if I was a bear and a madman on a bicycle disrupted my nocturnal peregrinations. Probably turn him into a snack. Soon, however, it's clear the bear is as twitchy as I am and has no plans of biting off my head because I next hear the snapping of twigs, which tells me he has abandoned the road.

Too close to home to want to turn back now, I take a deep breath and pedal hard past the stand of trees the bear entered. I ditch my bike once I reach the Oasis and jump into my car. Upon arriving at the scene of my near accident, I pan my headlights through the woods while making a three-point turn. Crafty bear—there's no sign of him. Yet when I drive a quarter mile back down the road, there he is again, sauntering down the centerline like before. He looks even bigger in the beam of my headlights, his haunches rippling with each ponderous stride. Wildlife rangers tell me they subtract between fifty and one hundred pounds whenever they receive reports of bear sightings from park visitors, so overblown are the weight estimates. Even so, I'd wager the bear weighs more than four hundred pounds. What's clear is that my bicycle and I would be a mangled mess right now if not for blessed moonlight and good timing.

I lay on the car horn, but the bear doesn't take notice or seem to care as he plods along. No amount of honking gets him to move out of harm's way until I climb out and begin yelling. The sound of a human voice delivering a good berating does the trick. The bear gives up the road at last and climbs a steep bank into the woods, glancing back at me once with a pouting look. I head home once again, satisfied to know that anyone else who is foolish enough to bicycle down the road tonight without a light won't meet with a surprise, and hope it is the last I'll see of him.

A bear cub weighs barely a pound when it is born. During its first weeks of life, spent in shaggy darkness with its mother, it will gain several more while nursing. Its first steps are a vertical ascent inside a standing hollow tree its mother has overwintered in—a birth canal of another sort once they both exit it in March. Next comes blinding daylight and a harrowing descent into the world below.

The mother will not have eaten in months, and in order to expel the fecal plug lodged at the end of her large intestine, she will consume what little vegetation is available in early spring. Opportunists by nature, she and her cub will prey little and forage much over the course of the growing season, filling 90 percent of their diet with berries, plants, insects, and nuts. Carrion makes up the rest unless an old or weak deer presents an easy target. The bond will last until the following summer, when the mother will chase off her yearling cub and mate again.

Never come between a mother bear and her young, warn the guidebooks. However, I did just this once while wading through a waist-high thicket of blueberry bushes. A sharp *whoof* sounded from somewhere out of sight as a bear cub appeared and scrambled past me up the wooded slope. According to popular notions, the mother ought to have come charging out of the trees like a hot-tempered Marine, but that isn't what happened. At first, what happened was nothing. The mother still wasn't visible, so trying to get a better view of the woods, I climbed onto a partially fallen tree jutting from the hypotenuse of the mountainside.

A mother black bear separated from her young, it turns out, does not roar. She does not bark or hiss or hunch her shoulders, hairs standing on end, even with her offspring in mortal danger. At least this one did not. When she came into view, she walked slowly toward me, avoiding eye contact while chomping the air in a manner that seemed almost comical. It was not a Hollywood-bear moment, even if the message she was sending was clear: it was time for me to leave.

Bear attacks, while rare, have taken place in the park, resulting in just two fatalities—a remarkable statistic given skyrocketing human visitation and a population density of two bears per square mile. Bears have swelled in number over the past several decades. While the era of tourists feeding bears through car windows is long over, thanks to public campaigns and stricter law enforcement, managing bears foremost means managing people and relying on them to make good decisions. They don't always.

One summer, when my sister and I were teenagers, we returned from two weeks at camp to discover a margarine container with holes in the lid sitting inside the refrigerator. The holes looked like teeth marks.

"That's a long story," said our mother when we asked her why there were holes in the lid of the margarine container. We were all ears. While my sister and I were away, she had gone camping in a state park with our father, who had wedged their cooler beneath a picnic table bench for the night, thinking that was enough to secure it. Hours later, a commotion outside their tent woke them. Unzipping the door, they looked out and saw a black bear making off with the cooler and a week's worth of groceries it contained. This bear was no rookie. It had already sampled the cooler's contents after undoing the latch and was now dragging it away with one paw curled nimbly inside one of the handles.

"Bob, do something. He's getting our food!" yelled our mother at our father. Tasked with convincing the bear to give up the thing it wanted most at that late hour, our father stepped outside the tent armed with only a flashlight. Waving it around accomplished nothing, so he shouted at the bear. Now he had its attention but wasn't sure what to do next. Then he thought to turn the beam of light onto his own face, at which point the bear immediately abandoned its spoils and fled. The cooler spent the rest of the night in the car, while our father afterward was left to wonder about his purported good looks, considering how easily his face had scared away the bear.

Our mother inspected the cooler in the morning and discovered only a single item had been molested. Her sense of frugality ran deep from having been brought up by a mother who had lived through the Great Depression and raised three daughters as a widow and on a country teacher's salary while living in a one-bedroom apartment. Thus, back into the cooler, and eventually the refrigerator, went the margarine container.

"I'm not eating from that," my sister announced when the story was over.

"Don't be so sensitive," replied our mother. "Besides, you already have. I put some on the sandwich you just ate."

A bear that enters a campground or picnic area in the Smokies and becomes habituated to human food may have to be captured and relocated. A last resort, it is hoped the disorienting experience of being trucked several counties away and facing other bears whose territory it has unwittingly invaded will discourage further such behavior. Sometimes the bear will find its way home, as one did after having been moved over a hundred miles away. If it has learned nothing and resumes old habits, it is put down.

I crossed paths with one particular bear so often during my first autumn in the mountains, recognizing her by her small size and shy temperament, I gave her a name. *Matilda* was the result of my having confused two songs Greg often sang: the well-known Australian ballad "Waltzing Matilda," which had nothing to do with bears, and "Waltzing with Bears," which did. It was unclear at first whether Matilda was a male or female, so I showed her to Edwin Dale, a backcountry US Forest Service ranger and former reproductive physiologist. Convinced that Matilda was a female, he pointed out how closely she stuck by her food source, a stand of white oaks where I often found her foraging, which suggested that she was pregnant.

A female bear's reproductive cycle involves an adaptation called delayed implantation, whereby a fertilized egg will multiply into a few hundred thousand cells before floating around the uterus in a suspended state. If a mated female gains sufficient weight by wintertime, the cells will attach to her uterine wall, but if food is scarce, her body will abort the fetus. A balance is struck in this way between the food supply and the bear population.

The number of black bears living in the southern Appalachians provides one measure of how well forests in the Smokies have recovered since the end of the logging era in the early twentieth century. Once on the verge of becoming extinct throughout the region because of deforestation, bears have rebounded with such success that by the early 1990s, they reached carrying capacity, or the maximum sustainable population size given available food and space. Wildlife biologists correlate this phenomenon with the maturation of oak forests. Acorns are high in carbohydrates, which turn into fat, and the year I got to know Matilda, there was a bumper crop of hard mast, supplying bears with more acorns than they could eat. One bear shot by a hunter outside the park weighed six hundred pounds and had a layer of fat five inches thick.

Our first few meetings could best be described as awkward. Too curious to make myself scarce, I'd watch Matilda as someone who lacks social graces does, not knowing when he has overstayed his welcome. Growing tired of my presence eventually, she would turn coyly away and shuffle off. But over time, she grew to tolerate me long enough that I could show her to coworkers and students.

The last time I saw her, she was busy as ever devouring acorns in preparation for winter. Bears eat 9 percent of their body weight each day on average in the fall. Accordingly, a bear weighing 150 pounds (roughly Matilda's weight) would need to consume the equivalent of fifty-four McDonald's Quarter Pounders each day. Were any creature able to survive on such a diet, bears arguably could, considering their hardy physique. Susceptible to few diseases, bears are also capable of healing quickly from injuries. One that suffered a broken femur when it was struck by an automobile near my hometown in Pennsylvania was walking again two weeks later. Once she entered her den, Matilda would not eat or drink all winter, and her body temperature would decrease to forty-five degrees. Burning up to four thousand calories a day while lying for months in a contorted position inside a hollow tree, giving birth, and then nursing her cub for a month or two more, she would lose up to 30 percent of her body weight. So this was important work she was doing by putting on weight. Her life, and her cub's, depended on it.

Which perhaps explains her reasons for doing what she did next: she charged me. Giving me fair warning, she first stamped the ground with her paw, her courteous way of signaling that I was in her space even at a distance of sixty feet and would I please leave. I didn't, not understanding at first what she was trying to tell me. Then she abruptly bounded straight toward me with her head down. She stopped after going several feet. I stood my ground and looked away. Matilda did the same. Had I wanted to tempt fate and test her patience further, she might have charged me again, coming closer but engaging in physical contact only as a last resort. To my surprise, she was the first to depart. Before doing so, however, she aimed her hindquarters in my direction—perhaps as a gesture of what she thought of me—and emptied her bowels.

The following spring Greg said he wanted to show me something he'd found in the woods. We scrambled up exposed bedrock on a knife-sharp ridge choked with greenbrier until we reached a level patch of earth no larger than a child's bedroom. A natural balcony surrounded by steep drop-offs on three sides offered a view of the forest below. It seemed the very picture of security. In the middle of it was what looked like a giant bird's nest made out of evergreen branches a male bear had torn from nearby saplings before settling in to spend the winter on open ground. The bear who'd made it was possibly Matilda's mate.

Though I never knowingly laid eyes on Matilda again, a researcher informed me years later that a nineteen-year-old black bear was living with her two cubs on the mountain just across the river. If it was Matilda, she'd managed to exceed the life expectancy of female black bears living in the wild by more than half a dozen years.

I dreamed one night I was a bear. My cub siblings and I were following our mother along the riverbank as motorists slowed down to point at us and stare. We moved fast and passed by our father, who sat beneath a tree teaching our youngest brother about the finer points of bear life. I felt strong and full of vigor in my dream, a sensation that brimmed inside me when I woke and lasted all day.

I visited friends in Asheville the following weekend and returned home by way of a curve-bedeviled stretch of Interstate 40, where the Pigeon River jags through the mountains. It was nighttime, and I watched in horror as a black bear stepped out of the darkness into the beams of an oncoming minivan several car lengths ahead of me and darted across the westbound lane. The bear pressed up against the concrete wall dividing the highway as the minivan driver and I blew past, neither of us having time to brake. "Go, go, go!" I screamed as if I were a sergeant barking orders to a fellow soldier while under enemy fire. I pulled onto the shoulder and shifted into reverse, scanning the road for signs of a dead or injured bear, though from what I could tell it had managed to scale the median blocking its path and get away.

Red wolves, rather than populating my dreams, sometimes woke me from them. Nearly driven to extinction throughout their home range in the Southeast a century ago, an experimental reintroduction program in the park made us neighbors for a time, and, day or night, I often heard one howling in the valley. Red wolf #538M was the largest wolf in the Smokies, weighing seventy-five pounds. During the monthlong period that the wolf took up residence in the woods behind the Oasis, the squeaky brakes on Jeff's pickup truck would sometimes set him howling.

I spotted the wolf in broad daylight once while returning home from work. A ball of fur dashed in front of my car just before I reached the driveway. Braking to a stop, I watched as he lingered at the edge of the woods. We studied one another for half a minute—a blip in the millennia of shared history binding together humans and canines in a complex web of relationships—before he loped away. I followed him on foot, searching for tracks or scat but could find nothing. It was as if he'd never been there. An hour later, Jeff spotted him through the living room window carrying in his mouth what looked like the leg of a wild hog.

Several weeks later, I was jolted awake in the middle of the night by a noise outside my bedroom window. Sitting up in bed, I listened as the wolf howled in the night, joined by a barred owl and caterwauling bobcat. The forest seemed united in ecstatic polyphony as their voices rose and fell in unison. The sound reverberated around my bedroom—a concert, it seemed, composed by the wild, for the wild, in the wild. Was this what the forest sounded like every night while I was lost in dreamland? Steve and Jeff the next morning said they hadn't heard a thing.

I accompanied a biologist on several occasions to inspect the leg traps he'd set for the wolf in hopes of evaluating its health. The wolf was too smart ever to get caught. We'd find paw prints around the spot where the device lay buried beneath the soil and the bait the biologist had placed gone. Or we'd find that another animal had sprung the trap, including once an opossum that was playing—well, possum—its mouth agape and long rows of teeth showing.

The experimental reintroduction program for the red wolf—the most endangered wolf species in the world—was cancelled the following year. Every litter born in the park died from parvovirus before biologists could locate and inoculate the pups to give them a fighting chance, and although the public was overwhelmingly in favor of the program, human generosity was in too short supply when it came to space. Despite its size, the national park wasn't large enough to support a small mammal population sufficient in density to sustain the wolves, which by nature do not recognize human boundaries. The wolves established home ranges well beyond the park's borders, where development was rampant. The wolves were recaptured and relocated to coastal North Carolina, their absence once more diminishing biodiversity in the Smokies and depriving the ecosystem of one of its top predators.

There were those neighbors too who, if they entered my dreams, did so in a nightmarish manner. Timber rattlesnakes populated Walker Valley, and though menacing in appearance, they were also beautiful. I visited a den where they lived year-round every so often, comforted by the knowledge that their docile behavior and reluctance to squander venom on something too large to eat diminished the chances that the worst would happen.

I offered to show the snakes to a group of visiting amateur photographers during a workshop conducted at the nature center. "Where do we go now?" several of them asked after I'd shuttled them to a photo shoot. Within plain sight of us was a pair of streams rushing through a forest paradise gilded with autumn colors, but they seemed to want something more. I thought of that morning's photo shoot in a meadow. Deer were grazing there, and the photographers did what photographers everywhere do, and what I'd done myself plenty of times: use a zoom lens to erase distance and make creatures that rely on space for survival to appear closer than they actually were. A contrived intimacy with wildness was better than none at all, but even better, I figured, would be an authentic close-up, in which case, showing the photographers the rattler den made perfect sense in my mind. I assured them that despite the absence of safety glass between us and our fanged subjects, I'd never once seen the snakes act defensively.

"They just lie there like sunbathers on a beach," I said. Judging by the looks on their faces, however, I might as well have suggested we go skydiving without parachutes. They began setting up their tripods close by the parking lot and didn't ask me for any more advice for the rest of the weekend. A visit with the neighbors was all I'd had in mind, though I'd clearly asked too much of the photographers. The snakes were my neighbors, not theirs, and it occurred to me how much my boundaries had begun to loosen and how comfortable I'd become with ambiguous borders.

The notion of extending hospitality to wild creatures, including potentially dangerous ones, had never occurred to me before moving to the Smokies. Indeed, I was in many ways *their* guest, not the other way around. And yet even within the constraints by which I abided in "my" territory, I still faced choices.

Paper wasps took up residence on the porch one spring, building their nest on the ceiling directly above the front door. On the day I discovered them, dozens of wasps stared down at me, inches from my face, and I braced for an attack that never came. The next day, still no attack, so I let them be. As weeks went by, I worried they might alarm guests, but no one ever noticed. It was a solitary gesture, letting the wasps live, and though they never threatened a soul, I wondered if my sense of hospitality had gone too far. If I kept on like this, would someone pay the price for my generosity come autumn when the wasps were likely to turn defensive and mean? I never found out, for the colony shoved off by midsummer and never returned.

I wondered how many other creatures had escaped my notice in my daily comings and goings and how often they took me as a threat. The traces they left behind in the form of tracks and scat piles proved they were all around, so why did we not cross paths more often? Why so little contact between us? To the coyote and the river otter and the bobcat I heard but never saw, I wanted to say: "Come let us break bread together and pass the cup, for I am full of goodwill." But they knew the real score and that I and my kind didn't really mean this. Those treaties were broken long ago, and a scrim has separated us ever since.

Hypocrisy lies at the heart of much of human diplomacy with wildlife. Occupying or obliterating habitat while refusing to share territory except perhaps with those species that are less troublesome, we come to revere the very creatures we've run out of our private kingdoms and confined to zoos, parks, or extinction. Robbing ourselves of ordinary encounters, we come to expect extraordinary ones and make much of them—the deer meeting our gaze, the hawk staring right through us—perhaps out of a need hidden deep in our subconscious to be reminded of what we've lost. Yet such encounters also provide us, if not an opportunity to restore and extend hospitality, then

Meeting the Neighbors

at least a fleeting moment when we find the distance between us and the Other erased. It can feel like grace.

At times, however, it can feel like something quite different.

After encountering the bear in the road late on that eventful summer night, I return home once more to find Jeff and Steve gone. Indoors, I go to my room and turn on my desk lamp, which feels more calming than acting like a fraidy cat and flipping on every switch in the house. With adrenaline still pumping through my veins and no one around to share what has just happened, I open my journal and begin a new entry: *A few seconds ago, I just about plowed into a bear. Jeff nearly stepped on a copperhead today. We are all inching our way toward that line, that no-man's-land, and, at least today, stopping just short.*

My heart eventually stops racing and I'm once more in possession of all my mental faculties. Almost bedtime, my thoughts turn to preparations I need to make before work tomorrow. It's then that I hear a faint scratching sound coming from the kitchen.

The first thought to enter my head is that I share a house with a pair of pranksters. Jeff, for one, has the uncanny ability to persuade people to believe whatever he tells them. One time he convinced a new teacher-naturalist that the well-known spherical landmark in downtown Knoxville, which rises over two hundred feet and resembles a giant disco ball, houses the Disco Music Hall of Fame. Our coworker repeated this piece of misinformation to guests until one woman broke the news to her: "Honey, no, that's the Sunsphere from the 1982 World's Fair."

Steve, for his part, believes humans ought to exercise the same powers of awareness as the rest of the animal kingdom and takes a special delight in hiding from his housemates and colleagues before springing upon them in surprise. Any time of day, one can count on him to lie in wait behind a closed door or on a darkened staircase or sneak up barefoot behind an unsuspecting victim. Not knowing Steve's whereabouts can be nerve racking, and the only way to beat him at his game is to adopt an animal-like alertness, constantly anticipating an attack, so that when he surprises you, which he will no doubt do, you do not have a heart attack but will instead maintain a stoical posture and reply, "I knew you were there, Steve"—even if you didn't.

It is with the scheming natures of my two housemates in mind that I creep out of my bedroom and steal toward the living room in the dark. Jeff or Steve, or likely both of them, I'm convinced, have come home and, finding all the lights turned off except the one in my bedroom, are plotting to scare the living daylights out of me. Instead of coming through the back door (too obvious), their plan is to enter through the kitchen window. The reason I know this is because I can hear them trying to remove a window screen on the front porch, which explains the scratching sound I'd heard. Conveniently for them, a table propped on the porch beneath the kitchen window will make for easy entry.

With my nerves still raw from my close brush with the bear, the timing of their prank is not ideal. Yet it appears I have the upper hand. Jeff and Steve think I'm in my bedroom, unaware that I'm crouching only a few feet away and preparing to give them a taste of their own medicine. I can practically taste the satisfaction it will bring.

I execute my plan perfectly, springing from floor to kitchen counter and then bellowing "Ha!" into their faces through the window screen. But my actions do not produce the expected result, and only dead silence hangs in the air. The next moment an exhalation of warm hairy breath carries through the mesh wires and meets my face.

My body does my thinking for me, giving involuntary instructions to waste no time leaping away from the window screen. The bear's instincts are the same. A jumble of noise tells me he's hopped off the table, whereupon I rush to the front door and fling it open as I flip on the porch light.

Mutual astonishment leaves us both speechless upon seeing one another. "You again," he must be thinking—as am I. Dazed-looking, he starts milling about in the yard as if trying to make sense of what has just occurred. "Go away!" I scream, finding my voice at last, and miraculously he does.

I race up the road in my car and find all my coworkers watching a movie in someone's apartment. "We have a situation," I tell them.

Steve and Jeff follow me back to the Oasis, where we keep vigil throughout the night, during which the bear visits us three more times. We bang pots and pans and light firecrackers, trying to scare him off. I dig my old wooden bow out of the closet before realizing blunt-tipped practice arrows will only bounce off his thick hide. The floor-to-ceiling living room windows are an especially vulnerable entry point, which the bear, circling the house, discovers around one o'clock and nearly penetrates. Not until morning will we remember Steve's .50 caliber flintlock rifle, which might have served as a last resort had the bear gotten inside.

Mast failure—in other words, a bad year for acorns, hickory nuts, and walnuts—provides one explanation for the bear's aggressive behavior. Another is that we'd cooked fish for supper and placed a fan in the window to air out the stench. Unknowingly having baited a hungry bear wandering down the road, we'd probably turned the Oasis into what it took for a giant salmon tin. The occasion marked the last time any of us would ever cook fish inside the house.

Hours into the night, I collapse into bed, hoping the bear has left for good. Steve heroically volunteers to sleep on the living room floor in case the bear returns, which it does one final time at four o'clock in the morning. In my half sleep, I listen as Steve resorts to the only defense any of us has left, which is to unleash his inner bear.

"Mmmmmrawrrrr!" he roars.

The long night's events have left me willing to surrender, if not the Oasis, then at least a few more inches of space separating me from the wild. Listening to Steve as he roars over and over, his voice neither deep nor scary but convincing enough for the bear, which at last departs, I erupt into laughter. It's this moment that punctuates my first year living in the woods, and as delirious laughter carries me off to sleep, I begin dreaming of a day when I, too, can speak in a language bears understand.

PART II

Heartwood

Winter Light

IF I WAS IN THE BUSINESS of naming colors, Noncommittal Gray is the one I'd choose to describe the sky this February afternoon. Visible only if I crane my neck from my perch on the Oasis couch—itself a homely shade of gray disguising its peerless qualities when measured by comfort—the clouds hold up a mirror to my disposition this past week, most of which I've spent curled up and shivering with the flu. Overcast skies arrived the same day illness did, and then yesterday, when I began feeling better and could sit upright, the sun showed its face. I'm happy the coincidence ends there, however, since clouds have returned accompanied by a dull colorless light glomming onto everything in sight.

Wintertime from my vantage point on the couch affords a view of the forest at its scruffiest, as if it were the morning after a wild party. The mess and clutter of wind-tossed trees and rotting wood are noticeable everywhere, and the veil of green that once hung from every rafter, concealing it all, is a distant memory. Time, meanwhile, plays tricks on my mind. The weeks stack up with a lifeless calm, and I begin suspecting that if winter exists—the kind where something—anything—happens, I must go looking for it. And then a nuthatch jeers from a nearby tree, waking up my senses, which finally take in what has been happening all along. Colors metastasize to reveal purple shoots of blackberry, ripened dogwood berries, and pale gold deadheads of last summer's wildflowers. And the bleached trunk of a sycamore, a denizen of the river corridor, catches my eye, offering a splash of something white in the absence of snow.

The fleeting character of winter in the Mountain South requires a person to catch quickly whatever evidence of it there is to find. On the coldest days when the river's surface freezes, ice crystals stitch together across the moving current, meeting in the middle in slower pockets. Mornings after it rains, fragile tendrils of ice poke out of the frozen ground. Warming by afternoon, the saturated earth turns into a soggy mess. The ice melts, the rains return, and the river roars like a jet taking off.

Once in a while it actually snows. Several weeks ago, five inches fell overnight in Walker Valley and twenty-six on Mt. LeConte. Subsequent road closures forced the cancelation of a trip with my students to the meadows in Cades Cove, so we plunged into the forest close by campus, pushing for hours through tree branches sagging under the heavy weight of melting snow. Howls of protest erupted each time a heavy clump descended from treetops and landed on top of someone's head with an audible smack. "Don't look up," I advised those who were tempted to do so, which was all of us. Keeping our heads down helped only a little since each time we crossed a stream, the falling snow bombs splashed ice-cold water in our faces.

I dared to glance up at one point and spotted a deer browsing ten yards away. A buck still wearing its antlers, it seemed unfazed by both our presence and the aerial assault and kept right on eating, granting us a momentary distraction from our collective discomfort. Back at campus we turned on one another, stripping the grassy play area bare, snowball by snowball, until each of us was wearing in water weight some portion of what the sky had dumped overnight. Somewhere in all of this was a lesson on the value of being wet, cold, miserable, and perfectly happy all at once.

Snow seldom lasts longer than a day at low elevations, though it's an ideal time for tracking wildlife when it does. While following an old wagon road carved into the mountainside in the nineteenth century, I came across a fresh set of bobcat prints pointing in the same direction I was going. Having no illusions about laying eyes on the bobcat who left them, I thought I might at least learn something about its habits and behavior by studying its trail. I tried getting inside its mind as I stepped where it had stepped and saw what it had seen, but then the tracks abruptly stopped. I looked around for the tree branch or boulder it had leaped to, but there weren't any close enough—unless it happened to be an Olympic-caliber bobcat—which maybe this one was, because when I made a wide circle around the last print in search of another, I couldn't find a single one. Was I blind, I wondered? Snowblind?

Winter seems predictable on the surface of things. The trees stand bare, and cold temperatures come. The forest plays possum, and sometimes it snows. We wait and wait and wait some more—for the next cold snap, warm spell, or first sign of spring. Then a bobcat vanishes into thin air, causing me to doubt my ability to detect what's going on right in front of me.

And a tree falls on a calm day when the wind isn't moving, shattering the quiet.

And the wind, when it blows, blows so fiercely it lifts the roof right off an outdoor shelter and drops it on the ground in one piece. Coworkers awakened during the night by the wind's fury responded in varying ways. Liz took cover in her bathroom, shielding her head tornado drill-style, too unnerved to grab a blanket from her bedroom, while Jan kept watch by her window all night, enjoying the show. The forest the next morning looked like a boneyard piled with the skeletal parts of hundreds of trees throttled by the wind.

Greg's sister, Ann, married our mutual friend Mark in eastern Pennsylvania in January. I sat in the backseat next to healthy, smiling Jonah, now nine months old and growing hair and putting on weight, during the long drive to the ceremony. In Virginia we counted five tractor-trailers toppled over by powerful winds the previous night. The windstorm's leftovers were still raging, and when we stopped to refuel and stepped out of the car, we felt its force. The sensation of it, combined with views of the snowcapped Shenandoah Mountains in the near distance, stirred something inside the new father. Raising his preemie son toward the sky in the palm of one hand, Greg shouted, "The wind! The mountains! Gird thy loins! We're going into battle!" I marveled at his display of wind-loving, fatherly affection for just a minute before darting back to the car.

Against my better judgment, I found Greg's fondness for wind compelling enough during the previous fall to be persuaded to climb trees with him at night during a windstorm. Not a fan of heights, my consolation came from the darkness obscuring the depths beneath us as we swayed back and forth, high in the branches of a pine tree like John Muir when he climbed a hundred foot all Douglas fir during a gale. The approaching cold front was a giant bellows pressing oxygen into our pores and grinding dust into our eyes. When I looked in the mirror the next morning, I found a leaf-sized piece of lichen tangled in my hair.

In the South it is possible to visit the North without actually stepping foot there. If rain is falling at lower elevations and temperatures are hovering just above freezing, snow is likely piling up higher in the mountains—a sight which, when viewed from a distance, gives them the appearance of a multilayered gown bearing tiers of brown and white. Drive from valley to mountaintop and you've got yourself the kind of winter that in New England is garden variety.

Ice and snow can last for weeks, sometimes months, in the high country, allowing those visiting it to exercise wintertime vocabulary, a rarer occurrence at low elevations. A colleague who had observed hoarfrost clinging to tree limbs along the loftiest ridgetops the previous day reported her sighting over breakfast. As we talked, I noticed a guest sitting nearby who seemed troubled by our conversation, her face scrunching into a frown at each mention of *hoarfrost*.

"Is something wrong?" I asked.

"No. Or yes. Maybe. I don't know," she said. "I'm trying to understand why you all keep talking about a 'whore fest' like it's perfectly normal."

For a brief moment, we were a table filled with arched eyebrows as each of us considered what the woman had been imagining. She felt much better once we explained what happens when water vapor freezes on trees. "But I still wouldn't put it past you all to talk about a whore fest," she said. "You naturalists are always talking about weird things."

Some years, signs of spring appear in lower elevations soon after winter has gotten underway. Trailing arbutus and daffodils can bloom as early as January. Toothwort, a member of the mustard family preferring conditions many plants find intolerable, typically sends up its first leaves before winter even starts. Wood frogs wait for a mild January night to risk limb and life to raccoons and other predators while engaging in orgies that would make the most seasoned naturalist blush. In the weeks preceding such nights, their antifreeze-like blood enables them to freeze internally without perishing. Where precisely they hole up is anybody's guess.

Actually, that was no longer true once a fifth grader showed me where in December. I had tasked her and her classmates with searching for terrestrial salamanders among a mixed stand of conifers and hardwoods. In the middle of the activity, she reported seeing leaves moving on the ground all by themselves. I asked her to show me the spot, figuring we'd find a beetle that had miraculously survived a spate of recent frosts. I raked away the leaves with my fingers but found no beetle, only bare topsoil, which was indeed moving before our very eyes. Gently tearing away the thick mat of humus, I uncovered an inch below the surface the orange back of a wood frog followed by its head and legs. The students and I were delighted, but not the frog. Having woken it from hibernation, we covered it back up and watched as it stirred the ground above it every few seconds, pulsing like a heart buried in the earth.

Winter brings apocalypse, which is to say revelations. I'm reminded of this each time I gaze into the woods and realize how much deeper into it I can see than I ever could in summer. The contours of the land revealed in the absence of tree leaves clarify my perception, as unaccounted-for boulders and mounds of earth that I didn't know were there prompt me to question how well I think I've come to know the place or myself. All of this is temporary, of course, for as soon as I've grown accustomed to winter the forest begins putting on spring's attire and covers itself up again.

But all this is premature. Today winter's oppressive sheen casts itself everywhere and nothing much is happening. Today I feel as if I've been on pause and am waiting for something or someone to press play. Today I'm wondering how soon is too soon for spring to arrive and just what to make of the wildflower species that have appeared earlier than expected. What I tell myself—illness having displaced anxieties over climate change for the time being—is that today I need one fewer cause for worry. I feel a little like a wood frog myself, not quite certain I'm ready to wake up and face reality.

Earlier this week, a woman I will call Linette, who works in the dining service on campus, served me her homemade tonic. She'd been making it all week for employees suffering from the flu, and after hearing that I, too, had become stricken, she handed me a mug full of a mysterious black liquid. "Drink it," she instructed, and because she possesses the authority of a woman more than twice my age, I obeyed. If the goal was to get my mind off one affliction by saddling me with another, her ploy succeeded in spades. A fire ignited in the back of my throat, causing me to gag and cough. I somehow managed not to spew it across the room.

"What did you put in this?" I asked. She recited the recipe from memory:

Mix and heat over stove:
1 teaspoon Black Pepper

1 teaspoon Sage
1 teaspoon Ginger
1 teaspoon Cinnamon
1 teaspoon Dittany
Several teaspoons Honey
Several teaspoons Lemon Juice
Half to three-quarters cup Moonshine

The last ingredient was not the legal potion distilleries market as "moonshine" to provide their product with an allure of illicitness, but the genuine article, concocted and sold to her by an undisclosed local source. Her husband used to make and sell quite a bit of it himself, she said. When I asked why he'd stopped, she replied in her thick mountain accent, "'Cuz it was illegal."

"But wasn't it illegal before?" I asked, my throat still burning.

"Of course. But the law wasn't after him then."

Linette insisted I take home in a saucepan the portion of the tonic I hadn't imbibed in her presence, and once more I obeyed. That was three days ago and it has been sitting in the Oasis refrigerator ever since. After making one final attempt at drinking it, I decided I was better off staying sick.

Prying myself off the couch, I make use of my legs for the first time in several hours. I fish the saucepan out of the refrigerator and carry it to the sink. Dogwood winter, blackberry winter, and whippoorwill winter are terms that describe the season according to whatever is blooming or active when snow falls after winter has ended, each one taught to me by Linette. We may yet experience one or more such weather events. Now I can add to my knowledge of mountain culture an elixir palatable only to the bravest soul. Despite its awful power, love and care were perhaps its main ingredients, and it's for this reason that I hesitate before tipping over the saucepan and watching a river of sludge, remedy for winter's malady, gush into the sink and circle the drain.

Border Crossings

THEY'RE ALL HERE BY NINE. Arriving in separate vehicles and coming from varying points of origin, each of the ten adults who signed up to spend the weekend backpacking with us, many for the first time in their lives, pull onto campus and unload their belongings. What each one wants, presumably, is a taste of wilderness under the guidance of a trained professional. While this describes my co-leader Jan far better than it does me, I'm all too happy to oblige and lend a hand. Among other things, it will mean getting to explore a part of the backcountry I rarely visit, during springtime no less when the eastern deciduous forest, land of transfixing wonder and beauty, is at its very finest.

Jan, in her well-practiced and quietly confident manner, greets each person as they enter the meeting room. Once we're all seated in a circle, she asks everyone to introduce themselves and share where they're from. Out-of-staters to the last one, and ranging in age from late twenties to early sixties, they seem to have an inkling of what "roughing it" means, even if they don't know what the journey ahead will require of them. What's certain is that right now is the most relaxed and rested any of us will feel all weekend.

We spend the rest of the morning packing food and gear before boarding a van and driving over an hour to the trailhead located on the flank of Kuwohi, the highest peak in the park. Green has begun creeping up the mountainside thousands of feet below us, but the forest surrounding us remains in the grip of winter. We will have crossed several borders by the time we complete the twenty-four trail miles on our three-day hike back to campus, the shifting of seasons just one of them.

The next one comes almost right away. After climbing half a mile up a paved trail we reach the mountaintop and the nearby observation tower, which we decide to skip since several miles lie between us and our campsite, and it's already midafternoon. We turn onto the Appalachian Trail, which doubles as the state line throughout much of the park, now walking with our left feet in North Carolina and our right feet in Tennessee.

Items we've distributed more or less evenly between us include meal ingredients, tents, ground cloths, water filters, stoves, cookware, and nylon bags for hanging anything harboring food odors out of reach of bears. Sleeping bags, chocolate bars, clothes, and sundries are each person's responsibility. Despite my best efforts to talk him out of it, a guest named Scott has insisted on carrying his own equipment, having informed me that he spent hundreds of dollars on new gear and didn't want to leave it behind. Scott is thirty-five; despite being a paramedic by trade, he doesn't seem in top physical condition. He keeps pace with the rest of the group for a while but soon stops to rest every thirty paces, then twenty, then ten.

"Doing okay?" I ask, though it's obvious he isn't. His face has turned the shade of a fire engine.

"Chest pains," he mutters between breaths. "I've got these chest pains."

I ask him to take off his pack. Once he does, I test its weight. "This feels like a ton of bricks," I tell him.

"It's not the pack," he insists. "I think it's something more serious."

It's clearly the pack, though I don't say so. Also a wounded pride and what I suspect is some nervousness about spending the night in the woods.

"I think I should go back before something bad happens to me," he says.

There is no polite way to tell him he's out of shape and has increased his discomfort by choosing to rely solely on himself rather than the group. No point either in arguing with a paramedic about medical symptoms that might be real but probably aren't. It's a fact that death from any number of causes is a possibility out here. Not long before I started working at the center, an elderly guest suffered a heart attack after climbing the walkway leading to the observation tower, now a quarter mile behind us. The staff naturalist leading the hike performed CPR until an ambulance arrived, but the man was gone. His wife said later she couldn't think of a more beautiful place for her husband to die.

Border Crossings

It's beautiful here, all right, I'm thinking as I consider what I will do if Scott keels over. If he does, I'm guessing it will be from embarrassment as much as anything else.

Twenty minutes have elapsed since we last saw the rest of the group. Jan, noticing we've fallen behind, comes walking back down the trail, and together we form a plan. I will accompany Scott back to the parking lot and find him a ride while she and the others press on. I'll catch up with them at the campsite or sooner if I make good time.

Hiding my backpack in the woods, I hoist Scott's onto my shoulders, an arrangement he seems perfectly fine with, and together we retrace our steps back to the trailhead. His backpack is so large that the hip belt won't clip around my waist, and with all that weight pressing down on my shoulders, staying upright is a challenge. It is grueling work, and I'm relieved when we reach the parking lot so I can take it off. When I do, it lands on the ground with a thud.

No ranger is in sight, though I find a friendly couple who agree to give Scott a lift back down the mountain where he can make arrangements to retrieve his automobile. His pack takes up the entirety of their trunk. He climbs into the backseat and stares straight ahead without returning my wave as the car pulls away. So begins and ends his first and perhaps last backpack trip.

My pack feels light as a feather by comparison when I relocate it. With the group an hour ahead of me by now, there's little point in hurrying to catch up. My map tells me I'll have cut in half the six-thousand-plus vertical feet between the mountaintop and sea level by the time I reach the campsite. Might as well enjoy myself getting there.

The wind sounds different—smells different—in the high country. The sun feels hotter and the shade cooler. Ubiquitous moisture has turned every plant and rock in sight damp with condensation. It's a quiet place where hardly a sound reaches my ears until a winter wren chatters its long, caffeinated song. Most activity going on this time of year is happening belowground, where seeds are getting ready to sprout and every living thing is preparing in its own time to take advantage of the short growing season that will soon begin.

I pass by mountain ash trees and spidery witch-hobble bushes. Where several large red spruce trees have been wrenched from the ground by the wind, their root balls form facades comprised of unearthed rocks and loose soil. The topsoil is so thin that bedrock is visible in many places. Despite this inhospitable environment, however, life has managed to take hold and flourish.

The vegetation growing on the highest peaks of the southern Appalachians has more in common with Canada than it does the American South. When more northerly regions became uninhabitable during the most recent ice age, species migrated southward to escape the cold. Once temperatures warmed, many made their permanent home among sky islands such as this one. Elevation mimics latitude in this way, which is one reason a variety of forest communities residing between Georgia and Canada dwell here within a single mountain range. It's also why no single forest exists in the Smokies but instead *forests*—multitudinous and knitted together, one morphing into the next. Five primary communities to be precise: pine-oak, cove hardwood, hemlock, northern hardwood, and spruce-fir.

The one inhabiting the high country is spruce-fir, and everywhere I look there is ample evidence that its character is not what it once was. Fraser firs have been all but wiped out by the balsam woolly adelgid, an invasive aphid-like insect unwittingly imported on Asian lumber. Where living fir trees once towered, now pale ghosts stand resolute against the sky. Red spruce trees are faring better, though acid rain and fog led to stunted growth and premature death before a years-long effort helped to begin cleaning up the air. Living a mile high and downwind of coal-fired power plants comes with risks, and climate change likely means further disruption lies ahead.

The ridgeline I'm walking along grows stingy on views, obstructed by magnificent spruce trunks and thickets of young firs filling the void left by dead parent trees. More than making up for it is the endless array of herbaceous plant life at my feet. It's as if the Appalachians were designed for the pleasure of the nearsighted by offering so many things to notice up close. The landscape as a whole offers the mirror opposite of spaces out West where plant life is less varied yet one's range of vision is vast owing to the relative absence of trees. In contrast, trees here are innumerable as grains of sand on a beach and blanket the earth for as far as the eyes can see, assuming I could see past those blocking the view.

A forest is more than the sum of its parts. It's the parts, though, that field guides tend to focus on. Most I'm familiar with single out each tree species while omitting any mention of the larger community to which they belong. The field guides I own likewise fall short in the sensory department, as if a tree's sole attributes were those attainable through sight alone. More rewarding might be a tack similar to the section called Tasting Notes in a book I own about Scotch whisky, which its author doubtless spent many enjoyable hours writing—taste just one quality he relied on to describe each of several hundred distillations. If I were to become an itinerant habitat junky, which perhaps I already have, I would create my own version and call them Sensory Notes, and begin with the spruce-fir:

> *Color:* Fecund darkness mixed with intermittent portals of light.
> *Nose:* Citrus. Intimations of musk and the Far North.
> *Palate:* Unrestrained. Bitter. Acidic.
> *Sound:* The sloughing of wind, the staccato of birds. Lengthy periods of quiet.
> *Body:* Broken yet robust.

Despite walking alone, I'm reminded again and again that I do not have the woods all to myself, as first one hiking party followed by another hoofs past. The seventy-two-mile stretch of the Appalachian Trail that runs through the national park unsurprisingly is the most popular backpacking trail in the Smokies. Springtime is when northbound thru-hikers pass through on their five-month trek from Springer Mountain, Georgia, to Mount Katahdin, Maine, which means the park's backcountry right now is busier than usual. Thru-hikers are a braver lot than I am. Though I have pondered from time to time whether I possess the stamina necessary for completing the trail's more than two thousand miles, the desire to find out has long eluded me. Most thru-hikers average fifteen to twenty miles per day, power-hikers as many as thirty, and though I've grown accustomed to hikes in excess of twenty miles, I'm content to take a week or more off afterward to absorb the experience and rest. Even much shorter hikes often leave me feeling that for all the miles I've logged and views I've laid eyes on, I have digested little. Move too fast through a landscape and one misses all its intricacies. The result is a kind of sensory indigestion I prefer to avoid.

Tonight I will sleep under a tarp on the bare ground while thru-hikers will sleep inside cramped shelters on wooden bunks. Shelters in the park were comprised for many years of three stone walls, with chain-link fencing covering the exposed side to keep out creatures of a distinctly large and carnivorous variety. The design worked well until some human occupants lacking sounder judgment began feeding bears through gaps in the fencing. While this guaranteed excellent photographic opportunities for those billeted inside, hikers who arrived late in the day and found the shelter filled to capacity had no choice but to sleep outside where the beggar bears roamed. As a result, the fencing on many shelters was removed to encourage better backcountry etiquette. Call it equal opportunity jeopardy since if one person should risk dismemberment, now everyone would.

I keep heading opposite the direction of thru-hikers, stepping aside to allow each one to pass without having to break stride since their task is far more daunting than mine. With solitude impossible to come by just now, I'll be glad to leave the busy A.T. behind once I reach the next junction and turn onto a different trail. Though solitude this deep in the woods may at first lead to loneliness, I've come to think of it as an essential ingredient of an authentic wilderness experience. It felt like unwelcome company on my first few solo outings and yet blossomed into something more companionable given enough time, becoming just one more border to cross.

A good omen: there's no sign of the group when I reach the junction, which tells me Jan and company are making excellent time.

My feet now planted firmly in Tennessee, I come to another boundary after descending a thousand feet in elevation or so, this one between forest communities. I've departed Canada and entered New England, or something very much like the northern hardwood forest found there, though with a southern twist. Representative overstory species appear, one after another, including Carolina silverbell, northern red oak, yellow buckeye, and black cherry, each towering trunk dwarfing me down on the forest floor. I mistake other trees much smaller in size for saplings before realizing they're mountain maples. Lacking in economic value, mountain maples are what foresters sometimes call a "trash tree," though I bet birds and other organisms would beg to differ. A member of the understory like dogwoods and American hollies, mountain maples don't seem interested in reaching canopy heights and make do with the scant light they receive in the shady depths, contributing to the forest's structural complexity.

The first time I heard of the terms overstory and understory—a forest's topmost layer and the layer beneath it, respectively—I instantly grew fond of them. The use of "story" to simultaneously describe both architecture and the passage of time—the scaffolding of a place as well as the events going on there—enlarged both my understanding of the forest and personhood. It called attention to what I hadn't noticed before but became plainly obvious, which was that venturing deeper into the woods often also means tracing a path into one's own hidden contours. To stretch the metaphor a bit further, the overstory is where one's dreams and ambition take conscious form, but the understory—the subconscious—is where the real action often happens.

The forest seems never to be in a hurry, though perhaps it is according to its own notions of time. Not in much of a hurry myself these past several hours, I glance at my watch and realize it's nearly mealtime. I quicken my pace when I recall that those who are ahead of me are carrying supper.

A steep mile-long descent commences, and I'm soon thick in the green part of the world that was visible from the trailhead. With winter above and behind me now, spring appears at my feet in the form of violets and trout lilies and at eye level where tree buds are starting to unfold. Another border crossed.

The last mile is always the hardest, even going downhill—or perhaps especially going downhill, given that my legs are doing all the work. Long gone is the endorphin rush I felt hours ago climbing the path to the mountaintop.

The trail levels out when I reach the foot of Goshen Ridge, and ahead I hear voices. I spot tents a minute later, and when I enter the campsite's tidy clearing, Jan and others extend warm greetings. Everyone is safe and sound. Not surprisingly, they've gotten along just fine without me.

Supper's waiting. Refried beans and rice with melted cheese and salsa and Fritos sprinkled on top. "Grab your bowl and come get some," says Jan, and I do.

We're slow to crawl out of our sleeping bags in the morning. Frayed nylon on one person's pack shows where mice chewed through to burgle a forgotten granola bar. We break camp after a breakfast of oatmeal and bagels. Groans issue from the mouths of several people when we shoulder our packs. Though today's mileage is greater than yesterday's, we are getting an earlier start. And despite the weight each of us carries on our backs, our task is a fairly joyous one. All we have to do is walk eight miles to our next campsite, nearly all of them downhill, through one of the most stunning forest communities on the planet.

A person might make a convincing case for despair in wintertime, I suppose. But to do so in springtime in a cove hardwood forest, found in protected valleys like this one where it is clear heaven of a certain kind exists on earth, would be unforgivable. Measured by their astounding biodiversity, cove hardwood forests are the rock stars of North American forest communities. Fewer than a dozen species of vascular plants dwell in a quarter-acre plot in a spruce-fir forest on average. In contrast, between forty and sixty species do in a cove hardwood forest, making any attempt at compiling Sensory Notes a prodigious challenge. Sheltered by surrounding mountain slopes that form a haven from exposure and heat—thus the "cove" part of the name—the soil here is damp, rich, and deep. It's as if sunlight has farther to travel to reach the forest floor, and little of it does through the dense canopy down to where the shade exudes a crepuscular quality.

I once assumed a forest was little more than a bunch of trees growing in the same place. Not that Johnny Appleseed had anything to do with it, but I figured the process was similar, with birds and wind doing the work of seed scattering. A tree could grow on one plot of ground as well as any other, and wherever a seed fell, it would take root. But this isn't how nature works. A host of factors determine why a tree thrives where it does, among them latitude, elevation, aspect, pitch, geologic history, temperature, and rainfall. The American basswood tree could not survive for very long the sun-bright existence to which Table Mountain pines have adapted on ridgetops. For a tree to not just survive but thrive, the right place is critical.

Yet places change over time. Were we able to time travel back to the close of the ice age sixteen thousand years ago, we would find ourselves standing in the thick of a spruce-fir forest. Only when temperatures began to climb did the boreal forest creep northward—upward, too, in the southern Appalachians—providing space for other forest communities to occupy. The eastern deciduous forest, of which the cove hardwood is a part, emerged soon afterward from pockets on the Cumberland Plateau as well as along the Atlantic coast where it had taken refuge from the cold, migrating northward at a rate of about half a mile every year.

The eastern deciduous forest in North America originated in China and India, back when continents in the northern hemisphere hugged the North Pole and Greenland's climate resembled New England's today. Long before the advent of the ice age, deciduous forests ringed the Arctic like hair on a friar's balding head. When subzero temperatures pushed them southward into Europe, they had nowhere to go because of the east–west orientation of the Alps, which blocked their passage. Many species died out as a result. But the northeast-southwest orientation of the Appalachian chain in North America formed an escape route. Continents drifted and seasons passed, millions of them. Older tree species survived and new ones evolved. Woody plants and wildflowers flourished. The story is one of constant change, making the notion of a forest fixed in a primeval state for all time a fairy tale. All the same, ecologists make a convincing case that for its biodiversity, bounty, beauty, and complexity, the eastern deciduous forest ranks among the greatest forests on earth.

Acquiring a layperson's fluency in forest ecology is one way I've deepened my sense of place while living and working in the mountains. But I've come to accept the fact that forest ecology doesn't excite everyone, having watched listeners' eyes glaze over while I enthused about the finer points of deep time. Early on, I was more interested in spotting one of the forest's celebrities, an expectation shaped in part by media images that seemed to suggest such places had little more to offer than a bear sighting. And yet just as fascinating once I took a closer look were a forest's set and stage design and the intricacies of the past still at work in the present.

In a cove hardwood forest, on the other hand, and during this time of year especially, my attention turns to other things. We move at a snail's pace, making progress in fits and starts because of the scores of wildflowers visible at our feet. My job of instructor in getting my companions to slow down and notice each bloom hardly seems necessary.

Today's education in the senses unfolds practically all by itself. Jan takes the lead once again, which grants me the luxury of poking along in the rear while adding each species to my growing list. There's wild geranium and mayapple, yellow trillium and painted trillium, spring beauty and bishop's cap, yellow mandarin and phlox, Solomon's seal and bellwort. Also jack-in-the-pulpit, wood anemone, Indian cucumber, lousewort, crested dwarf iris, foamflower, Solomon's plume, and numerous violet species. Growing in seeps is brook lettuce, an edible long favored in Cherokee culture, and, in bottomlands, fringed phacelia, which makes its own unique contribution to the carpet of paradise spread before us by cloaking acres upon acres of the forest floor with snow-white blossoms.

I drop to my knees and lean over, burying my nose in the phacelia in the manner of naturalist William Bartram, nicknamed Puc Puggy, or "flower sniffer," by the Seminoles when he traveled through their homeland in the late eighteenth century. An unwise move, I realize too late when the weight of my top-heavy pack shifts and pins my head to the ground. For all its charm, phacelia's aromatic output is nil, its efforts going into producing sheer numbers. My own clumsy efforts at righting myself meet with failure until I roll over and unclasp my hip belt and scramble to my feet, grateful that everyone is too enthralled by wildflowers to have noticed this rather undignified drama of man versus pack.

Shrubs, too, are blooming, including dog-hobble, maple-leaf viburnum, and sweetshrub, the latter nicknamed "booby-bush" by women who tucked its blossoms into their bosoms as a natural perfume. And sedges—grasslike plants with triangular stems—including Fraser's and crinkle-leaf. And trees, including dogwood, redbud, yellow buckeye, cucumber magnolia, and witch-hazel. And still more wildflowers: wild ginger, rue anemone, blue cohosh, bloodroot, showy orchis, hepatica, yellow star grass, sweet white trillium, hairy buttercup, sweet cicely—and on and on. Our botanical wealth today is great. We've turned into a posse of flower sniffers, paging through field guides and snapping photos while inching along. Over lunch, I tally up the blossoms we've spotted: forty-eight species. We've come during that magic window of time when spring ephemerals accomplish all their work, from germination to flowering to going to seed, once the danger of a killing frost has passed but before leaf-out has closed the canopy. Like guests who put hats and coats back on soon after arriving, many will show little evidence they were ever here a few short weeks from now.

Our attention eventually turns to the task of reaching today's destination and we establish a steadier rhythm in our step, breaking only for brief periods. An uphill climb empties my mind, and there's nothing for a time but the lung's bellows, wind in and wind out. We top one rise then another, until at last, we arrive at our campsite.

Supper is pizza cooked over a camp stove. Jan's technique is to dribble water into the frying pan and then quickly cover it with the lid. The resulting steam melts the cheese on the pita bread we use for crusts. I try my hand at it but pour in too much water, which turns several pizzas to mush. No one complains. The taste of salt and fat is more than enough to satisfy everyone's raging hunger. We settle around a campfire after dark, savoring the sensual delights of woodsmoke and starlight.

"This is what I call living," says Marie, a middle-aged woman who until now has kept mostly to herself.

"I could get used to it," agrees Stella, in her twenties and also on her first backpack trip.

"My mind agrees with you but not my body," says Ralph, a retiree from Ohio, as he grouses about his sore muscles while struggling to find a comfortable sitting position on the hard ground.

I picture Scott stepping out of the shadows after having changed his mind and tracing our steps through the woods, his pack lighter and his mind filled with faith that he isn't going to die but only experience a little misery on behalf of a greater good. He makes no such appearance, of course. Perhaps he's nursing a wounded ego in front of a television at this moment while surrounded by all the comforts of home.

It's suddenly time for stories, a fitting way to end the day. Jan recounts her stint in the Peace Corps, during which her mother back in Minnesota mailed boxes of Jell-O to her in sub-Saharan Tanzania, a thoughtful if futile gesture in the absence of refrigeration. Scott wasn't the only medical professional in the group. A woman and two men who traveled together from Indiana decline the opportunity to tell war stories from the emergency room where they work, and who can blame them? They seem content to stare into the fire and listen while others share.

When a lull falls over the group, I describe my first backpacking trip at Philmont Scout Ranch in New Mexico when I was a teenager and having to schlep fifty pounds of water to a dry campsite. I describe the art of the atomic wedgie, which involved us boys choosing a new victim each night around the campfire and yanking the elastic waistband of his underwear as we held him down until it tore free, and feeding mine into the flames when my turn came, a sacrifice made to the gods of mischief.

My most vivid memory of that ten-day trip occurred on the final night when we decided to forgo sleep and hike through the dark to a mountain-sized block of granite called the Tooth of Time, where we hoped to glimpse sunrise. Our plans changed around midnight. The heavens opened once we summited the mountain we'd spent several hours climbing, bringing rain and fog so thick that we couldn't see a dozen feet in front of us. Forced to pitch camp, we strung a tarp between four trees and piled underneath it in our sleeping bags. With no room except for my legs among all the bodies crammed under the tarp, I somehow managed to fall asleep with my head and torso sticking out in the pelting rain.

Hours into the soggiest night of my life, screams jolted all of us awake. In our collective confused state of mind, we couldn't figure out what was the matter until the beams of our flashlights revealed a most perplexing sight. The smallest boy in our group was lying on his back in the middle of all the bodies. Directly above him hung the sagging tarp, inside of which the weight of dozens of gallons of rainwater had pooled while we slept, pinning him to the ground as if by a giant thumb.

The situation called for immediate and heroic action. Scrambling out of our sleeping bags, we heaved against the tarp with our shoulders, trying to free our trapped comrade and put an end to his incessant screaming. Our mistake was failing to decide which direction to push the water and forgetting that it always runs downhill. Several boys were still lying in their sleeping bags, including Whistlin' Jake—so read the inscription on the jacket he wore at all times, awarded him in a whistling competition back in Pennsylvania. Jake was eighteen and exceeded the prescribed weight limit for trip participants by a hundred pounds. Earlier that week, he had suffered a minor case of hypothermia from profuse sweating. The pool of rainwater, once we managed to push it above our heads, tipped over the edge of the tarp and poured onto the sloped ground directly uphill of Jake, flooding his sleeping bag like an empty water balloon held under a spigot. Whistlin' Jake did not whistle at that moment. He screamed.

"Hell's the matter with you boys?! Packs on! We're leaving!" barked our crusty, cigar-chomping scoutmaster once the chaos subsided. Weary and drenched, we marched through the night until we reached the Tooth of Time, only to find it enshrouded in fog.

My point in sharing these recollections with everyone, if indeed there is a point, maybe is this: See, this isn't so bad. Whatever is ailing each of us—sore backs, aching shoulders, tired legs—must seem like nothing by comparison. After all, we haven't had a drop of rain or any thunderbolts, hypothermia, or flooded sleeping bags. And no atomic wedgies either.

Our campfire's smoldering embers grow dim, and one by one, everyone turns in for the night. Everyone except for me.

Too restless for sleep, I wait for the others to settle in their tents before going exploring. I tiptoe through the maze of tents down to the tiny creek bubbling past the perimeter of the campsite and step into the shallow streambed. Stones sparkle in the beam of my flashlight as salamanders creep among them, hunting for food. I hold out my palm and chase one into it with my other hand. It's a dusky, a member of the genus Plethodon that breathes through its skin. Less than half an inch long, he doesn't try to escape. I hold him up to my face and stare into his poppyseed-sized eyes. I bring him closer and then, without thinking, pop him into my mouth.

Instinct is working at this late hour more than reason. A predator's impulse is to stalk and capture, which for the moment describes me, even though I have no intention of finding out what effect salamander slime might have on the human digestive system. It's a strange sensation as I hold him in the warm cave of my mouth for several seconds before spitting him into my hand and returning him to the creek. Mystified, perhaps, but not visibly traumatized, he goes back to his business of securing a meal. Feeling swallowed up by the fullness of the day and the beauty on display at every turn, I crawl beneath my tarp and burrow deep into my sleeping bag, and within seconds I am fast asleep.

Birdsong high overhead. The sound of a tent door unzipping. The scent of charred wood and ripening body odors—my own, of course. More sensations invade my sleep and when I can't fight it any longer, I open my eyes. I poke my head out past the edge of the tarp and peer into the canopy without the aid of my glasses. Pillars of light mingle with a menagerie of shapeless leaves backlit by the morning sun, a blurrily beautiful sight seemingly reserved for those with poor eyesight. Subpar vision comes with few benefits, but this is one.

When I put my glasses on, it is clear why Cherokees call their homeland Shaconage, or "land of blue smoke," a name describing the natural haze noticeable on cloudless days like today. It's the dense broadleaf forest at work as millions of respiring trees release vapor into the air, a magic act made visible to human eyes. I try to picture what else must be going on in the forest. A doe dropping a fawn and warblers making ready to raise their first broods of the season. Emerald tiger beetles zipping over the ground and stag beetles plodding along like miniature rhinos. Morels poking up through leaf litter and ants at work pollinating trilliums and wild ginger. Busybodies ourselves, once we're all awake, we down granola and mugs of coffee and restuff our packs one final time.

We cover the first couple of miles of today's eight at a brisk pace. Though detecting a boundary between one forest community and another can require a watchful eye, there's no mistaking this one when we come around a bend. We've left the cove hardwood and entered a pine-oak forest. Bathed in warmer air, we find ourselves surrounded by hickories, mountain laurels, serviceberries, and other species accustomed to direct sunlight. I pluck a leaf off a sourwood sapling and chew it. The flavor is like green apples and better than a salamander. I tear another leaf into small pieces and offer them to my companions. Most decline though a few partake, their polite but strained reactions suggesting it is an acquired taste.

Fire has not visited this patch of forest in many years by all appearances, as evidenced by dozens of downed logs and an impenetrable shrub layer, all of which have primed it for ignition by a lightning strike. The native Southern pine beetle plays a vital role in the fire regime of pine-oak forests by periodically targeting pine stands and killing older trees. The resulting dead wood provides fuel for fire, which in turn spurs the regeneration of species such as Table Mountain pine, whose cones rely on intense heat to open and release seeds. That's how it worked for millennia, at any rate, before widespread fire suppression during the twentieth century threw the ancient balance out of whack. These days the park conducts prescribed burns in areas where it is needed and allows natural-caused fires to burn so long as they don't pose a threat to human life and structures. Instead of the enemy it was once believed to be, ecologists now recognize fire as a necessary aspect of forest life. Fire embodies the paradox of the unexpected guest who by introducing seeming chaos restores order.

I share this bit of native-born forest ingenuity with the group. But foremost on everyone's minds seems to be covering ground as swiftly as possible. It's understandable given the long automobile drive back home that lies ahead for everyone, along with the responsibilities awaiting them there. Escape has been only temporary, and a good thing, too, I suppose, since civilization will need our three Hoosiers stitching broken people back together come Monday morning.

A forest is as good a place as any to recall that a world without borders is a myth. All these porous boundaries we've crossed also serve as a reminder that borders, including many created by humans, aren't barriers so much as meeting points. One after another comes and goes as we wind our way down the mountain, entering and exiting various forest communities in quick succession as we move toward the most jarring one of all, where the trail ends.

Putting one foot in front of the other, we stop only to sip water and admire a pink lady's slipper, further evidence of the springtime forest as poetry incarnate. Before long we reach a bend in the trail that I recognize. We've now begun our final mile-long descent back into the world we left behind on Friday.

Hanging in the rear, I find my attention torn between where I am and what lies ahead. I try to hold thoughts of a hot shower and fresh food and a soft bed at bay, and when I hear traffic noise in the river valley below us, I feel the impulse to resist it all and preserve the present moment for as long as possible.

Only now that I'm about to part ways with it do I recognize a deeper in-the-marrow forest time I have entered over these past three days. We all have, I suspect, perhaps without fully realizing it. Like fire, a journey such as ours causes chaos of a certain kind by disrupting routines and posing challenges to mind and body. But, also like fire, it restores a sense of order by having granted us the chance to set aside the demands imposed by efficiency-loving human time and to get outside our heads and stop and smell the flowers. Even before we reach the trailhead and step onto campus, I feel it start to fade.

It evaporates further when we unpack our gear and say our goodbyes. Tomorrow I'll perhaps feel like Dorothy waking in her bed in Kansas and wonder if I've dreamed the whole thing up, at least until a pile of dirty laundry and a wildflower list several dozen species long tell me otherwise.

Skunked

AS BLOOD RUNS DOWN MY FOREHEAD, I stumble outdoors to retrieve a first aid kit from the trunk of my car. Only once I blunder smack into them do I notice the cloud of insects buffeting the air. Mercifully not the biting kind, they dance in midair swooping down and back up again in dizzying arcs, as dainty as fairies. Cupping a hand, I scoop one up. A female yellow stonefly settles on my palm, a swollen egg sack hanging from the tip of her abdomen. Within seconds she wings off to rejoin the mass mating ritual underway on this warm May evening.

On ordinary spring evenings—ones when I haven't suffered a self-inflicted head wound because of failing to notice the sharp corner of a bookshelf, as I did moments ago—I'm drawn outdoors often by what's coming in. A stonefly or caddisfly that's slipped beneath the window screen will orbit a light bulb in a wild frenzy, delivering news about the hatch occurring outside. A hatch likely means trout are biting like mad, and if there's still enough light in the sky I'll grab my fly rod and make haste for the river. In just this way I am something of a fair-weather fisherman, and also a lazy one, trying my luck most commonly when conditions are in my favor.

Just now I face a perplexing choice: whether to tend to the bloody inch-long incision in my scalp or head for the river. With sunset fast approaching there isn't enough time to do both before dark. Hatches can end as abruptly as they begin, so I must decide quickly. Figuring what's a little blood loss compared to missing a golden opportunity to catch trout, back indoors I go to fetch my rod.

Since digging it out of a closet in my parents' house several years ago, when I was first learning how to fly-fish, I have relied on my father's old two-piece rod which has remained on permanent loan to me. After fishing with it one recent afternoon, I laid it in the backseat of my car for the ride home, tip sticking out an open window. Halfway home, forgetting about the fragile cargo riding behind me, I rolled up the window turning it into a useless three-piece.

Luckily, an inexpensive replacement rod arrived in the mail just this morning. I tear open the package and join the five pieces together, tighten the reel to the reel seat, affix tippet to leader, and tie on a size 16 Parachute Adams. A Parachute Adams in my view resembles a microscopic whale spouting elk hair through a blowhole more than it does a yellow stonefly drying its wings, as it's meant to do. But if I've learned anything it's to not get hung up on trying to mimic whatever insect is hatching at the moment. Trout are intelligent creatures and routinely outsmart me regardless of which pattern I lay before them.

While dashing back outdoors into the swarm of sex-crazed stoneflies, I realize the manufacturer's plastic wrap is still covering the cork grip of the rod in my hand. Like my oozing scalp it will have to wait. I am about to make a blood offering of sorts to the Middle Prong in hopes that I will receive a blessing in return in the form of a trout, and I have no time to waste.

I step into the current in shorts and sandals, wading further in until I am knee deep, and make my first cast. As always, it is impossible to resist the expectation of feeling a tug on the end of my line or picturing the effervescent body of the fish I will hold in my hands if I land one. Often at such moments, however, something else takes over, which it does tonight. It is enough before long to feel joined with the activity swelling around me as the current pulses against my legs and the air practically thrums with the wingbeats of insects, as if the river and legion of stoneflies and trout breaking the surface right before my eyes are all part of a giant wave that keeps building and climbing toward its crest.

What I want more than anything suddenly is not to catch fish but to ride the wave for as long as I can.

I grew up in a musical family more than a fishing one. Fishing, though, is what you do when you find yourself living in a cabin in the mountains near the banks of a river teeming with trout. Even if fishing in the recent past led to failure and frustration on more occasions than you care to admit. Even if it is something you'd sworn you would never do again.

Fly-fishing for me has become largely an exercise in learning to fail well. But for a long time it amounted to failing miserably, as with many of the musical instruments I attempted to learn how to play in my youth. One way of charting the course of my upbringing would be to name which instrument I picked up at each age before setting it down, one after another, when even modest success eluded me despite hours of practice, until at last one seemed to stick. So it makes sense, I suppose, why I hesitated on the day I was handed a wholly different kind of instrument during a camping trip with friends in northern Michigan, since it too might lead to failure.

Along with his fly rod, my friend Mark gave me his waders, which were several sizes too large. I put them on anyway because the waters of the Manistee River were cold and impenetrably dark. I could count on one hand the number of times I'd gone fishing with my father and my uncles as a boy, always with spinner rods. My sole familiarity with fly-fishing came from watching my father practice his casts in our backyard. Misunderstanding how it worked, I couldn't fathom how fish were supposed to jump out of the water and latch onto the fly with quick precision as it whizzed past, making it seem that only by miracle could one ever catch anything. The way it actually works is by laying the line down on the surface of the water, again and again, until the artificial fly tempts a hungry trout to the surface. At the time, however, I assumed the near impossibility of success was the reason my father soon gave up fly-fishing, his rod never taking to his hands quite like the oboe that he played in symphony orchestras.

The difference between the musical instruments I'd tried to learn and a fly rod the first time I held one was that, with the latter, I met with almost instant success. Copying the motions I had seen Mark and Greg make while fly-fishing, I waved my casting arm slowly back and forth. To my amazement, after making only my second cast an invisible force pulled on the other end of the line. I held on as it squirmed and thrashed, obeying Mark's instructions to keep the tip pointed up and let out some line. Between the two of us, fish and fisherman, I had the advantage of strength and size, and a minute later I was holding a brook trout in my hands. Its sides sparkled with serpentine yellows and greens, a thing of beauty. I understood then why some people regard fly-fishing as a religion and knew that I wanted to join.

I dusted off my father's rod and vest on the next visit home and made use of them over the next eighteen months each time I found myself near trout waters. I deemed nearly every one of these outings a resounding success owing to the fact that I kept catching trout. All the signs kept pointing to proof of a minor miracle in light of my past failures handling musical instruments: I was a natural at this.

What I'd chalked up to my own prowess, however, turned out to be only a prolonged period of beginner's luck. Before long my luck changed. The fish seemed to—how else to put it—turn against me.

By now I had moved to the city where my ex-girlfriend was living, with plans of wooing her back. When that ended in failure and I began spending long days in the bowels of the doorframe factory, I coped by visiting a nearby river on weekends. My goal was to conquer its resident trout. Such occasions constituted my sole familiarity with fresh air and sunlight each week, which intensified the pressing need I felt to achieve quick results. But even though dozens of trout rose to the surface all around me, none would take my lure. Having learned to tie flies by now, I hated losing my painstaking creations on submerged rocks and overhanging tree branches more than I hated not catching fish. And soon I was spending more time scribbling onto a notepad my observations of the fishing life, what little I knew about it—which was little indeed—than I did actually fishing.

The bright idea I got one day, which was not a bright idea at all, was to bring along a cigar. I began smoking them out of boredom and because I'd noticed older fishermen doing so. The cigars, I figured, would help me look the part. With a stogie clenched between my teeth it seemed less likely I would be outed as the phony that I was.

A foreigner to the ways of trout, yet determined as ever to catch one, I plied the river one evening and returned the next to try again. That second evening I detected a stench so overwhelming that something dead nearby could be the only plausible explanation. I searched the riverbank but discovered only a deer carcass long since picked clean by vultures, and when I waded back into the river the smell was just as strong as before. No matter which direction I faced, upwind, downwind, it kept following me.

The conclusion I reached was that the river itself must be the cause. The river and its smug trout, which kept ignoring every fly I laid before them. I finally glanced down, at last spotting the culprit only inches from my face. Staring back at me from the breast pocket of my fishing vest was the cigar I'd half smoked the previous evening before stowing it away for today. Saturated at one end with day-old saliva and charred to a crisp on the other, it seemed an unholy thing and a sign pointing to everything that had poisoned fly-fishing for me over the past several months—my impatience, my entitled view toward catching fish, and now my inattention to the truth lying right beneath my nose.

I pitched the cigar into the bushes. Harder to address at just that moment, however, was the truth. And the truth was that the cigar wasn't all that stunk, because so did I. A wayward disciple of a tradition that demanded some small measure of humility, I had succeeded at little more than trying to force my will upon creatures and the places they inhabited. I didn't yet understand fly-fishing, and now I doubted I ever would.

Like the piano and saxophone and clarinet, a fly rod now numbered among the instruments I had quit out of frustration. There didn't seem to be any point to fishing if I couldn't catch fish, and since I had found time and again that I couldn't, why even bother? Several weeks later, however, I moved to the Smokies and began living in the Oasis, where the Middle Prong rolled by within shouting distance. Wild, not stocked, trout inhabited its every run and riffle. Giving up fishing suddenly felt as if I were abandoning the faith while residing in the church's manse.

Renewing my religious vows, as it were, and leaving cigars and notepads behind, I trudged dutifully to the river each evening and returned home empty-handed each time—skunked, as they say, though getting my ass whipped by the Middle Prong was more like it. Every third cast it seemed my line would catch on a tree branch, every fourth cast I would lose another fly, and every fifth cast the tippet would break. But rather than letting this stop me, I kept at it. I would perform my penance.

Fly-fishing in the Smokies rarely if ever involves the sort of grand gestures portrayed in movies and photographs wherein anglers strip dozens of feet of line while making graceful arcs over a wide, flat river. That would be out West where there is plenty of elbow room. Not so along the Middle Prong, where the cramped river corridor and overhanging vegetation restrict freedom of movement. Stalking and hunching behind boulders becomes necessary, which results in a sore back, knees, and neck. Yet I was doing the hard work now. I was paying my dues, even if I had nothing to show for it.

Then one evening I caught a fish, a silvery one a little longer than my hand, its cheeks streaked with red: a warpaint shiner. Minutes later I caught a rainbow trout. This one I also released, and cast again with less caution, eagerly awaiting another hit. The fly I had tied on was a store-bought Yallerhammer, a pattern I had never used before. I'd discovered the secret weapon at last. But on my next cast I snagged the fly on a limb, and while trying to free it I snapped the line. The only Yallerhammer in my possession fell into the water and disappeared along with all my hopes of catching another fish.

A wiser person in that moment would have called it a day and headed home filled with gratitude for having caught fish for the first time in over a year. But being neither wise nor grateful, I instead chose a scapegoat on which to take out my frustration. I removed my boot knife from its sheath, placed it on a boulder, and bashed it with a rock, over and over, until it broke in two.

Relieved that neither my housemates nor any students were around to witness my temper tantrum, I sat and stared at the river in doleful silence. A minute later a kingfisher plunged into the water and, as if mocking me for my idiot rage, flew off with a fish in its beak.

Summer arrived and we held a youth camp in partnership with the local chapter of a national trout organization. I took kids fishing in the backcountry, ostensibly as their "guide," even though I had little to teach and everything still to learn.

"You're not going to catch anything that way," I told the thirteen-year-old boy with a buzzcut who was under my supervision.

Ignoring me, Jackson kept dipping his line into the current like he was fishing in a barrel.

"You'll only scare off the fish standing that close," I said.

But Jackson instinctively knew something I did not because within seconds he'd hooked a trout and soon landed another using the same technique. I clammed up and watched, apprentice to a boy well under half my age who without uttering a word had schooled me in the ABCs of fly-fishing.

My own efforts continued to come to nothing and I sensed that I was approaching another crossroads. A glutton for punishment, I hadn't yet considered quitting like before. I instead began to pass up opportunities to fish, a break that felt more and more permanent as the weeks wore on. Times I contemplated heading for the river grew fewer, and the ache from my past failures slowly began to wear off.

Then Greg asked one day if I wanted to go fishing with him. No, I did not, in fact, want to go fishing. At all. My ambition and desire had withered to the point of vanishing altogether, and I was quite happy residing in a state of angler purgatory. Fly-fishing had begun with friendship, however, and I had no good reason to turn Greg down other than out of self-pity. So I agreed and nervously pieced together my rod and threaded the line through the eyeholes in preparation for another afternoon of defeat.

My nerves settled down somewhat by the time we waded into the stretch of water flowing past campus. While fishing a hundred yards upstream of him, I kept stealing glances to see if he was watching. Greg is a patient and skilled fly-fisher and I wanted him to notice how good my casts were. But the next time I looked he was busy removing the hook from a rainbow trout he'd just caught. I turned my attention back to what I was doing and saw that I had snagged my fly on a tree branch on the opposite side of the river, an all-too-familiar situation and a sure omen of worse things to come. Except when I pulled gently on the line I saw it wasn't connected to any tree branch, and I didn't recall casting in the direction where it was hung up.

My line now began moving all by itself, swaying to and fro in an inverted arc, the far end of it hovering for a moment in one place before it moved to another. Greg had stopped fishing and was staring too. I tried to understand how my line was levitating in midair. The physics of it didn't seem possible. At one end it was wound around the reel that was attached to the rod I clasped in my hands, while at the other end it appeared to be connected to nothing at all. And yet when I tugged on it, I felt it tug back as if by an invisible hand.

There comes a moment, or perhaps a series of moments, when you come to understand the natural world is not going to do what you want it to. That it exists not for the purpose of conforming to your will but for entirely different reasons, and that your will must bend toward it. A moment when you also realize you are never going to be an expert angler, nothing remotely of the sort, an acknowledgment which might make you a better one. A moment when you find you are happy to stand crotch deep in mountain water, no longer needing to achieve anything, win a trophy, or get a pat on the back, and when, contrary to everything you believe, you understand it is possible to feel satisfied, blessed even, to be a failure. A moment when you realize fly-fishing isn't a religion, or at least not one you believe in, but just some damn thing you do because you want to feel a part of a place, part of something bigger than yourself—an impulse that maybe has something religious about it after all.

That moment arrived for me when I reeled in the line, yard after yard, none of what was happening making any sense, until the far end came within reach and I saw the Parachute Adams, a luminous dragonfly latched onto it. As it hovered in the air, I am tempted to say we locked eyes in a mesmerizing me-and-you sort of way, and that is perhaps true—we did stare at one another—the bulbous green orbs protruding from its head impossible not to notice. But a dragonfly has thirty thousand eyes and I had only two, which made me only a single object among a great many within its vast range of vision. Having nabbed my fly out of the air on my last cast, the dragonfly was clinging to it in a death grip with all six of its legs, its corkscrew-sized body betraying a tremendous strength for its size. Were the Parachute Adams something the dragonfly could have digested I would have gladly relinquished it. I instead pinched the dragonfly's thorax between my thumb and finger and gently pulled until it released its grip.

After a second I let it go, freeing both it and me.

An injury sometimes can be a blessing in disguise. After all, if not for my mishap with the bookshelf I would not have known about the stonefly hatch. As night descends, insect activity dissipates like a musical note played pianissimo, moving bar by bar toward the instant when it will fade to black. With yellow stoneflies in flight all around me, I ride the moment awhile longer.

The wave finally breaks, though before it does my line jerks. I pull tight, my Parachute Adams having seduced a rainbow trout full of vigor and fight. Next time might be different and I'll get skunked. A year might go by without catching another fish. I remove the hook and lower the trout into the water where it darts from my hands like a ghost. Before heading indoors to tend to my wound, I keep still for a moment and try to discern the stoneflies against the darkening backdrop of the mountainside. But just like that they're gone.

In the Flow

FOR SOME REASON it wasn't until long after I had moved away that I learned the name of the stream closest to my boyhood home. Like other nearby moving bodies of water, it was simply "the creek," or *crick* as I called it back then. Thanks to a civics class I was required to take in junior high school, the names of many nearby streams and rivers were no mystery—Aultman Run, Kiskiminetas, and Two Lick among them. Neither were the Allegheny and Monongahela Rivers or the direction each one flowed before forming the Ohio River in Pittsburgh, almost two hours away. Only once I'd started living in the Smokies, where map study sparked my curiosity, did I seek out the name of the ribbon of water coursing through the place where I spent the first eighteen years of my life. A name calls a river out of the void of placeless scenery and compels a person to observe more closely as a result, if for no other reason than to see if the name fits. It was obvious on my next visit home that this one did: Crooked Creek.

In contrast, I learned the name of the river flowing past the Oasis and the learning center campus almost the minute I first laid eyes on it. A name that describes relationship rather than shape, the Middle Prong, anatomically speaking, supplies the valley it plunges through with a main artery while its tributaries act as veins. The Cherokee term for rivers is Yunwi Gunahita, or Long Man, wherein a river is "personified as a man with his head resting on the mountain and his feet stretching down to the lowlands, constantly speaking to those who can understand the message," according to James Mooney, one-time ethnologist of the Eastern Band of Cherokees. The Middle Prong has got the mountain part covered, though it could hardly be considered long at a span of just five miles. One of three forks forming the Little River, all of which meet half a mile downstream of the Oasis, and taking into consideration how far it must go to reach the Gulf of Mexico, it is but a strand of hair on the Long Man's head.

European Americans who moved into the southern Appalachians called tributaries smaller than the Middle Prong "branches," a fitting term given that on maps, the main channel of a river resembles the trunk of a tree and its conjoining parts twigs. Enlarge your scope, however, and the trunk becomes only a branch of a still larger river. The Tennessee River, into which the Little River flows, becomes in just this way yet one more branch of the mighty Mississippi, which itself is but a droplet running down the face of a planet whose mainstay is *water water water*. So endowed with moving water are the Appalachians that they hold more miles of streams than Alaska—at one-third the size. Many streams throughout the ancient chain barely support life today, owing to acid leaching from abandoned coal mines, and hundreds of miles more lie buried under rocks and soil because of the destructive mining practice known as mountaintop removal. While the nearly three thousand miles of streams in the Smokies are spared a fate such as these, none flows freely to the ocean. All are dammed and thus damned to one degree or another somewhere downstream.

Like the forest of which it is a part, the Middle Prong plays an omnipresent role in the lives of creatures inhabiting Walker Valley, mine included. Its voice, rarely out of hearing range, is audible when I go to bed and when I wake. It grows louder if a climb a ridge, becoming a chorus of voices whenever I cross paths with one of the dozens of tributaries fattening it. Though never silent, it gets quiet during dry spells before roaring back after rains. I realized early on that making headspace for it was essential if I didn't want to be driven mad by its ceaseless chatter.

A river begins in the ocean or the heavens or perhaps both—a chicken-or-egg question better left to hydrologists to figure out. One thing is certain: an awful lot of rain falls in the Smokies. More than fifty inches accumulate in the low elevations every year, and nearly twice that among the highest peaks, making much of the habitat within the national park a temperate rainforest. Air currents charge eastward or sally up from the Gulf and blow across the Tennessee River Valley or creep in from the Atlantic during hurricane season and grind to a halt upon colliding with the mountains. Rainfall is just one reason for the lush plant life here—slope, aspect, shade, and absorption and retention rates are others—but it's a big one. No rain, no Smokies; know rain, know the Smokies.

If rain threatens to spoil a hike I've planned for the weekend, I usually go anyway. The forecast is wrong as often as not, and, either way, solitude is virtually guaranteed because everyone else will have stayed home. Times when a rainstorm turns the trail into a roiling creek, I also get to have the satisfaction of knowing I'm the only person deranged enough not to have done the same. The price I pay for this comes when the elements find flaws in even the best raingear money can buy, which they inevitably do. The rain will eventually stop, however, awakening the natural bouquet of the drenched forest, much like what happens when adding a splash of water to a glass of Scotch. The perfume filling my nostrils at such moments adds days or possibly weeks to my lifespan, or so I tell myself at day's end as a pile of sopping clothes amasses at my feet.

The role a mountain plays in the rain cycle is an extraordinary one. As rainwater collects on the forest floor, pools behind miniature dams comprised of leaves and twigs, and breaks free to run in rivulets downhill, it has to keep moving, keep going someplace—and that's when something astonishing occurs: it disappears. What doesn't run into the nearest branch finds pores in the earth's skin and continues gravity's path of least resistance into a belowground labyrinth inaccessible to human eyes. Then, after a time and in a different location, something equally astonishing occurs: the rainwater resurfaces, now as spring water.

The Middle Prong, like any river, has to come from someplace, which seems obvious. But try picturing with any degree of detail what the inside of a mountain looks like. I'm aware that something called the water table exists down there where fissures in bedrock store rainwater deep underground and that gravity has a large say about when it reappears. But how a mountain can contain a lake's worth of water and not belch it out all at once after a heavy drinking session for me takes more than a little imagination and guesswork.

The earth, at any rate, leaks up and down the river valley, and in one place where it does so, I fill my water bottle several times each day. "Bottled at the source," read the labels on inexpensive store-bought water bottles, which makes me wonder exactly where they mean. A factory spigot? Luckily for me, my source lies at my feet where the mountains give liberally and no middleman is necessary. I stumbled upon a spring once while hiking in the Blue Ridge Mountains in Virginia. The area looked clean and seldom visited, so I knelt to drink. It was a hot day, and upon submerging my face in the cool water, I spotted a frog staring back at me. A good sign, I decided, since amphibians thrive in only the cleanest water. While revisiting the area several months later, I came across a brook that I assumed was fed by the same spring and followed it downstream to the place where it joined the Shenandoah River. Then I reversed course and traced it back toward its source, sure that I would locate it like before. I discovered a source all right—a dozen of them, in fact—each trickle of water threading into the woods from a dozen different springs. But the frog-guarded one I never found again.

Springs can yield surprises, which makes inspecting them periodically a wise practice. The one I drink from comes with a concrete catch basin planted at a low point in the mountain. A buried pipe leads from the basin to the exit point twenty feet away where the water pulses out. Boards covering the basin keep leaves from falling in, but as the boards begin to age and rot they sometimes no longer fit securely. After filling my bottle one day, I noticed that the water smelled unseemly and peeked inside the basin. Floating inside it was an unidentifiable creature, its fur detached from its body and its pinkish-white skin shining like the surface of the moon. An alien from outer space, I deduced, until I removed the carcass and saw that it was a drowned squirrel. I let the spring flush clean for several weeks before daring to drink from it again.

Another potential hazard: what you might find after filling a water bottle at night. Groping my way to the spring late one evening, I topped off my bottle and stowed it in my pack for the following day. When I tilted the bottle to my lips in the morning, I noticed something with tiny legs and eyes tumbling around inside it. Salamanders, like frogs, indicate clean water, assuming they are alive. This one was not. *Salamander killer*, my coworkers muttered for days afterward in mock disapproval. Thereafter, as with bicycling at night in bear country, a flashlight accompanied me whenever I visited the spring after nightfall.

A spring drinker's chief concern is suffering from symptoms caused by giardia. Fear of ingesting the bacteria that causes severe intestinal distress is why anyone with good judgment purifies water in places where human feet or animals have trod. "Boil All Water" declare the signs at Appalachian Trail shelters—for the simple reason that some hikers lack enough sense to defecate downhill of their water source. While this is reason enough for many people to eschew drinking from springs altogether, springs have served as the primary source of water for humans for thousands of years and do so still in many parts of the world. Although giardia is often called "beaver fever," according to biologists, it is likely that humans themselves introduced it to the environment. The best antidote to uncertainty about the security of one's water source is an old one: prevention through protection.

The origins of the Middle Prong are many, its rebirth happening all the time. The Appalachian Mountains were first etched by moving water beginning two hundred million years ago in the Paleozoic Era, and erosion has been stealing them away bit by bit ever since, using rivers as its chief accomplices. It seems almost possible while standing beside a moving body of water to experience time as a physical property. A woman who worked at the nature center for many years liked to tell students that if they dipped their toes in the Middle Prong, they were bound to return one day. She knew it was true of herself, once having lived in the logging town upriver in pre-park days only to return to Walker Valley decades later to feed hungry mouths in our dining hall.

The river corridor becomes a virtual highway of activity during the warmer months. Rough-winged swallows perform artful displays of fast-food consumption, combining in-flight acrobatics with the terrorizing of insect life. Louisiana waterthrushes build their nests on tributaries and flute their syrupy melodies. Kingfishers perch on branches like sentinels, their blue-and-white plumage not easily detectable by prey below, while great blue herons heave overhead toward favorite fishing spots upstream. Northern water snakes rule rock crevices and detritus piled up during high water, though closer inspection sometimes reveals a copperhead or rattlesnake coiled among tufts of grass on rock islands—swimmers beware. If a smooth gray rock suddenly moves, producing a pair of eyes and whiskers, and disappears as quickly as it showed itself, it's a river otter. Beaver sign shows up every few years along flatter stretches of water, though laying eyes on one is rare. Bank beavers, as they're called, figured out long ago that it's smarter to make a home in cavities along the stream margins since no amount of engineering has thus far dammed the fast-moving Middle Prong with any success. Along those same stretches lurk hellbenders, North America's largest salamander and elsewhere called Allegheny alligators, which shelter beneath submerged boulders and wait until nightfall to hunt for supper. Growing to almost two feet in length, they've rightfully earned the nickname "snot otters" for their skin, which oozes a sticky brown mucous.

Also living in the underwater world are darters, chubs, shiners, daces, hog suckers, and sculpins, each species securing its own niche. During the spring spawn, river chubs build stone mounds in shallow riffles alongside other males, around which male Tennessee shiners cluster in their own mating ritual, turning pockets of the river bright red. Trout, the largest of the bunch, occupy fast-moving runs to feed, sharking mayflies and stoneflies during a hatch. Whatever the species—rainbow, brown, or brook—it is a trout's fate to move without ceasing and without necessarily getting anywhere or wanting to, taking for a meal whatever insect comes its way.

Abandoned spiderwebs provide a record of recent hatches by means of the insect carcasses suspended in them. Mayflies live for a year or two in a thin sliver of hospitable space a millimeter high called the boundary layer, which lies between the surface of a rock and the current skimming over it. As with stoneflies, when a mayfly larva becomes a winged adult, it spends a single libidinous day as a mouthless terrestrial bound to the task of mating before it dies. And so it is that these innumerable insects, which collectively make up what may be the greatest biomass of any creature in the river, live the most fleeting existence of any river inhabitant as members of the Order *Ephemeroptera*.

Fly-fishers make frequent use of the river, casting their lines in the same overfished pools. More than a few of them stop by the nature center campus to inquire about where the best holes are located, which, because I am neither an expert nor a dispenser of secrets, always elicits the same response: "Tell me when you find one." Because the river is too rocky for kayaking most of the time, brave souls are obliged to wait for high water, at which point they must contend with continuous Class III & IV rapids. This didn't stop Steve from running the river at whitewater level while balancing atop a poor man's kayak (a.k.a. inner tube), his eyes as wide as hubcaps as he bounced on the waves with Jeff following along in his pickup in case Steve went overboard. A land mammal by choice as much as by birth, I hurried home to avoid having to witness Steve's drowning firsthand, an event that fortunately never occurred.

Suspicious persons have been known to make use of the river corridor, at least according to law enforcement. My dentist tells me he was once accosted by an FBI agent while fly-fishing on the Middle Prong. A man in full military camouflage stepped out from behind a tree to inquire whether he was involved in the narcotics ring then known to be using family-friendly tourist towns in the Smokies as stopover points between Florida and New York City. On the contrary, he was merely out fishing while taking a break from staring into people's mouths. A newcomer to the area at the time, my dentist was meanwhile suspected by some local residents of working as an undercover FBI agent investigating the drug ring. Several years passed before they let him clean their teeth, and the number of criminals apprehended along the Middle Prong to my knowledge remains zero.

The sole evidence of crime I've encountered along the river is a money bag stolen from a local church, which I spotted one day while out for a jog. My discovery called to mind the cleansing power rivers hold in the human imagination, in this case the expectation that one can count on a river to cover up misdeeds and wash away anxieties. What the thieves failed to account for is that a real river has a mind of its own and will often disappoint one's expectations. After removing the cash, they disposed of the money bag in a body of water as transparent as glass and in the shallowest of channels where it was easy to spot, when they should have chosen a lake.

Humans have permanently altered the Middle Prong in many places, especially along its more accessible lower reaches. Prior to the industrial logging era, people used the river for splash-logging, a practice that involved dynamiting boulders in order to float logs downstream unimpeded by large obstacles. Despite possessing this knowledge, I assumed early on that the river appeared as it had for centuries, overlooking jagged rocks indicating the presence of now long-gone boulders known exclusively by those who lived here in former times. Farther upstream the river was left largely untouched, however, and retains its original character where house-sized blocks of Precambrian sandstone form dusk at midday, producing baritone notes as the current squeezes between them.

I take students to the river during classes on stream ecology. Learning is living, and the best way to know a river is to get in one. Picture a high school student wading into the Middle Prong with timid curiosity while trying to keep her brand-name jeans, rolled up to her knees, from getting wet. Now see her placing her feet on large submerged rocks instead of smaller, less slippery stones—a common rookie mistake. Visualize her mouth falling open as she loses her balance and tumbles backward into the never-warm water. Her scream when it comes might be heard a mile away if not for the sound of the current drowning her out. Multiply this scenario by ten or twelve, and the entire class has by now given new meaning to the term "immersive education." I've never once witnessed a student sulking after falling in. Like moths to a flame, they are drawn back in again to test their balancing skills and are shocked and delighted with equal measure when they once more fail.

Once the chaos subsides, we get to work with seine nets and hand nets, catching critters and placing them in a shallow tub. Later we take a closer look in the science lab aided by a microscope connected to a camera that projects images onto a screen for all to see. As a water penny moves slowly across a petri dish, its translucent undercarriage becomes visible under a bright light. A water strider, or Jesus Christ bug, won't keep still and darts around on the surface of the shallow water. A dragonfly larva demonstrates how it propels itself when it forces water out of its rear end. Enlarged onto the screen, each invertebrate in turn becomes a monster, a celebrity, and an indicator of exceptional water quality all in one.

"This has been the best day of my life ever," said a bright-eyed ten-year-old boy walking behind me at the end of one such afternoon. "Ever!" he repeated, in case anyone had missed his point.

Perhaps a bit of an overstatement, I thought, until another boy, also drenched from head to foot, chimed in.

"I'd say it's been the best day for me in maybe, well, a decade," he said. "It's definitely been better than the day I was born. That wasn't exactly what I'd call a fun experience."

High humidity combined with high temperatures in summertime becomes so stifling it turns the Oasis into a sauna. In the absence of air conditioning inside the house, the air sticks to one's skin like dog breath. My first summer, I would come home each evening and sit as motionless as possible, desperate to cool down. An hour would pass while I continued to pour with sweat, my brain about to melt and every square inch of my skin begging for mercy. I finally got enough sense to jump in the river at the end of each day. The relief was instant and long-lasting and made me wonder why I hadn't done this from the start.

The lingering memory of summer's heat perhaps explains what motivated me to practice what the Cherokee call "going to water." Whereas traditional tribal customs might include rising before dawn, praying, and walking several miles to a special location, my quasi-redneck version involved merely submerging my entire body in the Middle Prong one day each month over the course of a year. I say merely, but only in summer and early fall did this ever prove easy. As the water temperature turned frigid, I donned fleeces and wool socks before coaxing myself ankle-deep into the current—stupid, stupid, I'd scold myself through chattering teeth—and then, only when I could no longer feel my feet, I'd plunge in and scramble out as quickly as possible. Though there are saner ways of becoming familiar with a body of water, few that I know of are quite so invigorating. My boss, Ken, has adhered to the twelve-month plan for many years running, and so has the delivery man, who claims he's never gotten sick since beginning the regimen. For me, though, one year was enough.

The color of the Middle Prong is as elusive at times as the dragonflies haunting it. Overhanging leaves and the sun's reflection obscure it for much of the year, but in wintertime, jade bejewels deep pockets of water. Jason, a colleague to whom I often turn for explanations of natural events, tells me this is because cold water lacks the ability to hold molecules in suspension, a state which affords it unparalleled transparency. If the water looks clearer during this time of year, the sounds it makes seem clearer too. Vox omnia, or "all voices," gurgle, chatter, murmur, and laugh, causing me to turn my head and look for whoever is conversing nearby when nobody is there.

As summer passes and early fall arrives, the river level drops. "The rocks are up again," someone will wisecrack. Even then, the white noise of the river remains perceptible, barely, its hushed movements as reassuring as a child's noisemaking in the next room, which signals she's okay. Too loud or too quiet, and you begin thinking something must be wrong when the opposite is true: there isn't a single thing wrong, nothing of the sort, with the way the river sighs one day and has a tantrum the next.

It was during such moments that I got an inkling I was becoming a part of the place. An exchange was underway that had begun rooting me to the rhythm, tempo, and harmonies of the few square miles of the earth I inhabited. I was giving it my attention as it flooded my senses day after day, shaping me, asking for something, and giving even more. More time—more river—would go by, and the connection would deepen, such that if I ever left this place, I knew a little piece of me would stay behind. And wasn't that the point, really, that we should all feel at home someplace and claim it as our own, even while knowing it isn't really ours and will long outlive us?

A different kind of exchange takes place between the river and the forest each day. I assumed for a long time that partially submerged rocks encircled by wet rings just above the water line indicated the river level was dropping. This was true, though only to a point, because the next morning, in the absence of any precipitation, the river had returned close to its previous depth. I turned again to Jason, who explained that trees, as they photosynthesize during daytime hours, take up water that would otherwise filter through the soil and enter the river. Then at night, when the trees aren't drinking, groundwater makes its way back to the river. It is for this reason that one can find branches running in the morning, dry by afternoon, and running again by the next morning. The tradeoff is that during major rain events when the river gets its big britches on, as the saying goes, the conversation becomes one way, as attested by the battered trunks of trees anchored to its banks.

Shallow channels of the river flow sideways around rocks during prolonged dry periods, the water's depth not high enough to rush around them for the time being. The humbled current must go around them now, whitewater no longer white, and white noise barely audible. The fish must think the sky is falling. While watching the level drop day after day, it's tempting to believe it will actually happen this time, the river will finally run dry. It never does, of course. The radiant sky, blue for days on end, grays over at last and the rain begins to fall. It falls and falls, gushing off mountainsides and pouring into the river as if from a thousand broken bathtub spigots, the waning ended and the waxing commencing once more.

Sometimes when it rains, it keeps on raining, rains some more, doesn't stop, doesn't seem to know how. Two, maybe three, times a year, this occurs. The Middle Prong dons its big britches and my students and I steer clear. The rain sometimes won't stop even then, and before you know it a flood is underway. A rock—a very big one—is reliable at such times. A rock is a rock after all. One can't count on a tree to stay put forever. But a rock is immovable and thus a permanent fixture on the landscape, or so I once believed.

I've come to depend on particular river rocks for the comfortable sit-spots they provide when my mind more than my body needs a good rinsing. The river is so full of large rocks that I've found it impossible to memorize their precise arrangement, even along short stretches of water. A general impression of the pattern they make forms in my mind even so. Move them around and it would be like Steve or Jeff pranking me by rearranging my dresser drawers and leaving me to guess where all my socks have gone.

Dislodging a large rock isn't easy. I learned this firsthand when Mark and Rob, another college friend, were visiting and we tried pushing over one that was sitting on the riverbank. The boulder was there and we had nothing better to do. We figured we couldn't harm it, just help it take a short journey—one of about four feet—which boulders rarely get to make after all. And anyway, the park service had harassed the rock once already decades earlier during the construction of the bridge it sat beneath.

Mark shoved first. Not surprisingly, the boulder did not budge. All three of us pushed, grinding our heels into the ground, without success. A sense of personal mythology and grandeur might have helped our efforts, but this wasn't Mt. Everest we were climbing. It was just a rock we were trying to push over and not even a very big one compared to other potential candidates. For half an hour all that mattered to us was moving the rock. "We need a tree branch," said Rob, and a fallen one was conscripted into service as a fulcrum. We shoved with all our might, and when the boulder finally moved it did not roll so much as plop. I would understand later the disappointment that sometimes accompanies rock-tipping when a boulder used by my fellow naturalists for jumping into our favorite swimming hole was found shoved into it by an unknown assailant.

Every rock in the Middle Prong, large or small, is on a journey. Few reside where they did before the last flood, and now they wait for another, the permanence of their current location just an illusion. In May I witnessed what old-timers call a century flood when all but the biggest rocks were moved once more. Boulders the size of picnic tables tumbled end over end alongside sections of asphalt torn from the road by the frothing current. Farther upstream the river gouged a trench in a gravel roadbed two feet deep, washing away thousands of taxpayer dollars. A culvert wrenched out of the ground by the force of the water lay as twisted and battered as a discarded beer can.

I went in search of my coworkers Jaimie and her husband Michael. While Jaimie kept students occupied at a safe distance away from the river, Michael and I formed a search party and bicycled up the road, now a secondary stream eighteen inches deep. We found a man stranded with his truck on the far side of the ripped-out culvert.

"Call my wife and tell her I'm all right, will you?" he asked, giving us her number. A day would pass before park rangers, stretched thin by more pressing emergencies, put a temporary bridge in place so the man could rescue his truck.

Not every manmade object damaged or relocated by the river was a total loss. A log bridge washed away by the floodwater was found deposited on the road half a mile downstream. Six of us hoisted one end into the bed of a pickup truck with the aid of a hydraulic jack before dragging it back to campus.

Stand on the banks of a mountain river in flood if you ever get the chance and listen closely. As the swollen river rages on, even once the sun comes out, your heart will begin to race. You'll hear what you think at first must be only in your head, as I did on the day the Middle Prong flooded: the sound of muffled thunder. Not a cloud in the sky, yet there it is all the same. It's the sound boulders make as dozens of them somersault over and over in the brown abyss. Afterward, when the water level returns to normal, everything will appear unrecognizable. But for now the boulders hurtle invisibly through the valley as the current spits water droplets backlit by the sun and birds keep their distance—which you should be doing, too, while wondering what it's like down there where the fish and crawdads must be hanging on for dear life and how they'll possibly survive all this tumult, though you know they will—they've been doing this for a long time, since before the dams went up and just like they will after they're gone—and perhaps it will cross your mind that it doesn't make sense, this violence that's nevertheless beautiful—and that you're not worthy of this abundance and overflowing of riches imparted by the river, which you welcome anyway, still a novice like me, perhaps, to the workings of Creation.

Stepping Out

ON HIKING DAY, at a quarter before eight in the morning, I meet a handful of students at the weather station on campus. A dozen middle schoolers from Tallahassee who never laid eyes on mountains before this week will follow me into the backcountry several hours from now, nerves and all. But first there are the vital signs of the valley to take.

"Good morning," I venture.

No response. One boy's finger is shoved up his nostril, and the nose of another is running like a faucet. No one's brain seems to be working quite yet, mine included.

Nothing fancy, the weather station contains several inexpensive analog instruments housed inside a wooden box perched on four legs. I unlatch the doors and coax a shy student into reading the thermometer (51°F) and hygrometer (90 percent humidity). Another writes down the data, which the students will announce to the rest of their class during breakfast. We estimate the wind speed by blowing soap bubbles into the air and comparing their movements with the illustrations in the charmingly unsophisticated Beaufort wind scale. The barometer, unchanged since yesterday, confirms that another clear day lies ahead.

When a jangle of steel announces the start of breakfast, we make a beeline for the dining hall. A girl and boy inside take turns reading aloud the menu, then everyone reads in unison this morning's words of inspiration written on a poster in large lettering: *A trail is not the shortest distance between two points, but perhaps the best: a road built only for the traffic of boots and thoughts* (author unknown). Next comes a moment of silence reserved for anyone wishing to express reverence and gratitude in their own headspace—that rarest of events when you can hear a pin drop in a room crammed with people. Afterward student volunteers get busy fetching platters of eggs and pancakes for their tablemates. Barely a minute into the meal, the sound of a small dam bursting open erupts as an upended pitcher of orange juice gushes across a tabletop and floods onto the floor. In typical school cafeteria fashion, a chorus of voices rises to a crescendo in response to the commotion, and I head for the mop room with my mouth full of eggs. We are all of us wide awake now.

Following the weather report, food waste is collected from each table in a bucket and weighed on a scale. This meal's total is half a pound, which, divided by the number of students in the room, equals perhaps twenty milk-soaked cornflakes per person. The data point is recorded onto a graph alongside others from previous meals. Taken altogether, the lines on the graph approximate today's hike: up one meal, down the next, and back up again before trending downward—valleys and peaks all in a row, which provides visible cues for students to strive toward a common goal of minimizing waste.

Half an hour later, our lunches packed and water bottles filled, we gather once more. Time now to introduce everyone's favorite topic: how to go to the bathroom in the woods. Enter Stanley the Shovel, a nickname of unknown origin given to the metal trowel each teacher-naturalist carries in their pack, including the one I hold up for everyone to see.

"If you gotta borrow Stanley, first find a private spot with a nice view," I say. "Then dig a hole about five inches deep and five inches wide. Or wider, depending on your aim."

Going Number One requires less explanation. My coworker Mary invites those who have never urinated in the woods to join the Number One Club and get comfortable with the idea of doing so today—a ploy, above all, to persuade kids to hydrate. All of this talk about pooping and peeing elicits a few chuckles but mostly mute stares of disbelief. By way of encouraging anyone who is nervous about going without the use of a toilet, I tell them about the Walker Sisters, exemplars of girl power and descendants of early settlers who continued living on their land for several decades after it was incorporated into the national park. Famous in their day for bucking newfangled trends such as electricity and indoor plumbing, the five unmarried siblings chose to forgo the use of an outhouse as well, relying instead on the

Stepping Out   121

forest for privacy and dried corn husks for toilet paper. Going a single day without the luxury of a porcelain throne—perhaps the one time in their lives many students will do so—should seem easy by comparison.

A final flurry of shoelace tightening and herding to the bathroom commences before we head outdoors in our hiking groups. Once outside, I point out the mountain visible across the river and explain that its top is several hundred feet lower than the one we're about to climb. Gasps issue from several mouths. The eight miles that lie ahead must seem like a death march in the imaginations of eleven-year-olds. Yet already this week they have accomplished things many never dreamed themselves capable of: sleeping in a strange bed away from home and their families, liking different food, braving a cold river while netting fish, walking in the nighttime forest without the aid of a flashlight, and spending nearly every waking minute outdoors—much of the time while wearing wide-eyed expressions of delight. When I start up the trail, I'm not surprised to find them right on my heels.

A series of switchbacks usher us to an overlook where a break in the thick tree cover affords us a rare view. Inches from our feet a scree slope angles down close to the spot where we were standing just moments ago. Giant domes of mountains rise in the near distance and the roar of the river carries to our ears. Cameras click and eyes widen at the sight of scaffolds of green framed by blue sky. Then we're off again.

"Has anyone ever fallen off the mountain?" says a voice behind me. Kelsey, the girl asking it, means the one beneath our feet.

"Sure," I say calmly.

"Did they die?"

"Trees caught them before they made it very far. So, no. They just got a few bumps and bruises."

The trees below us are spaced so closely together that even a stone rolling down the mountainside wouldn't get very far. The footing is tricky and the trail rather narrow in places, however, and we pass several steep drop-offs before long. More questions from Kelsey, each one on the same theme: *This is dangerous. Should we really be doing this?* Children, octogenarians, and others in between have sustained insect stings and minor injuries during classes I've taught outdoors, but no one has ever broken a bone, been struck by lightning, become hypothermic, suffered a concussion or bear attack or snake bite, drowned, or perished. As it happens, the forest is a fairly hospitable place. Accidents are more likely to occur back in civilization, where we accept many potential perils as normal—owning a pet, for instance, or chewing gum—and let down our guard. But rather than relying on words, I let our feet, which keep propelling us forward, provide an answer: *Of course, we should.*

We come to a waterfall where a mossy jungle clings to a vertical world. Creek water pours over bedrock, writing in cursive as it runs past our feet. I demonstrate how to make face paint using river stones and everyone begins streaking their cheeks in color. So absorbed are the students by the sensations ignited in them by the spectacle of this place that if I were to yell, "Free puppies for everyone!" I doubt a single student would pay me any mind.

Though a week provides little time to get to know my students' backgrounds, I'm aware of how foreign their new environment must feel compared to their usual everyday experience—one without electronics, and where temperatures are too hot or too cold and they must learn to take care of their needs while facing their fears largely on their own. For many, I'm sure, giving up creature comforts in exchange for physical hardship makes no earthly sense. "Builds moral fiber!" as my old scoutmaster would say, and he would be right. But such platitudes fall flat to anyone who has been conditioned to believe their future success depends on their ability to perform well on standardized exams. So instead of preaching the benefits of roughing it, it's the experience itself, honed by self-reliance and teamwork, I let speak. Besides, a mountain seems less intimidating after climbing one. A student bound to a wheelchair all his young life participated in a hike I once led with sixth graders. He was eager for a hike on four wheels, so his classmates took turns pushing from behind and pulling in front using wooden rickshaw-type arms connected to his wheelchair while he pointed out obstacles and shouted directions. In one impossibly steep section, I turned my head to see him resolutely peering into the woody abyss below. Should he have tumbled over the edge, he would have incurred far more than bumps and bruises. Biting my lip, I watched his helpers steer him safely past the spot, and by the time we crested the mountain, the word "can't" was perhaps forever erased from everyone's vocabulary.

The woods, I have to remind myself constantly, aren't experienced by everyone in the same way. A Black student who knows the history of lynching may not embrace it with the same peace of mind as someone less aware of the darker chapters in our nation's history or the privileges they've inherited from society. For a variety of reasons, parents of minority students may be disinclined to send their children away into the company of total strangers. Neglect, trauma, and a thousand other circumstances can mark a person's life. Often in this spot, I think of Star, a thirteen-year-old girl a head taller and a year older than her classmates, who came here with her class last year. As she stared at the cascading water, her teacher informed me that Star's mother made her turn tricks in their trailer park for older male "uncles" in order to make ends meet. Whether a hike in the forest taught her something about how to endure her precarious situation, I can't say. Perhaps at the very least, it showed her that beauty exists in the world should she go looking for it.

Regardless of each person's circumstance, one we are all sharing today is the arduous task of hoofing through the forest. Survival isn't the point, and least of all is it to toughen up kids in boot-camp fashion when facing adversity is already a daily reality for some of them. The point of our hike remains to be seen. Such is the elusive and humbling nature of my role as their instructor. Rather than doing the work for them, my job is to play midwife to whatever the day will bring.

Next comes a miniature chasm separating us from the far side of the creek. One at a time, we leap across, our feet finding traction on bedrock threaded by milky veins of quartzite. We climb another series of switchbacks steeper than the first and come to an old railroad grade.

"Congratulations. We've made it one mile," I announce when we pause to catch our breaths. In the silence that follows I can almost make out the sound of a dozen hearts sinking. Then the protests begin.

"Only one? It felt like five." Fortunately, the day is not yet ripe for mutiny. I suggest that perhaps we should call it quits and return to campus. The students consider this for a moment—a very brief moment—before unanimously deciding to keep going. First devouring granola bars and guzzling copious amounts of water, we press on, reverse psychology having fulfilled its function. From now on, no one will be pushing them up the mountain but themselves.

It is impossible in the tactile world we've entered to avoid coming into contact with something leafy. Feisty dog-hobble shrubs grow so thick in places that we can't see our feet. A bonanza of rhododendron crowds the path and brushes against our faces. Greenbrier vines and hemlock boughs do as well, but above all, rhododendron, the leather-leaved shrub which, if the forest were a party, would play the extreme extrovert by being everywhere at once.

Calling the path we're following a "trail" would be generous. Abandoned by loggers and later by trail crews, we make the best use we can out of what the wilderness hasn't swallowed up. The trees these days fall by themselves, and where they fall, there they lie. All manner of them choke our forward progress, forcing us to step over them here, duck under them there. Their sheer variety could fill a field guide. Dead trees lying flat or slouching against living ones. Leaning dead trees refusing to yield to gravity. Dead trees propped up by limbs poking into the ground like giant hypodermic needles. Standing dead trees, sitting ones. Dead trees as hard as stone. (Speaking of rock-hard trees, I once led a hike in this area in winter when snow-laden limbs drooped low across the path such that I had no choice but to put my head down and plow forward like a running back to clear the way for others following behind. In just this way I managed to ram headfirst into a concealed tree trunk lying horizontally across the path. *Idiot Naturalist Knocks Self Out, Strands Children in Wilderness* ran the news headline in my throbbing head when I came to. I gathered my glasses and hat, which had been flung into the snow from the force of the impact. "Um, watch your heads," I hollered back to my followers, who were none the wiser.) Dead trees shredded by woodpeckers. Dead moss-covered trees. Slippery dead trees shorn of their bark. Trees that appear to be dead until closer inspection reveals a slender green wand signaling a breath of life.

This is to say nothing of living trees growing everywhere. Nor of a sizable patch of poison ivy the path wends through—one place where it would be unwise to borrow Stanley the Shovel. I take a minute to explain that poison ivy often grows where people have disturbed the ground. Acting like nature's band-aid, it helps keep humans away until the natural process of succession introduces the next generation of plant life and reestablishes the forest. Though it isn't what they expected to hear, the students seem willing to entertain the possibility that poison ivy isn't the enemy we often think it is.

Around the next bend, cries of fascination and disgust break forth behind me. Glistening in the morning sun atop a mat of pine duff sits a fine specimen of scat, or "dookie" in the parlance of schoolkids. Black hair intertwined with pine needles gives it the appearance somewhat of a braid cut from a stylish human head. Huddling around it, we try to unravel the mystery: Who left it? How long ago? What creature did the hair belong to before becoming another's meal? Fresh signs of rooting nearby indicate wild hogs have been active in the area. Though it's unlikely that we will lay eyes on a hog today or the coyote that digested one, the evidence left behind provides us with a window through which to peer into the secretive life of the forest. It won't be the last time students will contemplate the subject of poop, a fact of creaturely existence that a hike manages to make a little less uncomfortable to talk about. At tonight's campfire they will learn the "Scat Rap" composed some years ago on campus and chant the chorus loudly into the night:

It starts with an S and ends with a T,
It comes out of you and it comes out of me.
I know what you're thinking, but don't call it that!
Be scientific and call it scat!

We sample the forest's smorgasbord of flavors as we encounter them: eastern hemlock needles, partridgeberry berries, and sourwood leaves. We find remnants of old logging equipment, including a steel cable used to drag logs down steep mountainsides to waiting railcars. Rusting and half-buried, it looks like an industrial-strength grapevine poking out of the ground.

While I'm helping kids balance on a slick log at another stream crossing, I notice a boy pick up a rock and strike a tree with it. It takes me several minutes to help everyone over the creek, and all the while, he keeps mercilessly hammering away at the tree until he has gouged a hole in the trunk and exposed the inner bark. Other boys have crowded around to witness the spectacle. It's Trevor, of course, a tall boy held back a grade who has made it his personal mission this week to test the patience of every adult in his presence. Senseless acts of destruction are practically a rite of passage for a boy his age, and the tree will likely see worse in its lifetime. It is the violent brazenness with which he is going about his vigilante performance that I instead find unnerving. It's not hard picturing him growing up to become a narcissist or self-hater who beats up on his girlfriend and the world, and while imagining this possible future, I become filled with the urge to grab him by the scruff of his neck and drop-kick him back into the fourth grade.

Not for legal reasons alone do I refrain from doing this, for I, too, once had a destructive streak not unlike Trevor's. One of my chief passions during the week I spent at McKeever in the sixth grade, besides ignoring whatever assignment I'd been given to do, was rocking standing dead trees back and forth until they crashed to the ground. Despite the risk this involved, including when the top half of a dead pine tree broke off and nearly landed on me, pushing over trees made me feel alive, as if I could cause something to happen in the world. The remarkably patient pair of young women who were my instructors never once upbraided me for reckless behavior or hurting Mother Nature. One of them asked if I knew what purpose dead trees served and which creatures depended on them for survival, and after graciously prompting me with a few answers, let me decide for myself whether to keep knocking them over. Before the end of the week, I stopped of my own accord.

Trevor notices me watching him but not reacting. I can see there isn't any malice in his eyes, just dumb ignorance and a lost faraway look. His face registers a hint of understanding over the damage he has caused even before I tell him that exposing the inner bark risks disease and premature death for the tree. Figuring he has likely heard plenty of lectures in his short lifetime and doesn't need another, I leave it at that, playing the role of good cop for now.

We march on. More stream crossings, more wet logs and rocks, until a hole in the ground captures everyone's attention. Several boys are convinced that it's a snake hole, and when I ask what they mean, they look at me like I'm stupid for asking. Duh, it's where a snake made its home, they say. I'm tempted to throw cold water on their theory. Snakes don't dig holes, after all—how could they? But as with my former destructive streak, I had my own version of snake holes when I was a child. Mine was a skunk-rabbit, which I owe to my father who reinforced my belief in their existence each time he claimed to have spotted one on road trips. My sister and I always looked to see if we, too, could glimpse the elusive creature created in his imagination and recreated in ours, but the skunk-rabbit always slinked out of view before we could spot it. We eventually realized it was our father's way of distracting us whenever we were fighting with one another. But that such a thing might exist was reason enough to keep looking for it because even in the skunk-rabbit's absence, our search for it led to noticing things on the landscape that we would otherwise have missed.

In a way skunk-rabbits have remained inhabitants of the forest for me ever since. "Unless you become like little children, you will never enter the kingdom of heaven," says the Book of Matthew, which I don't think means that humans ought to be compliant and unquestioning—an impossibility anyway, especially for children, whose nature is to be curious and ask why. A kingdom in its own right, the forest works much the same way, and I think it is impossible to experience it fully without seeing it in part through child-like eyes. At some point, though, scientific inquiry becomes necessary, at the very least to counter a propensity for ignoring evidence and clinging to convenient explanations that deter one from further investigation.

"So what did the snake use to dig with?" I ask, inviting the boys to furnish evidence backing up their claim. A brief reconsideration of their assumptions quickly leads to a different and far more plausible conclusion: perhaps a rodent excavated the tunnel before a snake carried out a home invasion and made off with one in its belly.

Conversation among the students soon turns to video games, movies, sports—and then the inevitable questions come: *How far have we gone? When's lunch? Can we take a break?* Beauty and suffering go hand in hand, and after climbing steadily uphill over the past several hours, the way has grown steep. Wilderness is a setting ripe for suffering and some of that is going on now, though a mild discomfort born of unfamiliar sensations would be more accurate. When complaints grow more vocal, I consider delivering a back-in-my-day speech to help put things in perspective, but when I was their age I complained plenty too. My colleague Michael believes that in the event of a nuclear holocaust, cockroaches and children will be all that's left of the world. I think he might be on to something. Kids are tough and often don't know any better than just to keep on putting one foot in front of the other.

When we stop for lunch at last, there isn't rejoicing among the students so much as a collective collapsing onto the ground. Within seconds they haul themselves onto logs and tear into their sandwiches like jackals. Naomi, their classroom teacher, and I exchange pleased looks when Trevor elects to sit with other kids rather than by himself. In the hour that has passed since he assaulted the tree, he has behaved downright gentlemanly, even assisting other kids at creek crossings.

Once everyone finishes eating, we watch him organize a game of Camouflage, likely the first time in his life he has done anything of the sort. Kelsey, playing the hunter, closes her eyes and counts to thirty as the others scramble to hide in the woods and peek out from behind tree trunks just enough so she has a chance of spotting them. Scanning the woods without moving from her position, she points when she sees someone, picking off Jaden, Blake, Aaliyah, and Sidney one by one.

"Migrate!" she yells, closing her eyes once more, and those still uncaught move nearer and hide again. Whatever veil still separates each child from their surroundings, if there is any, has utterly vanished. Complete immersion in the present moment is all there is as the scene unfolds: a pair of eyes searching the forest, a half dozen more staring back, the thrill felt by each child who evades detection, and the exhilaration the hunter experiences each time she spots her prey.

Ten minutes later, Kelsey has caught all of her classmates except one: Trevor, who is beaming. Though it's his turn to play the hunter during round two, he hands over the role to an eager classmate out of a desire to hide again and keep a good thing going. I'm not so naive as to believe the changes I'm witnessing in his behavior are permanent. His social graces are lacking to a severe degree, and hard days no doubt lie ahead. It's heartening all the same to witness this other way of being in the world he has discovered, a version of himself those back home may not at first recognize or affirm when he returns there at week's end, yet which his fellow students and Naomi will help nurture.

The forest presents an altogether different character when we resume our hike. The sound of the creek has disappeared and oaks and mountain laurels have replaced tulip trees and rhododendron. Walking now on a ridgeline, we're no longer glimpsing up at the forest from a valley floor but peering down into one. Beneath our feet is a bona fide trail, wide and level and maintained by the park service. But the hardest part is still to come.

It begins soon enough with another climb, the final one. Thin tree cover on the nose of a finger ridge provides views of a mammoth ridgeline in the distance, atop which runs the Appalachian Trail. "Look! There's Thunderhead Mountain and Rocky Top and Devil's Courthouse," I enthuse, but no one is the least bit interested. All everyone wants is to get up this mountain.

And at last, we do. Though no magnificent vistas await us and no angelic choir breaks into song, the group feels a palpable sense of accomplishment, and congratulations are in order. Naomi has been hiking quietly at the back of the line all this time, and I catch her smiling.

Teaching in a public school very often means facing the pressures of shifting curriculum standards, larger class sizes, deteriorating student behavior, overbearing or unsupportive parents and administrators, and uncertainties over her and her students' safety. Less and less often, she told me earlier in the week, does it mean getting to actually *teach*. That is, to mentor, inspire, guide her students toward self-knowledge, and grant them the freedom to follow curiosity and a line of inquiry for however long as it takes. Kind and patient, she also said that working with kids was why she chose the teaching profession and why she stays; to help them stretch and grow and to nurture them into becoming responsible citizens and lifelong learners.

Despite her frustrations with modern schooling and the limitations she labors under, this week has provided a rare occasion to forgo abstractions, confining schedules, and teaching to the test in exchange for something more holistic. Outside of their routines, her students' usual roles have fallen away. No one's the troublemaker, overachiever, or verbose or quiet or wimpy kid just now. She no longer quite fits the mold of authority figure herself now that her students have seen her perspire and struggle up the same mountain they have. Everything has been turned upside down.

The culminating moment of the day has arrived and everyone sits on the ground awaiting instructions. For the next couple of miles, all of it downhill, the students will follow a narrow winding footpath through more territory they have never before stepped foot in—alone this time. I will depart first and their teacher last, with each student spaced several minutes apart in between us when their turn comes. None of us will see another soul until we all reach the gathering point, where I will be waiting for everyone.

I study their faces while explaining all of this and think about parents who struggle to shield their children from risks in a world growing more beyond their control every day. Most children will experience wilderness only vicariously through movies and their imaginations, absent actual sanctuaries that remind us we will never fully wrestle nature under human control. It's humbling to recall that the parents of those seated before me have entrusted me with the task of giving their children a taste of the real thing. If modern cultural narratives say that kids don't belong in unpredictable and fearsome wilderness, counternarratives rooted deeper in time and in cultures the world over say they do, and it's one they are living today to the fullest.

Trust is an essential ingredient of the Solo Walk. And because it would take only one kid breaking that trust for parents and school administrators to question our judgment and thus rob future students of having such an opportunity, my eyes settle on Trevor. If there is any lingering desire inside him to cause drama or disrupt another student's experience, the Solo Walk would be the time to do it. I have never chosen not to trust a student, however, and today will be no different. All I can detect is some nerves and excitement he's perhaps feeling over braving the wilderness on his own. Besides, it's kids like him who have never been granted such trust who need it most.

Don't leave the trail or make lots of noise, I advise the students. Don't stop until you reach the end, but don't turn the Solo Walk into a race either. Life so often moves too fast, and yet all we have to do is be present, see what we see, and feel what we feel. I feel a little like a self-help guru telling them this, and too often, I fail to heed my own advice. A media-saturated world vying for our attention awaits each one of us. What's the use in rushing back to all that? Before us awaits the gifts afforded by solitude, including perhaps encounters with the oft hidden depths of human existence some of us may not be aware are possible. Given such a potent opportunity, it's no wonder students on past Solo Walks told me afterward about transcendent experiences they had that would be best described as religious.

Though incurring an injury during the Solo Walk is possible, chances are slim the worst will happen, so it's pointless discussing every conceivable hazard. Tripping carries the greatest likelihood, and to curtail anyone from overreacting should they get hurt, I paint a picture with words.

"Say you fall and land on a sharp stick, and it impales your chest. Breaks ribs. Goes through the right ventricle of your heart and protrudes out your back, causing blood to spurt like Old Faithful." Hand motions I make help illustrate this most improbable scene. "I can see why *maybe* then you would want to stop and call for help. I'll be happy to put a band-aid on it for you. But first, try rubbing some dirt in it and see if that works."

Teachers aren't supposed to talk this way, and at first the students look perplexed. But by the time I'm finished, Trevor, Kelsey, and the others, all of them smirking, get my point: don't make excuses for yourself unless it's for real because you are tougher than you think. I will tell them later about the timber rattlesnake lazing in the middle of the gathering spot at the end of one Solo Walk I led. Another group of students hiking in the opposite direction with their teacher-naturalist that day soon arrived, eventually bringing the number of people converging on the spot to more than fifty. Glenn Rice, a teacher who, over his forty-year career, brought thousands of students to the woods from Birmingham, Alabama, was last to arrive. Not a fan of snakes, he knew he would have to answer to his students' parents back home if they became alarmed upon hearing news about their youngster sharing cramped quarters with a venomous reptile. But he said only, "Well, the snake was here first," and watched with the rest of us as the snake meandered through the throng of students eating their lunches in attentive silence, never once rattling.

The phantom goals of ultimate safety and comfort that society tells us to strive for, we have had no choice but to give up today. In their place we've found something more authentic and harmonious, perhaps foremost a creatureliness commensurate with our surroundings. We have grown hungry and tired, found countless obstacles blocking our passage, and might still encounter wild beasts lying in our path. But whatever comes, we will make do. We will adjust to whatever tempo and rhythm the forest requires. We otherwise demand so much of the world through our habits and appetites and the human systems supporting them, blind to the sacrifices we expect the earth and other people to make on our behalf, often while asking little of ourselves. The fact is that the future promises increasing discomfort for us all—more for some than for others—and that those who believe the future will inevitably keep getting better are bound to meet with disappointment. During my time living and teaching in the woods, I've grown more comfortable with being uncomfortable and expecting less, in part because "less" so often is more. Shining examples of this are my students who today have stepped outside their comfort zones and, by virtue of stepping outside them, have seen them expand.

Hikes like ours today provide a chance to consider the boundaries of my own comfort zone. I came to feel at home in the forest early in life, thanks to the Boy Scouts, parents who took me camping, and the woods behind my house. My knee-jerk resistance to discomfort and growth often instead has to do with my role as an educator. The expertise I've gained sometimes carries the temptation to wield knowledge as power and use it for the sake of using it, needlessly filling up space with the sound of my voice, such as those occasions when I waxed on about the forest rather than letting the forest itself do most of the talking while students investigated it. A similar temptation is making students unnecessarily reliant on me as their leader out of a need to feel indispensable, when handing over the reins to students and embracing the mild chaos that sometimes ensues would have accomplished loads more. Sharing expert knowledge is indeed necessary at times to the extent that it helps them flourish but determining when to hold back and let students struggle requires constant mindful effort. It turns out I need my students just as much as they need me. Above all, I need them to help renew my sense of wonder and keep me alert to what I might otherwise take for granted. Plans go sideways, I make mistakes, and I watch with a mix of envy and humility as a newly hired teacher-naturalist younger than I am does a superior job fertilizing students' imaginations. I keep going, learn to provide fewer answers, ask better questions, and recognize moments when it's best to step out of the way of my students and let them lead.

Now is one of those times. My role as Beatrice, Dante's guide on the journey to paradise, has abruptly come to an end. Time to let go and allow Trevor and each of the others to take over. Instinct will be their only guide now. Though they don't yet know it, they are about to have their socks blown off, their circuitry permanently rewired, their senses prodded by sensations they have never experienced before. By the time they finish the Solo Walk, none of them will be the same person they were when they began. They will come to a new understanding of something about themselves and the world. Who more than children are open to taking such a step?

"Happy trails," I say before turning and walking off down the trail.

Alone now and no longer a child myself, not by a long shot, I wonder: What about me? How open am I to change and the discomforts that come with it? For in just a few weeks, I will move out of the mountains and trade my hiking boots for a pair of cycling shoes.

Interlude: Making Tracks

AT THE END OF MY SECOND YEAR working at Tremont, I bid goodbye to my coworkers and moved east to live near friends who had invited me to help them launch a bicycle courier company. Seth and Rachel lived six hours away in central North Carolina, and though I didn't relish the thought of leaving the mountains—for good, I assumed at the time—I decided to scratch an itch I'd begun having for other adventures. As it turned out, the next three years would teach me a good deal about the worth of the work I'd left behind. Time and again I would be reminded of the rare gift I'd received by getting to live in the Smokies, an experience that would in turn show me the value of the national park as a measuring stick as I encountered an altogether different landscape.

The differences between my old and new surroundings were jarring. The Piedmont region was flat and hot, and though bicyclists seemed to outnumber motorists in the small town where I rented a room in a house on a side street, I found myself residing in what sounded like a noise factory. Goodbye to darkness too. A streetlight cast a yellow glow around my room at night, and the only way I could fall asleep was by draping a rolled-up T-shirt across my face. Before long I began regarding every sliver of light and nighttime noise—automotive engines accelerating, house doors slamming shut—as if it were an invasive species intent on ruining my peace of mind. Mountain life had spoiled me good.

Customers were few in the early days of the bicycle delivery business. Finding temp work at a copy shop to help make ends meet, I was soon spending evenings duplicating seven-hundred-page legal documents. Though I saved money by bicycling everywhere, there were other prices to pay. While pedaling to work one day, a minivan pulled alongside me, the door slid open, and a posse of teenage boys began pelting me with eggs. Now a newly minted martyr for the bicycling cause, I returned home to scrub raw eggs out of my clothes and hair and explain to my boss on the phone why I was going to be late.

Several nights later, as I was staring mindlessly out the window of the copy shop, a pair of teacher-naturalists with whom I'd worked in the Smokies who were in town for a conference came striding down the sidewalk. The two women looked cheery and appealingly unhip on the main street of a college town. Suddenly feeling out of place in nice work clothes rather than hiking boots and Carhartts, my first instinct was to hide, but they'd already spotted me through the plate-glass window and came inside to deliver hugs and news from the mountains. Doubts immediately formed in my mind about what I was doing here and why I'd left Tremont.

My next part-time job was at UPS, where instead of getting to drive a big brown truck, I was put in charge of the customer service desk. Another disappointment: rather than a pair of brown shorts and a brown shirt, I was given a clip-on tie and an oversized button-down shirt with shirttails that reached to my knees and bunched inside my pants like a cloth diaper. It didn't take long to figure out that manning the customer service desk was the worst possible job to have at UPS. Lines grew so long they stretched out the door, and I couldn't figure out how to operate the arcane computer program that tabulated the weight and cost of packages, a task my supervisor had never explained to me. Outright ignoring me most days, she would stop by wearing a look of disgust on her face only to click a few buttons on the keyboard and get the line of customers moving again.

I succeeded one day in getting her attention and asked her to show me how to operate the program.

"What are you saying?" she said with exasperation.

"I'm saying I would like you to show me how it works."

"They told me you were smart. Said you had a college degree. That you were a genius."

Understanding finally why she hadn't bothered to train me on something

Interlude: Making Tracks

a genius ought to have easily grasped, I assured her that I was not a genius in case this wasn't abundantly clear by now, and at last she explained how the system worked. The best part of my job was lifting boxes onto the conveyor belt, a task reminiscent of the countless times I'd stacked firewood in the mountains. I would have lifted boxes all day if they would have let me. Thanksgiving arrived and the company gave each employee a frozen turkey. I placed mine in the backseat of my car and headed to Pennsylvania.

Seth and Rachel were sympathetic when I had to quit the business to pay my bills. I quit UPS as well upon landing a full-time position with an outfit that advocated for a better understanding of learning differences in children. Decent yet mindless work, my sole duties were to make database entries and answer the phone. Growing bored from sitting all day, I gazed out the window and drank excessive amounts of caffeine to stay awake. To counter its effects, I retreated to the supply room to do pushups, nervous about getting caught. I wondered what superpower other people with desk jobs possessed and why I was incapable of finding any fulfillment in mine—unless they, too, perhaps pined for something else out there beyond the bricks and mortar of office life, such as I had once had and found myself longing for again.

Another reason I left the mountains was to pursue my dream of performing as a singer-songwriter, which I had little chance of doing while living in the boonies. I rented studio time to record an album of original songs and spent more money I didn't have getting the recording mixed by an industry professional. Lacking representation, a record label, and a marketing plan, I paid bills by performing as often as possible, which was less gratifying than I'd pictured. Though I had developed a certain level of comfort in front of audiences in my youth while performing in bands and orchestras, now I was alone onstage. And while I had a passable singing voice, I found playing guitar while trying to remember the lyrics and not look stupid doing it nerve racking. I could never figure out what to do with my eyes. Close them? Stare at the floor? My musician father had nerves of steel, but I hadn't acquired those genes. After eight months of gigging in coffee shops and bars, I'd spent nearly every dollar I earned renting a sound system because purchasing one was too expensive. It seemed clear I was never going to earn a living doing this, a conclusion I reached with some relief.

On weekends, I escaped to a forest several miles outside town. The pine-oak forest ubiquitous throughout the Piedmont region didn't match the definition of "deciduous" that I carried in my mind, even if Lucy Braun's *Deciduous Forests of Eastern North America*, the seminal work on that subject, assured me it met the criteria. The trees there were as tall as ship masts, towering over a soft carpet of pine needles and a persimmon tree whose fruit I collected in winter. Maybe I could get used to this, I tried convincing myself.

I moved west at the end of the following summer—one incremental step back toward the mountains, I realized later—for graduate school. Greensboro was a bigger town yet had a family atmosphere with barking dogs, cookouts, and friendly professors. My fellow students and I hiked together on weekends and gorged ourselves afterward at a cheap Chinese buffet. Traffic noise rattled around my room and streetlights shone in my window at night, and I kept draping a shirt across my face so I could fall asleep.

Though I had spent more time away from the mountains than I had lived there by now, I still felt out of place and was beginning to think I wasn't cut out for town life. I'd grown accustomed in the woods to talking out loud to myself without fear of being overheard. In my new neighborhood there was no hope of that without being mistaken for a loon, so I took walks around the block at night just to hear myself think. Nighttime afforded, if not audible, then at least visual relief from sensory overload, even though something akin to sensory deprivation was what I was also experiencing. Wild plants seemed few and far between in a region stamped with a heavy human presence, and those I could name were scarcer still. Also missing was a river and anything like the daily mental rinsing the Middle Prong had once provided.

Around people, too, I often felt out of place and said the wrong thing. At a party, someone complained about having stepped in dog shit, at which point it seemed only natural to chime in about the fascinating subject of scat and what one could learn about the animal that left it by studying its droppings.

"Bear scat doesn't smell as bad as you might think," I began. "Not if the bear was eating acorns. Looks nasty and kind of pureed-looking, like baby food. But the smell really isn't bad. And without smelling it, how do you know for certain what the bear ate? Know what I mean?"

No one else standing in the circle of people knew what I meant. At all.

"You picked up poop with your hands and you smelled it?" said a woman with revulsion.

Only now did it occur to me that what was an ordinary topic of conversation at the nature center was here and everywhere else in the world a breach of civilized social discourse. Aghast faces were staring at me, but it was too late to turn back.

"Um, no. What I did was poke it with a stick. And then I smelled it."

Time and again, I struggled to explain what I'd done for a living in the woods. I knew it sounded to many listeners like little more than year-round summer camp and "young person's" work undertaken by outdoorsy types until they got serious about their future. Such was the case at many outdoor schools around the country owing to the challenges of providing a living wage for those who performed a service society deemed inessential, perhaps even frivolous. My old job had indeed consisted of summer camp, including a week reserved for adults to encounter the natural world among their peers. Such programs had always felt like time well spent, and as with those conducted during the school year, I'd begun to wonder if someday they might represent the norm for a grade school education and beyond rather than the exception. Learning outdoors opens the mind as well as the heart and senses, inducing the kind of curiosity that is often difficult to cultivate in conventional settings. What looks like child's play to some observers is, in fact, a more soulful engagement with the world, including through the hardships often experienced outdoors. For some kids, the forest is safer than home and the center provides the one place in their lives where they are served three square meals a day. According to numerous studies, not only does outdoor education improve health and well-being and even help increase test scores among students, but it also punctures the solipsism felt by many students and adults alike who feel isolated and swept away by the frenetic pace of their lives. It provides a glimpse of harmony and wholeness and sparks a sense of wonder and belonging. A democratizing place that demands by turns independence and cooperation, the forest is where human beings are formed and citizens made. If going to the woods where nothing stands between oneself and raw, unbridled Creation achieves little according to modern standards of success, it is also an act that ignites a desire to save nature and take immense delight in it.

It had been good hard work, and, despite the lousy pay, it had yielded the reward of knowing I was making a difference in people's lives. Articulating this in a succinct fashion, on the other hand, proved difficult. Before polite nods were extended and the conversation moved on to another topic, often all I could manage was a vague appeal for greater respect for nature centers and the work my colleagues were carrying out in my absence.

Meanwhile I kept evaluating the Piedmont region with its sizable human population against my former home in the mountains. While this was hardly fair, given the pristine character of the Smokies, I discovered that my experience living there had afforded me a baseline for gauging the ecological integrity of other landscapes. Plenty of unruly wildness could still be found, and yet what had replaced much of the pine-oak forest left much to be desired. Asphalt deserts smothered vast areas of fertile ground, and many open spaces suffered from neglect, having been swallowed up by kudzu and privet monocultures that choked out native biodiversity. The longleaf pine forest residing further south, which had once stretched from Texas to the Atlantic coast, had nearly vanished.

Nothing about these observations was particularly original. I was merely seeing my surroundings through a pair of lenses I hadn't possessed before living in the Smokies and taking note of the natural world's erasure and what had taken its place. I could no longer take for granted that current conditions were as they had always been or represented what was best for the land and the people living on it. The Smokies, by contrast, constitute a landscape that suffered devastation yet have more or less recovered under the protection of national park status. They are a thriving embodiment of the power of rewilding, which, even if not every place could or should be a national park, is possible anywhere if self-willed nature is given a chance to live up to its full potential and humans commit themselves to restoring ecological balance.

An older gentleman I met envied the time I'd spent living in the mountains. "You lived *in* the national park and you *left*?" he said to me during a rails-to-trails work project I volunteered for—evidence itself that to a certain extent rewilding was already underway in the region. For good measure, he bonked me gently on the head with the butt of his fist, knocking enough sense into me to wonder if I should go back and if there was a way. Luckily, I managed to secure my old job in the mountains for the summer season, and a year later, following graduation, I returned for another. One last hurrah, I assumed, before I would teach freshman composition in the fall. Coming back to the mountains felt each time like slipping on a comfortable pair of old shoes, and when a full-time position with a promotion became available at the center, I decided to stay.

"Ah! The Oasis! They may have ripped out its heart, but they haven't taken its soul," said Mickey Larkins, a schoolteacher near retirement age who helped out each summer. His fondness for the house, where he could often be found napping on the world's most comfortable couch, was limitless. Several lamentable changes had occurred since the previous summer. The Oasis got central air and heating, making the woodstove unnecessary in cold weather, plus new carpeting and a fresh coat of interior paint. In danger of becoming downright civilized, it nonetheless retained much of its original character and charm despite efforts to modernize it. One thing I hadn't missed was the mold.

Taming of another sort had taken place at horse stables located on a winding road near the county line. I'd long admired the absence of a railing on

Interlude: Making Tracks

the platform the horses stood upon, which was positioned on a steep bank above the road and nearly jutted out over it. No railing meant that knowing where the platform ended was left up to the horses' good judgment. It also meant that driving past the spot brought a person into sudden view of the rear ends of half a dozen horses, any one of which was likely to wind up a hood ornament should it take a false backward step. Now that a railing had been installed, motorists would henceforth be deprived of a rather thrilling driving experience.

Steve had moved away around the same time I had, lured by another outdoor school in California before pushing on to Australia to play professional poker and eventually landing in Utah, where he ran a survival school. Jeff got back on the bus with the traveling graduate program with which he'd studied as a student. Jan fulfilled a lifelong dream by moving to Alaska, while Rebecca and Greg relocated to Minnesota after completing graduate studies in social work and forestry, respectively. Before long, Jonah had a sister on the way.

A person slips away to the desert or forest, perhaps at first for escape, and comes away with newfound insight or wisdom to impart to others. In the heart of unfamiliar ground is found a lick of flame to carry back to one's people as fire for the betterment of all. At least that's how it has worked in many cultures over the centuries. I'd done just the opposite by returning to the wilderness, perhaps to stay, and without much wisdom to speak of—just a deeper appreciation for environmental education and the knowledge that the Piedmont region, grading freshman papers, and anything approximating a "normal" job didn't suit me. By one measure, I was escaping all over again. By another, however, escape would be impossible, what with guests from every walk of life arriving at my doorstep each week. Despite once more living miles apart from cities and major cultural centers, it felt as if I was in the middle of everything, or everything that mattered to me, here on ground that was at once familiar and full of mystery. The sound of the Middle Prong again filled my ears. A curtain of darkness descended at night that was so perfect I couldn't make out my hand when holding it in front of my face. I no longer had to cover my face with a shirt to fall asleep. And come fall, there was the welcome sound of school buses filled with excited students heaving up the valley.

It is cooler tonight, following a string of unusually warm early autumn nights. I now live in a private apartment on campus, having moved up the road at the end of summer. Next door sit three more apartments connected by a roof, which my new neighbor and colleague Adam christened "the kennels," and there we are at our doors each morning to begin another workday, ready to be unleashed into our half-million-acre classroom.

Numbering among my new nonhuman neighbors is a screech owl with an affinity for mocking human rules by perching on the park service's "Private Residence" sign posted outside my living room window. A crate containing walnuts I collected from the woods sat on my tiny front porch for a time, attracting mice, which in turn attracted copperheads and water snakes until I thought it wise to move it. Other wildlife make themselves feel right at home. A skunk enticed by the scent of brownies baking in the oven one night climbed onto my porch and stared at me through the screen door. I nearly stepped on it several nights later when exiting my back door on my way to the laundry room. Thereafter I resorted to knocking on my door while still inside before venturing outdoors after dark in hopes of avoiding any further close calls.

A commotion outside tonight tells me another neighbor is once more on the prowl. A raccoon has been showing up around the same time each evening lately to rummage through the recycling containers on my back porch in search of nonexistent morsels to feed to her young. (Is it a she? I picture a negligent male off at the bar, leaving his mate to care for the kids.) Busy mom, she's behind schedule tonight by several hours. A friend who insisted on conducting a reading of medicine cards for me some time ago reached the conclusion that my "special animal" is the raccoon, whose primary trait, she told me, is generosity. I understand this to be less a description of my character than an aspiration to live up to someday. Just what it means to catch one's special animal in the act of attempted robbery I can't say, other than how satisfying it feels. Turning on the porch light, I open the door, and at the sight of me, she clambers off the stack of crates and slips away between the porch railings.

Around midnight I hear her once more as I'm lying in bed. Reluctant to get up and go through the same motions all over again, I recall the night when I was a teenager and woke to the screams of an animal out in the dark. The screaming went on and on, and when I went outside with a flashlight, I found a large raccoon lying in the road, its rear legs crushed by an automobile. By the time I returned with a shovel to put it out of its misery, it was already dead. I dug a hole in the lawn and buried it, though, as it turned out, not deep enough. Blood oozed from the ground for days afterward, turning that corner of the yard into a scene from a slasher movie.

Wondering if she's going to keep me up all night, I rise and tiptoe to the

Interlude: Making Tracks

backdoor. For a split second, I consider whether it is instead one of my new coworkers out there in the dark since several of them have a fondness for pranks rivaling that of my former Oasis housemates. But it's her, all right. When I swing open the door, she's standing less than two feet away and facing toward me. Meeting up close like this isn't what either of us expected, and when I crouch down to meet her at eye level, we are closer still. For whatever reason, I have no fear of being bitten, just as she seems to have little fear of me.

It seems only appropriate to close the physical distance between us further by reaching my hand out to her. Because how very good it is to be back in the mountains, here where mutual curiosity can take strange turns, and with my special animal the raccoon acting as an unexpected welcoming party no less. In gratitude, I touch her gently on the forehead with my index and middle fingers like a priest making a blessing. Perhaps it is best that she does not return the gesture and only delivers a wide-eyed stare for several seconds before bolting into the night.

PART III
Second Growth

Beethoven's Lowliest Disciples

ON A WARM EARLY AUTUMN NIGHT, with a rhythm section of katydids already going strong in the trees, the time has come for making music. All that's missing is a melody, and on almost a weekly basis, the duty falls on me to find one in the company of students gathered around a campfire. Both the audience and setting are poles apart from the cafés and bars where I once performed, which is just fine because I seem incapable of remembering the lyrics to more than three or four songs on any given night. Luckily for me, that's all there will be time for tonight.

Everyone is all ears when I strum the first chord of "The Crawdad Song," a jaunty early twentieth-century number with roots in Black Southern culture. Next is the "Scat Rap," followed by a retelling of the Cherokee origin story about the first fire, carried by Water Spider across the great river and placed in the center of a council house—a round structure much like the one we've assembled in—to bring light and warmth to all the world's creatures. As something of a variety show host, I do my best to shatter any illusion that I'm the star by coaxing my listeners into becoming my fellow performers.

My audience tonight is a group of high school students, a tougher crowd than most. The looks on several faces tell me what they're thinking as I begin another song: *This is all so very, very cringy.* True, but only to a point. While the vast repertoire of campfire songs includes some that have outworn their welcome—which is why there will be no singing "Kumbaya" tonight or any night—others possess a timeless quality easier to detect here in the woods, far removed from whatever happens to be fashionable at the moment.

For the umpteenth time, I am reminded that keeping a stringed instrument in tune before a blazing campfire is an exercise in futility, though if anyone notices, they aren't saying. I sidle up to the front row, trying to make eye contact with a pair of teenage boys who won't join in. Hard to tell whether it's fear of embarrassment or contempt that has set their faces to stone. Detached irony and coolness also tend to keep even the best songs and skits at arm's length. With my hands busy around the neck of the guitar, I convey as best I can that it's okay for them to let their guard down because what happens in the woods stays in the woods. They aren't buying it, but braver souls go all in, granting their classmates permission to make the most of this opportunity to express unbridled enthusiasm before their peers. Campfires after all are a unique space in which each person, whatever they're going through, is invited to get over themselves and be swept away by odes of joy.

The quick and easy way of lighting a campfire, and the only method I've ever relied on, is to hold a match to a stick of store-bought fire starter or the homemade variety consisting of dryer lint and melted wax packed into an empty egg carton. Steve's technique, on the other hand, was as old school as it comes. Without speaking, he would kneel before his audience and spin a hand drill made of a dried yucca stalk between his palms. After a good deal of concentration and effort, a tiny lump of hot coal would form, which he slipped into a wad of tinder fashioned out of the inner bark of a tulip or basswood tree. Cupping the tinder in both hands, he would walk slowly around the circle of puzzled onlookers while gently blowing on the coal until smoke poured out and a ball of fire sprang to life in his palm. Hands plus wood plus oxygen equaled fire: that was the simple yet painstaking formula. Watching him do it was like witnessing the birth of civilization.

Besides campfires, birthdays also mark occasions when my musical duties are called upon. Thanks to long-standing tradition, it isn't the standard happy birthday song I'll sing if other musicians on our staff such as my supervisor John are unavailable, but "Cut the Cake" by Tina Liza Jones. This occurs most often during breakfast, before we go our separate ways on the trail, which means I am faced with the challenge of leading a legion of comatose young people in song barely an hour after we've all crawled out of bed. Making music around a campfire by contrast offers a chance to watch a kind of subtle magic unfold. Learning how to summon it came through watching others do it and then doing what any artist does: crib the parts that suited me, tailor them to my needs, and make up the rest.

Whatever my audience's mood is from week to week, fire is the potent force holding everyone's attention. Once one is burning, it's rare for anyone to get up and leave except to pee. It's as if the earth's molten eye has been made visible, and once you've looked, there is little chance of turning away.

And then there are those sloppy nights when fierce wind and rain drive us indoors, where we huddle around a dimmer version of the great eye—a lantern placed in the center of our human circle—as we wait for the overhead lights in the next room to wink out. But it's no matter because at such moments, just as we do now, we still have firelight glowing in the dark. We still have the music and each other.

Music and nature became intertwined early on in my life. The sound of musical instruments reverberated around the house as often as did birdsong. Trees visible through every window were the backdrop for whatever someone was playing at the moment, whether it was my mother's piano, my sister's violin, or my father's oboe. Symphonic works poured out of the stereo most evenings, and whenever we attended one of my father's concerts, some of them held outdoors, I would hear one in person, perhaps "The Four Seasons" or "Waltz of the Flowers" or "Appalachian Spring." Years would pass before I became acquainted with Beethoven's epistolary rumination: "Who can express the ecstasy of the woods!" But that it was a composer who made the remark made perfect sense.

I remember my parents lamenting the diminishment of music education in public schools owing to budget cuts and increased classroom time needed for what were deemed to be more academically rigorous subjects. Though band and choir were electives a student might choose, the intrinsic worth of music was seldom acknowledged in many quarters, even if each student came automatically equipped with an instrument—their voice—free of charge to taxpayers. With music teachers for parents, however, I didn't have a choice whether to play an instrument, only which one. Self-discipline, or something approximating it, was thus instilled in me at a young age through time set aside for practice at the end of each school day. When I picked up the guitar—the first instrument I ever played that served my own ends rather than a conductor's—practicing took on a different character. Because I wasn't required to practice, I practiced as often as I could. And with no external pressure to succeed and all those strings available at my fingertips, experimentation became possible for the first time.

The result, for a long while, was the musical equivalent of a toddler's fingerpainting. My bedroom walls helped in this regard by insulating me from the imagined prejudice of anyone within hearing range. Privacy was in short supply once I began college, however, and I easily became self-conscious about being overheard, so I took my guitar outdoors to sit alone beneath a tree. Now that I was released from the threat of embarrassment, my guitar became an enchantress and I her obedient disciple. My mind went blank, my muscles relaxed, and I lost track of time and myself. I knew I was never going to achieve the results of a guy my age who I spotted in a park wooing three girls at once as his fingers slid effortlessly up and down the fretboard of his guitar, much to the delight of his adoring audience. That was just as well because it was discovery rather than romance I was after. Along the way, while playing my instrument day after day, I realized making music was always a form of practice, even onstage, and that practice, in my case, would never make perfect.

At least in theory, a musical instrument sounds better when played in the setting where its parts originated, much like seafood is supposed to taste better by the ocean. A guitar relies on unfilled space to resonate by means of its hollow body, which in certain ways mimics a tree whose heartwood has rotted away. Conversely, my father's oboe resembles the heartwood itself, so dense are its fibers and so narrow the channel through which sound spills out. Unlike in a concert hall, the sound musical instruments produce when played outdoors dissipates quickly, but in a forest, trees provide a surface off of which sound can bounce. And for wild animals the forest of course *is* the concert hall.

Chances of hearing wildlife sound off are rarer than they once were now that the North American landscape has become largely devoid of euphonic creatures such as elk and wolves, though birds still provide one such means. I am not a very skilled birder, which I attribute in part to the difficulty of spotting birds in the dense Appalachian jungle. The health and population size of ovenbirds, for example, depends on the very thing that makes them hard to spot: large contiguous forests. I've learned to identify many birds by ear as a result. This isn't hard to do in many cases, as most birds occupy the range of soprano in the forest choir. The dawn chorus heard each spring provides an opportunity to learn several birdsongs at once, as one species followed by another raises its voice until the listener is immersed in a frenzy of sound. A lot is left up to the imagination when song is all a person can rely on for identification, which for me leads to a welcome sort of anthropomorphizing. The eastern wood peewee seems to pity itself, so sweet and melancholy is its song. The winter wren has no equal for a conversationalist as dozens of notes spill out of its throat in rapid-fire succession. And the veery's ethereal melody, like that of its close relative the wood thrush, sounds as if it originated in another world. I watched a brown bird with a speckled breast hop along a fallen tree trunk as I ate my lunch one afternoon on the Appalachian Trail. It never sang, and though I'd never seen a bird like this one before, I thought I ought to know what it was. A guidebook later told me it was a veery.

There is the veery that appeared in the woods that day, and there are the unseen veeries whose songs tunnel their way to my ears from the forest's secret crannies. But as with radio personalities whose faces don't seem to match their voices when I glimpse their photographs, I find it difficult to reconcile them. My mind instead wants to accommodate two veeries, one seen and one heard. If someday I have the chance to observe a veery while it is singing, the divide will at last be bridged. But if that day never comes, I suppose there are worse things than stubbornly populating the woods with twice the number of veeries actually living there.

Whether birds sing to establish territory, find a mate, express joie de vivre, or some combination thereof, they seem incapable of making music grating to human ears (though the grackle and European starling come close). The same cannot be said of humans of course. If there is one place where crooning minus any suggestion of talent or good taste is pardonable, however, it's the woods where renegade behavior has long found refuge.

I spent a weekend camping and fishing in the Big Creek area of the park with Seth, owner of the bicycle cargo company I once worked for. After fishing all day, we returned to our campsite after dark to eat a late supper and relax by the fire. Just when we were thinking about turning in for the night, a stranger entered the ring of firelight and asked if he could join us. I feared he might be the annoying, jabbering drunken type. But he wasn't annoying or drunk, and soon his buddy, a survival instructor in the Air Force like him, came over. Then so did a third skinnier man who wasn't with the two servicemen. His name was Jake and he wasn't annoying, not yet anyway, though he was certainly drunk.

Jake had a guitar and he knew a song—one song—which began:

Now there's a man you'll hear about
Most anywhere you go,

And his holdings are in Texas
And his name is Diamond Joe.

Upon reaching the end of the fourth verse, he forgot the words and stopped singing. John, the first Air Force guy, informed us that he had recently returned from active duty and was on his way to Maine to teach in a military survival school. He asked about our favorite books, musicians, and political views. "No need to hold back, you won't offend anyone here," he said. Caleb had also served in Iraq. He handed each of us a bottle of homebrew, and we soon learned that he had once made moonshine, too, true to his Tennessee roots, before getting caught. After reprimanding him, his superior officers thought it wise to sample the fruits of his labors and complimented him on his fine-tasting potion.

"I've got it. Verse five," Jake announced. He made it as far as verse eight, slurring his words as he sang before pausing and starting over from the top. An interminable amount of time passed before he reached the final verse, though possibly there were many more and he'd only run out of steam.

"Don't you know how to play any other songs?" John asked.

"'Diamond Joe' is all I need to know," said Jake. "By the way, for your information, I was born right here in Haywood County. Native son!"

He again started at verse one, searching in the dim firelight for the correct fingerings and not always finding them. Jake could barely hold a tune, which was just one source of discomfort he was inflicting upon us. Another was the Homeric length of the ballad he was butchering. Lyric recall was for him like pushing a wheelbarrow up a steep hillside, momentum made possible only by starting over, and over, and over. No one complained when he fell silent after reaching verse ten or twelve. I'd lost count.

Caleb coaxed the guitar out of Jake's hands and fingered a chord. Several songs later it was my turn. Jake by this point had lost in the dark the only guitar pick he had in his possession. Ripping the tab off a can of beer as a replacement, I played one of the only songs whose lyrics I could remember at that hour and the only country song I'd ever had a hand in writing, "Devil's Elbow," about a dangerous curve on a road covered by a reservoir in my home county up north.

I handed the guitar back to Caleb. Everyone knew the chorus to "Paradise" by John Prine. When we ran out of songs with words we could remember, we made one up, a blues progression I picked on guitar while Caleb played harmonica. The harmonica also belonged to Jake, who had played it without regard to key or volume or even if it was right side up before Caleb convinced him to hand it over.

"Did I mention that I'm a proud native of Haywood County?" Jake said.

"Indeed, you did. You, sir, are in fact its hidden talent," Caleb said.

Caleb was an excellent liar.

"One thing's for sure," I said. "The finest show going on tonight in Haywood County happens to be right here." This was certainly stretching the truth, considering that it was Saturday and we were in the heart of Appalachia, where string band music was as ubiquitous as moss.

My grave error was releasing custody of the guitar back into the hands of its owner, who immediately launched into the only song he knew how to play. A dozen or more verses passed by at such a volume that carrying on a conversation became impossible. Life resembles a country song when a man loses his wife, his job, his truck, and his dog, as the old saying goes. Our lot just now was losing our patience and sanity. John finally succeeded in getting Jake to stop singing long enough for him to recite some of the words, which were growing less intelligible with each verse:

Now his bread it was corn dodger
And his meat you couldn't chaw
He nearly drove me crazy
With the wagging of his jaw.

"What's corn dodger anyway?" John asked. No one knew. Frustrated by our inability to return to our discussion about books, his next ploy was to prevent Jake from resuming his torturous musical performance by trying to argue with him, to no avail. When Jake started playing once more, John reached out his hand and wrapped it around the neck of the guitar to mute the strings.

The evening was perhaps on the brink of taking a surly turn. As a survival expert, John was presumably also skilled in methods of dispatching a person in the quietest way possible and erasing any signs of their whereabouts. He had passed around his pair of night vision goggles earlier in the evening, lending us each a surreal view of the nighttime woods. He'd also let slip about the gun stowed in his pickup. Whatever other tools of his trade he had with him was anybody's guess. All of this was lost on Jake, of course, who kept right on singing while strumming the muted strings.

Giving up, John released his grip and put his head in his hands. There would be no violence tonight, nor any more conversation among fellow travelers. Nothing but the strains of "Diamond Joe," the life's joy of Haywood County's proudest native, filling the smoke-filled air.

The wind picked up and trees began to sway around four o'clock in the morning. We all scrambled for our tents. I zipped up the fly on mine just as the sky opened up and a hard rain obliterated our campfire. The party was over for everyone except Jake, who climbed behind the wheel of his car, against our protestations, and returned to whichever mountain hollow had loosed him upon the world.

A pair of musicians who regularly performs for Tremont students has a dream, which is to perform "Rocky Top" on the crest of the mountain for which the song is named. It's a rather ambitious goal considering the length of the journey and height of the mountain, not to mention the band's instruments: Joan plays the banjo, which is light and easy to carry, but Jerry plays the upright bass, which is not. Less daunting was the plan Greg hatched on the porch of the Oasis while our friend Mark was visiting. Before we could change our minds, we climbed into Mark's car and headed for Kuwohi. We lacked common sense to drive over an hour to the park's highest peak, where the visibility of 150 miles that we might have glimpsed in daylight would be reduced to nothing, but this fact never crossed our minds. Mark retrieved his banjo from the trunk when we reached the empty parking lot, slung it over his shoulder, and tore up the path, plucking as he went. Twenty minutes later we reached the observation tower and stared out at a starless ocean of darkness and invisible million-dollar views as a soundtrack both familiar and strange at that high elevation rang in our ears.

Just weeks earlier, on a camping trip in Michigan, Rob and I were picking guitars on the riverbank when a beaver darted into the current inches away from our feet, moving through the water like an inverted shadow under a cloudless sky. Perhaps the percussion of our feet had disturbed it, or maybe it was the vibrations coming from our instruments that had summoned it from its lair much like a pounding rain draws earthworms to the surface. Episodes such as these remind me of music's capacity to find incarnation in lofty places and low ones, invited out of the formless void as a way of not just spending but keeping time.

My father was born into a working-class family on the Pennsylvania-Ohio border three months before Japan bombed Pearl Harbor. Clouds of smoke billowing from the town's steel mill filled the valley day and night, erasing views of the east hill from the west hill where they lived. For a long time, the only future my father could picture for himself was in the factory where he worked for a couple of summers and where his father was a machinist and foreman. "Nine days since last fatality," read a sign posted in the smelting section of the plant the summer his next youngest brother also worked there. When my father showed an aptitude for music in high school, his parents saved money to buy him a saxophone, at which he excelled. As for what his teachers thought of his otherwise dim academic prospects, one would tell my grandmother with pity and condescension, "At least Bobby will always have his music." He enrolled in college nonetheless, the first in his family to do so.

He took a job following graduation teaching band at a rural high school where his blue-collar sensibilities landed him in trouble. Preferring to spend his lunch hour in a bar among laborers and waitresses, several of whom he would trade Christmas cards with over the next thirty years, he was reprimanded by the school's principal for dining in a less-than-respectable establishment, and at year's end he resigned from his position. Numerous extended family members of his had worked in coal mines scattered throughout the region, and now he considered doing the same. Short in stature, he'd learned coal companies sought men his size to crawl into the tightest, most dangerous spaces. Before accepting a position, however, he followed the advice of his instructor in the oboe, an instrument he'd been playing for less than a year, and applied to graduate school.

Invited to audition at Juilliard, my father bought a bus ticket to Manhattan and spent the night in a YMCA. He climbed aboard a subway train the next morning for the first time and got off at the wrong stop. Finding himself the only White person among a sea of Black faces in 1960s Harlem, he asked for directions in a bar and walked twenty blocks south, arriving for his audition with five minutes to spare. After one of the most nerve-racking moments in his life, and feeling certain he had bombed his only chance to impress jury members, he returned to Grand Central Station and found he'd missed his bus. He watched two movies in a nearby theater and afterward tried to fall asleep on a bench only to be awakened at regular intervals by police officers who rapped on the soles of his shoes with their batons.

A letter arrived several weeks later informing him of his admittance into North America's premier music conservatory. Instead of digging coal, he was soon riding the elevator with a twenty-something Itzhak Perlman and attending rehearsals of the New York Philharmonic led by Leonard Bernstein, who impressed my father with his ability to address child audiences with as much respect as he did adults. His new instructor, an acclaimed oboist who was a better performer than he was a teacher, would point to my father whenever words failed to describe the timbre he wanted his other students to produce on their instruments.

"Like him," his instructor would say. "I want you to play like him."

Upon completing his studies, my father declined an invitation to join an avant-garde musical group that would achieve national fame, having married my mother by this point and desiring a stable family life over one spent on the road as a touring musician. Never looking back, he spent the next three decades teaching at his undergraduate alma mater and performing in symphony orchestras and woodwind quintets.

I spotted my father during his performances by his shock of gray hair visible in the center of the orchestra, the traditional seat of the principal oboist. The first note wafting into the hall once the musicians strode onto the stage and began to tune was always his, an A pitch furnished most reliably on the oboe. It was the sound the Duck makes in Prokofiev's "Peter and the Wolf," which a 1909 music dictionary describes this way: "While capable of expressing grief and pathos under certain conditions, it is more often used in pastoral scenes to suggest rural simplicity and gayety." Except for the metal keys, every part of the oboe is wooden, including the double-reed mouthpiece—wood on wood, as it were—which, because they wore out after just one use, my father spent hours crafting by hand each week for himself and his students. In each performance I heard, it was as if the entire ensemble surrounding him onstage was tuning to the forest.

Of the many sonic gifts I received during a childhood resonant with the mellifluous strains of the oboe, a sound that drifted up through the heating vents and into my bedroom whenever my father practiced in the basement, the most memorable came during a camping trip when I was seven or eight years old. Because my father's rigorous performance schedule required daily preparation, his oboe went almost everywhere he did, including on vacation. Needing privacy to concentrate, he would sneak away for a few moments of solitude, often unnoticed by my sister and me. On one such morning, while I was sitting in the dirt trying to turn a stick into a spear, I heard a noise coming from the woods. My sister was curled up with a book, and my father, I assumed, was on a walk with my mother. One birdlike musical note followed another and another until a series of notes floated through the trees. The sound was familiar, though I couldn't identify what was making it or where it was coming from. The sensation it produced warmed the back of my neck and slid down my spine. The Maestro had a word not yet in my vocabulary for what I was experiencing: *ecstasy*.

Obedient children do as they're told and stay put. But the sound coming from the forest was calling to me, so off I went in search of it, filled with a desire stronger than any fear of getting lost. The sun shone down and pine needles crunched under my feet. The music seemed to bounce off every tree trunk at once. I came to a clearing. On the far side of it was a tree stump, the biggest I'd ever laid eyes on, and on the stump sat a man with his back to me.

When the man brought the instrument in his hands away from his lips, the sound stopped, but the spell did not break. A sense of wonder can descend upon a child in any number of ways. Something scratches at the surface of things trying to get after some underlying mystery, and though an explanation is furnished—in my case, the realization that the man was my father—the mystery isn't explained away. It is instead made complete.

Today when I hear an oboe, including on one of my father's recordings, bucolic harmony isn't all that comes to mind. So too does a life that might have been for my father as well as for me and what might have become of it once time moved on. Shuttered steel mills and abandoned coal mines now pepper the landscape in the region where I spent my youth, monuments to a past that's unlikely to return. The forest meanwhile has crept back into places where it was once pushed out. Omnipresent in every corner of the state named for it, the forest that one time resembled a tragic finale has instead insisted on becoming an overture.

Another campfire is burning. We make less than perfect candidates for those who would answer Ludwig von Beethoven's inquiry, though we come close a few times. It is enough to enact a ritual common in every culture and era of human history, keeping the oral tradition alive in spite of ourselves.

Gathered around me are children, parents, and grandparents, each of them here for another chapter in the saga of people-meet-woods known as Family Camp. When a young woman begins to sing, it is impossible not to fall a little in love—with her voice, with the stars and wind, with the many pairs of eyes reflecting firelight and the people they belong to as flames turn pinewood into ashes. We are all of us keeping time, or maybe we're just lost in it. Playing along, I conjure the spirit of wood as best I know how out of the assemblage of fibers and steel in my hands, whose center is hollow yet leaks magic if I place my fingers just right. When the song finishes the memory stays close, an echo of what took place here last week, or last year, or long ago. It's easy to confuse these things. Music is like a dream.

Balancing Acts

MY FAMILY'S ROOTS in North America lie entirely within western Pennsylvania, going back six generations on my father's side and eleven on my mother's, but I have a few loose ties to southern Appalachia. One aunt married a man from Asheville and another once headed the nursing department at Western Carolina University situated in the shadow of the Smokies. My family went on vacations within the region until this aunt's death when I was seven, which I guess allows me to claim a personal connection with the place I now call home. Even so, I didn't grow up here, and not one of the cemeteries scattered across the mountains contains the gravesite of a blood relative. Nor can I trace a line of kinship like the boy from Oregon who visited the national park to see the cabin his great-great-great-great-great-grandfather built by hand. However long I stay, I will never be from here. In someone's eyes, I will always be an outsider.

Every so often I spot a pickup truck sporting a bumper sticker that reads "Teach a Yankee How to Drive: Point His Car North." The intended target of this blunt message no doubt includes the maddeningly high number of vacationers who clog the roads every spring, summer, and fall, especially those who chose to stay. The resentment some native-born residents feel toward well-to-do newcomers who alter local culture by making housing prices unaffordable is understandable. But whatever the reason for the message, I don't take it personally. As one more damn Yankee taking up space, I find myself in familiar company, historically speaking, given that many European migrants to the region first resided in Pennsylvania before pushing southward. The way I figure it, I'm merely a couple of centuries late getting here.

Too young to have remembered much about the character of the mountains from childhood visits, I was struck upon moving to the Smokies by how much they reminded me of my native Alleghenies. As with northern Appalachia, the southern part of the mountain range is marked by shady hollows and walls of green emblematic of the eastern deciduous forest, only on a larger scale. The local dialect also offers something familiar. For the first time since leaving home, I heard people using the term "you'uns"—the solution throughout Appalachia for the plural address of "you" as well as a habit I picked up as a kid before my mother put a stop to it. I started saying "you'uns" again and adopted other phrases and patterns of speech. Before long, family members and friends were telling me I was starting to talk funny.

Talking funny is relative, however. "You talked funny when you first got here," said Robin, a retired schoolteacher and park volunteer who grew up nearby, by the end of my first year. "Now you talk like one of us."

I seem to fit in for the most part and am forgiven when I don't, Southern hospitality being alive and well and East Tennesseans numbering among the friendliest people anywhere. If I stick out from time to time, the reason often has less to do with my geographical origins than it does my job title and line of work, both of which include that slippery word: the *environment*.

There were times early on when a stranger would ask what I did for a living, and upon explaining that I was an environmental educator, I'd realize too late I had stumbled into a minefield. One man I met outside the park, when I told him where I worked, said radar technology was so good these days that it could detect where the largest remaining reserves of gold are buried.

"Only you can't mine it because it's against the law. Bet you can't guess where," he said.

"I give up."

"National parks," he said. His tone of voice made it clear how unjust he thought it was that the federal government was preventing him from pursuing whatever get-rich-quick scheme he had in mind. I kept quiet while absorbing this odd bit of news, which sounded a little far-fetched. The man was entitled to his opinion and no one had appointed me in charge of debunking conspiracy theories. I was off duty besides, so there was no need to go opening my mouth. Though, of course, I did.

"So the gold belongs to everyone then," I said. "And because every US

Balancing Acts

citizen owns the parks, no one has to go digging it up." I then expounded on the merits of lush forests, unpolluted rivers, staggering biodiversity, rich cultural heritage, and countless other treasures found within national parks, against which the worth of any precious metals paled in comparison. I probably sounded to the man like a sanctimonious upstart, a communist, or worse.

My monologue was on the verge of slipping into the old narrative whereby an outsider swoops in to inform the locals that their values are upside down and how they really ought to go about things. Something akin to this was the perception of the work we carried out at the nature center among a few people I'd met who had never stepped foot there. It was far from accurate. We weren't a faceless organization based in faraway Washington, DC, after all, but a local outfit staffed in part by people who had been born and raised in the area. Educating rather than agitating was our purpose, and the kinds of dialogue I'd seen unfold at the nature center among people who in other settings might have regarded one another with suspicion had always struck me as a missing piece in wider debates about the environment. Besides, our clothes were too sweat-stained and our boots and fingernails too dirty for anyone to mistake us for elitists.

Time to parley, I thought, before our conversation took a nosedive. But a minute later the debate fizzled on its own and I learned the man was as much a native to the region as I was: he was from Chicago.

To the extent that the "environment" is a dirty word for some people, its inclusion in my job title is something I learned to accept as an occupational hazard. A person wishing to avoid having to deal with other humans might land a job patrolling the backcountry in Denali or Gates of the Arctic, rarely coming into contact with another soul, but in a national park overflowing with people such as the Smokies, misanthropes need not apply. Given enough patience and curiosity, one might eventually learn to accept and even appreciate that one's fellow humans are as fascinating as plant life. Throw a modicum of affection and magnanimity into the mix and it's possible to avoid murderous feelings when one is pushed to the brink. My task as an educator was ambitious from the start, since it meant reaching out not only to the informed, open-minded, and polite individuals, but also to those who were disagreeable and had an axe to grind, within reason.

"What is this place?" asked a fisherman in his fifties who stumbled upon campus. Standing in the autumn light outside the dining hall where I'd run into him, I furnished a quick explanation and watched his face sour the moment the dreaded word *environmental* escaped my lips. Suddenly he was off and away, describing for me in accusatory tones a recent day he'd spent fishing, which "environmentalists" had spoiled when they shouted "Stop cruelty to animals!" along with a series of expletives through an open car window as they passed by.

"These extreme environmentalists believe a rock or wood tick has as much right to be here as I do!" he lamented while delivering his tirade.

The animal rights movement differs from the environmental movement in many respects and is often at odds with it. Sportsmen, moreover, were among those who in the early twentieth century laid the foundations for the modern conservation movement of which the environmental movement that began decades later can be thought of as a conjoining stream. But it wasn't the right time for a history lesson. The guy was pissed off and was taking a kind of mad pleasure in targeting me between the crosshairs of his rage. Guilty by association and lumped in with opinionated, patchouli-wearing earth muffins everywhere, real or imagined, he expected me to answer for his critic's rude behavior.

Recalling author and fly-fisherman David James Duncan's retort when an animal rights activist leveled a similar accusation at him, I suggested the fisherman tell his critics that he was an "insect-rights activist." By using artificial flies resembling living insects, he would teach trout a valuable lesson about devouring defenseless mayflies, over which no animal rights group I knew of ever expressed any concern.

The blank stare that the fisherman issued in response said he wasn't in the mood for levity. In a last-ditch attempt in search of common ground, I told him I knew anglers who were also environmentalists and believed both interests went hand in hand. The quizzical look on his face told me he'd never considered this possibility. Though finished with his spleen-venting, he nevertheless was not ready to dispense with a bogeyman and easily identifiable adversary in the culture wars, because next he turned his back on me and walked away.

Larry was someone with whom I fell into debates on a regular basis, always against my will. Like me he was a member of our local volunteer fire department, and after meetings while several of us chatted outside the fire hall, he would make his views known about one topic or another related to the environment, and then wait to see how I reacted. It seemed to be his hope that as the nearest stand-in for whatever definition of an environmentalist he carried in his mind—owing to my place of employment, which he knew little about—I would become outraged by whatever came out of his mouth. During one humorless rant, he described his solution for tackling the country's garbage problem, which was to turn the largest open pit on the continent—the Grand Canyon—into a landfill.

"Ain't nothing but a useless hole in the ground just sitting there doing nothing," he said, trying to bait me.

Never having seen the Grand Canyon, and thinking I might like to someday, his plan didn't seem like a very good one to me.

"I don't know, Larry. Seems like an awfully long distance to haul trash," I said.

More satisfying responses always crossed my mind later, such as telling him we could all save fuel costs by dumping garbage in our local national park. Or, because there was little point in trying to out-redneck him, I might have informed him about his political tribe's past leadership in environmental stewardship as exemplified by Teddy Roosevelt, Barry Goldwater, and Russell Kirk. Or maybe I should have just told him to shove it.

Larry's tactic was always to have the last word before roaring off in his pickup. How satisfying it must have been for him to speak his mind not by shouting at his television or trolling faceless strangers on the internet, if that was what he did, but by baiting an in-the-flesh member of the opposition. Only I didn't fit the mold as well as Larry hoped. I'd grown up in a devout household and was raised by parents who held education, nature, and the arts in high regard. Though I had numerous friends who held progressive views and often voiced them loudly, our values and politics were solidly conservative, and over time I found things to both like and dislike about each political party. It made sense why placing restraints on human excess was necessary, including by regulating industry and creating public lands. And it made no sense at all, given the passage in Psalms about the earth belonging not to man but to a loving Creator, when a neighbor bulldozed his woods to drill a gas well, leaving behind an ugly scar.

But Larry wanted to do battle, not share backstories. Though I considered it a twisted sort of compliment that he'd deemed me a worthy adversary, his broadsides quickly grew tiresome, and when he tried to start an argument the next time I saw him, I took a different approach by inviting him to come hiking with me.

The idea didn't exactly thrill me. Nor did Larry's ample midriff give me much confidence that he would survive such an ordeal. On the other hand, a hike was like a legal form of kidnapping: with just one way in and out, and no means of escape, speaking our minds and listening to one another would be unavoidable. It might also succeed in getting him to slow down his chattering mind long enough to hear the wind in the trees and feel the blood pounding behind his eyes. If play helped break down barriers between children, why not also purportedly grown men?

Shock registered on Larry's face at my invitation. I'd cornered him, and for the first time he didn't know what to say. Perhaps he was trying to figure out if I was making a peace offering or trying to lure him into the woods where I'd leave him for the bears, a not-unappealing notion. He never took me up on my offer, but neither did he ever again press me into debate, and thereafter when our eyes met at fire department meetings, he always delivered a friendly nod.

An environmentalist, in my understanding, is someone who cares about the condition of the air, water, soil, food, habitat, and actual places upon which their survival depends. We are each of us environmentalists then (though we may prefer other titles: farmer, hunter, fisher, gardener, even consumer). The image of an environmentalist that comes to mind for many people is often quite different, of course. It is instead a self-anointed High Priest of the Environment pushing a one-size-fits-all orthodoxy while casting judgment on other people's habits and behavior. A friend of mine has a knack for living up to the stereotype.

"Burning trash is wrong, pure and simple," she proclaimed one day with a clenched fist.

She was understandably concerned about the degraded air quality throughout the southern Appalachian region, which for many years ranked among the worst in the nation. Burning trash pumps particulate matter into the atmosphere and contributes to the smog hovering over the mountains and the Appalachian plateau west of the national park. While the vast majority of the polluted air in the Smokies derives from coal-fired power plants peppered throughout the Tennessee Valley, her point was that the average citizen had the power to avoid making it worse. The problem was that by leaving no room for debate, she made debate inevitable.

I told her about my grandmother, who burned trash out in the countryside where she lived because garbage service wasn't available. I also questioned her assumption that having one's garbage trucked to a landfill was somehow a morally superior act. By one measure, people whose yards were cluttered with junk lived with more honesty than those who looked down on them while paying a third party to haul their household waste to a growing mountain of trash located in someone else's neighborhood. Notions of self-sufficiency rooted in necessity were lost on my friend, however. She'd been raised in the suburbs where burning trash was an unforgivable sin against the environment. I then pointed out that even though her workplace was located just a few miles from her home on a quiet road, her daily habit was to drive to work, thereby unnecessarily pumping carbon into the atmosphere.

"Okay, you have a point," she relented.

Larry would have loved this. Catching a High Priest of the Environment in an act of hypocrisy was a real coup d'état. But whatever satisfaction I felt over exposing her blind spot was tempered by the knowledge that if it were possible to keep a ledger tallying each person's transgressions against "the environment," we would all be declared guilty. That some people think in such terms as committing a sin against a personified Mother Earth or Gaia serves as a reminder of the profound cultural differences concerning the treatment of the natural world that have developed in the United States since its founding. One of the most famous episodes exposing the division occurred in the early twentieth century between Gifford Pinchot, who spoke on behalf of utilitarian conservationist principles, and John Muir, who championed wilderness preservation. Pinchot's view won out with the damming of Hetch Hetchy Valley in Yosemite National Park, a spectacular glacier-carved valley that supplied drinking water for San Francisco and which Muir had passionately advocated for, ending the friendship once shared between the two visionaries.

The politicization of the environment deepened in the 1960s with industry's opposition to regulations resulting from the publication of Rachel Carson's landmark book *Silent Spring*. Carson called for a reduction rather than an outright ban on the use of the insecticide DDT, which lodges itself in the fatty tissues of animals and causes cancer and genetic damage and can wipe out wildlife populations. She nonetheless made enemies merely by questioning an unchecked faith in technological progress that resulted in harm to both human health and the rest of nature. President Reagan exacerbated the polarization in the 1980s when he appointed James Watt secretary of the Department of the Interior. Watt was openly hostile toward the concerns of environmentalists and dismissive of long-established bipartisan efforts on behalf of land conservation and regulation, becoming the most powerful federal official at the time to turn the environment into a political wedge issue.

Advocates for the environment themselves played a part in polarization. Predictions of environmental collapse from overpopulation proved false, providing fuel for those who accused eco-activists of fearmongering. Cultural and generational shifts were other factors. Attendees of the first Earth Day rally in 1970 were largely young people who were perceived by older generations to be privileged, overeducated critics of the Vietnam War in search of another issue to protest. And in the following decades, many conservation organizations adopted strategies that favored a top-down approach, alienating local citizens and bolstering the impression that environmentalists were out of touch with ordinary people, further widening the rift.

Corporate greed and cultural grievances stoked by elected officials seeking to gain political advantage continue to play an outsized role in creating divisions, and though few people today would claim not to care about the environment, ordinary citizens have been living with the discord wrought by this mired history ever since. Most everyone claims to be "for" the environment. Arguments instead often revolve around its relative health. The patient isn't actually sick and climate change isn't real or can't be helped, insist opponents of legislative action, often while ignoring scientific findings: witness how resilient it is. Or if it is sick, new legislation and the enforcement of current laws aren't the way to restore it to health. Definitions themselves get rewritten if they stand in the way of "progress," and self-serving lines of reasoning are proffered as fact: there isn't any genuine wilderness anymore, maybe there never was, nor even anything called "nature" existing outside the bounds of human life, since we humans are ourselves part of nature, in which case, whatever we do is "natural" in the long run. All the while, the patient gets even sicker and the climate warmer, and environmental injustices, which disproportionately affect communities of color and the poor, go ignored.

On and on go the debates, divisions, and distortions, wending their way through culture and into local communities, including my corner of the globe, where animosities rear their heads on occasion. Misidentified at times for partisans pushing a political agenda, environmental educators get caught in the crossfire, leading some to ponder whether a term other than the "environment" should be used to describe the work we do. But it's possible sometimes to find unexpected allies.

I attended a party at the invitation of Tammy, a tough outspoken member of our food service staff who had grown up in the area. This was not the kind of party offering wine pairings and polite conversation, but one that might instead have reached its climax by doing donuts in the backyard and conducting target practice with empties. Just an average Friday night in the Tennessee hills, in other words.

"These the tree huggers?" sneered a man when we entered the house.

Already well into his first six-pack, he appeared to have no plans of slowing down. It was obvious to everyone present what he meant: *here come the High Priests of the Environment*. A buddy of his standing across the room snickered. Our perceived reputation had obviously preceded us.

Though hardly one of the more disparaging labels in the English lexicon, "tree hugger" is a term meant to cause insult depending on who is wielding it. At best, it describes a sentimental nature lover, friend to every ant and worm, and at worst, a purist who wants to lock up the natural world while living in denial of their impact on it. Tammy herself often used the term when referring to us educators in a tone that was part scornful, part teasing. It was her way of putting us in our place and reminding those of us who were not from here that we were outsiders. She lived in a mountain hollow one did not venture into uninvited after dark, where her equally hard-living neighbors were known to possess an old-fashioned sense of justice. We took the name-calling in stride because, as a rule, Tammy wasn't someone you wanted to lock horns with.

The way the man was employing the term was all scorn and no play, and now his friend was throwing it around too. Refusing to address any of us directly, both talked about us as if we weren't even in the room. As contempt grew in their voices, I thought of asking them if they understood what we did for a living—that we introduced people to the woods, children mainly, and tried to contribute in our way to the well-being of the planet. I wanted to ask them too about what their contribution to the world was besides taking up space. But this was not my turf and the first man had at least four inches on me.

Tammy acted like nothing unusual was going on, and I started to wonder why she had bothered to invite us. Despite the countless hours she'd spent feeding our guests over the years, seeing the joy on their faces and hearing their stories during mealtimes, it had never been clear what she really thought of our work at the center. I knew just a little bit about her background: after quitting school and running away from home as a teenager, she'd joined a strip club circuit on the West Coast before returning to the mountains to cook meals at the center and eventually earn her GED. I often found her by the river on summer days, feet in the water, a smile on her face. Her demeanor could turn in an instant, leaving you to wonder whether you were her friend or foe. Just now, it seemed as if her reason for bringing us to the party was another way of putting us in our place.

The two men were only getting louder and all but outright announcing their disdain for us and our kind, calling us tree huggers this and tree huggers that. Awkward guests thrown into mixed company, we huddled in pairs trying to ignore them. Tammy kept ignoring the insults, too, until she abruptly turned and faced off with both men.

"They aren't tree huggers," she said. "They are *environmental educators*." The way she enunciated the phrase left no doubt about where she stood on the matter. The room went quiet, and for the rest of the evening, neither man uttered an audible word.

On the following Monday morning, we entered the dining hall to mop floors and get ready for school students who would soon arrive. The light was on in the back of the kitchen and soon Tammy came out to greet us.

"*My* tree huggers," she said with a mischievous grin.

Though environmental education has its detractors and critics who rob one's energies if one isn't careful, the work doesn't wait. It goes on, even on behalf of naysayers and unwilling shipmates. When I am frustrated at times by the slow nature of education measured against the urgencies regarding any number of issues related to the environment, even to the point of wanting to press people into taking immediate action, holler at them, wake them up, I recall the catastrophist creed I once lived by and how fruitless it was as a motivator, how impoverishing to the spirit it turned out to be. I recall that one of the most effective tools available to me as an educator is conversation, as well as the immense reward of getting to work in a field that brings me into dialogue with a broad cross section of America. That we humans must devise armor for defense in war, having no shell for protection, tells me we're not cut out for it, which makes dialogue indispensable and vulnerability a gift. The most fruitful dialogue of all is the one I've seen take place between people and wild places—a give-and-take that turns those who are estranged from Creation into coparticipants with it.

I witnessed a curious sight one afternoon while thinking about the acrobatics I've performed trying to reach the seemingly unreachable. Students fresh off the bus from Cincinnati were taking their seats inside an outdoor shelter. A wasp lumbered lazily overhead, making for the large opening in the roof through which smoke escapes during campfire programs. It moved slowly, even for a wasp, and then I understood why: trailing behind it, tethered by a foot-long strand of gossamer, was a spider. Having blundered into the arachnid's web, so I gathered, the wasp struggled under the weight of its passenger as it attempted to make its escape. The spider meanwhile was going on the ride of its life. When at last the wasp breached the gap in the roof, the gossamer caught on the edge of a wooden shingle and broke, freeing the wasp and allowing the spider to scramble for terra firma—neither one any worse for the wear and each now in possession of a loftier vantage point from which to glimpse the world.

Watching the scene unfold, I couldn't decide which creature I identified with most. Wasp or spider. Overburdened pilot struggling to mount the air on the oddest of journeys or its clueless and thoroughly mystified passenger. The range of choices seemed incomplete, I realized, upon returning my gaze to the expectant young people seated before me who were waiting their turn to make the forest their home for the week, for there was my answer.

End of the Road

AN AMBULANCE RACES up the road with sirens blaring, shattering the calm inside my living room. A passing vehicle of any type often catches my attention on quiet afternoons like this one when I'm at home, providing the only drama I'm likely to experience all day. An emergency vehicle in response mode is unnerving, and when I go to the window and peer across the river to the road on the other side, I spot a pickup truck tearing after the ambulance. It belongs to my coworker Charlie, an emergency medical responder like me and a fellow member of our local volunteer fire department. Between us, he is by far the more active member. Except in cases of large structure fires and wildland blazes, the department seems to get along just fine without me. A good thing, too, since I live the furthest away and thus without fail am always the last person to arrive on the scene of every fire I've fought.

Radio transmissions at my place are spottier than at the Oasis where Charlie lives. But just now I don't need a radio to tell me something is going on. I get in my car and drive up the road as fast as legally possible while dodging potholes and tripod-wielding nature photographers, expecting to find the scene of an accident as I round each curve. I never do and come to the spot several miles later where the gravel road dead-ends. Though I've only just arrived, already the ambulance is pulling away and speeding in the direction I just came from.

The expression on Charlie's face tells me whatever he saw wasn't pretty. Pieces of evidence left behind provide clues about what happened. Piled in the middle of the road are a pair of jeans, a button-down shirt, and a T-shirt stained with a fist-sized splotch of blood. Each article of clothing bears a long incision mark so neat it's as if invisible zippers rather than scissors were used to expose the victim's injuries. Nearby sits a pair of cowboy boots, also split wide open.

I learn that the victim is a middle-aged man who was riding his horse stone drunk and fell off. As he lay on the ground his horse tripped over him and lost its balance, falling onto his chest. The human ribcage is not designed to withstand the weight of a thousand-pound animal, so the man's internal injuries are presumed to be severe.

Charlie says little as he packs away his medical supplies. Before I turn to go, I watch a park ranger donning rubber gloves lift the man's clothing one article at a time and drop them into a garbage bag. The victim, if he makes it, would be hard-pressed to find any further use for them.

Other accidents have occurred here at the end of the road, a popular spot where visitors spread a picnic blanket or explore the trails on foot or horseback. A fisherman in his fifties once blundered into a yellow jacket nest and suffered anaphylaxis, and a woman hiking with her husband was struck on the head by a falling tree. If death is a kind of wilderness, it is one that some have entered in this spot, as both the fisherman and the woman did, and also, I learn several days later, the man crushed by his horse.

Every couple of weeks I notice a rusting yellow Subaru parked near the river, recognizing it by the strips of red translucent tape covering a broken taillight. Sometimes I spot its driver, an old man who looks lost in thought as he walks along the road while gazing intently at the ground. Not once have I ever seen him look up. Nearby trails afford more privacy than the road does, and I often wonder at people who come to the woods only to stick close by the world of pavement and gravel. Perhaps in the man's case it's that he has found his mind can wander more freely without suffering interruptions from passersby or his feet having to negotiate obstacles. I choose this method myself on days when my body feels worn down but my mind needs physical movement to sort itself out.

I cross paths with the man one day doing just this, noticing him almost at the last moment. We seem to share a common affection for the river, and

End of the Road

so I want to say hello, find out his name, and learn his story and destination. Not the end of the road, I hope, which he won't reach by nightfall at the pace he's going. He shows no signs of noticing me as we pass one another, even though I'm the only person besides him out on the road today.

I don't see the old man the next week or the week after that. Weeks pass and the man still doesn't show.

Several months go by and our office receives a telephone call from a woman asking permission to hold a memorial service at the end of the road. Her father died recently, she says, and requested in his will that his ashes be scattered there. Because permission is not ours to grant, she is advised to contact park headquarters. This all comes to me secondhand. Did you catch his name? I ask. No one did, not that it would help since I never learned the name of the owner of the yellow Subaru with the broken taillight, though I'm sure it was him.

On a sunny spring morning I am standing over a wild hog caught in a trap I set the night before, awaiting the moment of its death. So that it suffers as little as possible, Rick, the park wildlife biologist sent to dispatch it, takes his time getting a bead on the sweet spot north of its snout and south of its eyes as he aims his handgun.

The trap is constructed out of chain-link fencing and rebar and is slightly larger than a refrigerator laid on its side. Whenever fresh hog sign appears in the flats next to the river where hogs like to root, I bait the trap with corn kernels. If I catch one, which isn't often, I call the wildlife office and someone comes to finish the job. Wild hog sign is unmistakable. The earth looks rototilled where they plow up the ground in search of grubs, salamanders, tubers, small mammals, or any other defenseless thing they find to eat. Large patches of forest floor that would otherwise be blanketed by woodland plants instead lie bare, marking where the bristle-backed hogs have denuded the herb layer and made a mess of the place.

An adult female hog is capable of bearing a litter of five or so shoats every nine months. Sixteen months after birth each female shoat in turn is able to reproduce. Female black bears, their chief competitor for food, and natives to the region, unlike hogs, mature at age three and have a pair of cubs every other year on average. The math, in other words, is tilted heavily in favor of wild hogs. Every living thing has a place on earth, but theirs is not here. The juvenile shoat that's about to die is descended from a strain of hogs introduced from Europe. Here by no fault of its own, its bad luck was to have been born on the wrong continent and caught in a trap set by my hand.

I have grown to admire wild hogs and wish they could live in harmony with their adopted home in North America, yet after a century they haven't even come close. I wish too that cougars and wolves still populated the mountains so humans would not have to act as the sole check and balance on invasive hogs. Wishes mean little at the present moment, however, and doing nothing would cause worse violence by granting them open season on the mountains and their native inhabitants. Neither choice—destroying the hogs or permitting them to exercise destruction—is an easy one.

As Rick waits for the hog to relax, it springs forward and butts the door of the trap hard with its head. The chain-link fencing gives a little upon impact and shows a bowl-shaped dent. Then the hog stands still, waiting for whatever is about to come next. Rick rests the heels of his palms on top of the cage and pokes the muzzle of his handgun between the wires. A minute passes and my heart begins to race. It's worse when you are the one who is only watching.

When the shot comes, the hog's forelegs and then its hind legs buckle. Then it is still as blood weeps from the hole in its skull.

Nearly every spring a pair of phoebes builds a nest on top of the light fixture on my back porch and makes another attempt at raising their young. Not once have they succeeded. One year they got as far as finishing construction before leaving the nest for parts unknown. Another year they hung around long enough to lay eggs, then abandoned them for reasons I never understood. The eggs, which I found decaying among a patchwork of delicately woven pine needles and grass, looked like stones plucked from the riverbed.

The phoebes passed up my porch altogether one spring in favor of some other location, but the next year they were back. Whether it was the same pair or not, I couldn't tell, though I had a good feeling this time.

Though phoebes are a commensal species and thus accustomed to living in close proximity to humans, I made a point of using my back porch as little as possible to help give them a fighting chance. On May 30, two weeks after I discovered their first clutch of eggs lying broken on the ground, I spotted the pair taking turns sitting on freshly laid eggs. Not hung up about a little thing such as death, the pair had quickly gotten back to work. The new eggs hatched by June 6, and the fuzzy chicks had grown considerably in size by June 9. Four days later one opened its eyes. Cries rose up whenever one of their parents returned with food, a noise I relied on to measure their progress each evening when I sat down for supper.

A couple of days went by and something felt odd. My kitchen was too quiet, and I realized I had not heard the chicks' cries or spotted the parents winging to their nest at all that day or the day before. I crept onto the porch and peeked into the nest. Figuring I'd find it empty, a sign that the chicks had fledged, even though it seemed too soon for that, I found two motionless chicks and three others that had been shoved out of the nest. All of them were dead, their wet feathers matted against their lifeless bodies, and their oversized eyes shut tight.

I telephoned Paul, a park scientist, in search of an explanation. Things were going so well, I told him. Sickness might have infected the nestlings, he said, or maybe the mother died, or something had scared the parents away. Or perhaps they were bad parents who hadn't figured out how to raise their young.

Bad bird parents. That was a new one for me. Butterfly weed and sumac were in bloom, spring morphing into summer. Death seemed out of place for that time of year, and for a long time a dismal silence hung over my back porch.

Not long before the baby phoebes perished a rat snake died near the edge of the woods. Thinking back upon it later, I realized even one fewer predator in the area hadn't improved the chicks' chances for survival. The snake's death was slow in coming. As it writhed on the ground, still alive, insects crawled into its eyes. Weeks after it expired and its flesh was consumed and bones carried off by rodents, a dark stain marked the location of its final days and decomposition. I thought of the spot as a death shadow. Or was it a life shadow? I couldn't make up my mind.

Forests teeming with an astonishing diversity of life also produce a great magnitude and variety of deaths. The tiny "junkyard bug," a type of lacewing, butchers its prey before attaching disemboweled snail shells and the severed heads of beetles to its back. Seen through a microscope it resembles a Colonel Kurtz in miniature. One explanation is biological and makes plain sense: whatever lives eventually dies, and everything has to eat. Making peace with such facts seems like a job better suited to mystics and the long-lived, however, neither of which so far describes me.

I spent two weeks as a teenager with my uncle, aunt, and cousin outside Anchorage, Alaska, where they live. Following military service in Vietnam, my father's youngest brother had settled there to work for the Army as an engineer. After retiring, he and my aunt ran a nature center in the Chugach Mountains. The sockeye salmon run was underway on rivers throughout the region during my visit, and my uncle and I fished for them at every opportunity. During a side trip to Valdez, we watched silver salmon jump out of the water as we stood on the shores of the bay, which 260,000 barrels of oil leaking from the *Exxon Valdez* would blacken several months later in what at the time was the worst oil spill in US history.

Years later my sister moved to Alaska where she married and had two daughters, providing me with several good reasons to make another visit. I looked forward to fishing with my uncle again once the summer season in the Smokies ended, but my timing was off. By late August the sockeyes had nearly finished their journey up the main river channels, turned bloodred, and begun spawning. No longer hunting for food, they were busy hollowing out nests in gravel beds where females would lay legions of eggs and males fertilize them. Embryos would hatch and develop into alevins—newly spawned, yolk-carrying fish—and then emerge as fry and feed off organic matter, including parts of their parents' decaying bodies. After a year they would migrate to the sea and mature into adults.

Fishing for them with my uncle would have to wait until the next trip, though we both knew it couldn't. A year earlier he had received a diagnosis of pancreatic cancer.

The presence of sockeyes migrating to their natal streams meant bears were feeding, and since hikers and piscatorial grizzlies don't mix, several trails running through Chugach State Park were closed to the public. One of the perks of being my aunt and uncle's nephew, however, was benefiting from certain privileges they alone possessed. My uncle had erected a yurt in a section that was currently closed and suggested I camp there. I would have the entire area to myself.

"Just remember, anywhere there's a beaver pond or feeder stream there are salmon, and where there are salmon there are bears," he warned. It was as if I was about to enter graduate studies in getting along in bear country.

I shouldered my pack and headed down the trail behind the nature center, passing by a giant cottonwood with a man-sized hole in the base of its trunk I remembered seeing as a teenager. Sitka spruce trees cast dark shadows across the narrowing path. I kept a sharp lookout, knowing I did not reside at the top of the food chain in this place. Under my uncle's recommendation, I'd decided against carrying a firearm for protection. An avid hunter in his youth, he had come to believe taking firearms into bear country can do more harm than good as an insurance policy. One reason was that gun accidents occur far more often than do encounters with bears. Another was because most people's aim is poor and a wounded bear is far less predictable than a healthy one. While my aim had been pretty good when I learned to shoot a .22 as a Boy Scout, I was eager to give my full attention to my surroundings without the distraction of a loaded weapon strapped to my chest. I left bear bells behind as well, not wanting to sound like a Christmas elf jingling down the trail, and so too pepper spray since I might end up blinding myself if the wind was wrong. Relying on my wits and making noise while coming around blind corners would have to suffice.

At the intersection I turned down the closed section of trail and came to a boardwalk leading over the lower end of a beaver pond. Last time I'd seen it the wooden planks were six feet lower. Over the years my uncle had built, rebuilt, and once more rebuilt the boardwalk each time beavers flooded it. His latest design was holding fast.

Where the boardwalk began, I noticed the first set of bear prints in a patch of mud. Scavenging magpies were perched on snags poking out of the saturated ground, another sign that bears were active in the area. My senses now on high alert, I started across the boardwalk. Butted up against it, on the pond side, was a beaver dam within such close reach that I could have leaped onto it without getting my feet wet. I was, in effect, standing on the dam already since the tree shoots and branches the beavers used to construct it were piled beneath the boardwalk's wooden planks and spilled out the other side.

A violent splash sounded on my right where water poured through a breach in the dam and gushed into the woods. There in the current, inches from my feet, were the sockeyes. Each one was a moving muscle smelling its way forward, waiting behind another for its turn to wrestle through the breach. After swimming for miles through a watery galaxy clouded with glacial silt the consistency of powdered milk, their sides scoured by sharp pebbles, gills aching from lack of purer oxygen, they had reached their childhood home, only to find themselves several sizes too large, like giants crashing around a toy-sized house. Green shimmered on their cheeks except for one gray-faced salmon whose facial scales had rubbed off from trying to force its way through the web of sticks. Across each one's flanks blazed an indelible red, bringing to mind distant stars that burn brightest just before going out.

Here in their geriatric breeding grounds, the sockeyes would mate and die—or die trying if they didn't first make it through the breach. It had not rained in a week and the stream was getting lower by the day. For the sockeyes, water was the sand running out of their hourglass.

One sockeye with a pronounced hooked snout was stuck in a tangle of beaver-chewed limbs. Only a foot away was the pond it was struggling toward—the pond itself acting like a cup of cold water just out of reach of a man dying of thirst. It couldn't move backward or forward, so badly was it snared. Lying in a maze of limbs, the sockeye looked weary, spent. If the bear whose paw prints I'd spotted found it, it was done for.

I am one who rarely feels tempted to meddle in the affairs of the natural world. But watching a two-foot-long salmon labor in vain in four inches of water changes things. A biological imperative mandated that the fish keep trying against impossible odds to wriggle free, while an inborn sense of rectitude perhaps explains why I felt compelled to do what I did next. Removing my pack, I rolled up my sleeve and lay face down on the boardwalk, and reached a hand under the sockeye's belly. I pulled sticks out of the way using my free hand and lifted the fish over the boardwalk and dam, releasing it in the deep pool of water where it swam off effortlessly. Moments later another salmon took the first one's place and got stuck. This one too I hoisted over the barrier and lowered into the pool. Each fish felt limp in my hands when I held it, as if giving itself over to me in sacrifice.

Though nothing quite within the range of my senses alerted me to it, the presence of an unseen predator hung in the air, something telling me it was close by. Then there it was: a rustle in the trees and a flash of brown fur. According to my uncle, a yearling grizzly was active in the area after becoming orphaned earlier that summer when its mother was killed by an automobile. The yearling, fifty feet away and moving toward the far side of the pool, looked several sizes bigger than the largest black bear I'd ever laid eyes on in the Smokies. It had come to kill and eat, but I had shown up first, and as quickly as it had arrived, it disappeared into the trees. I shouldered my pack and pushed on toward the yurt half a mile away.

Returning to the pond the next day to refill my water bottles, I discovered salmon carcasses littering the area, seven in all. A head was the only thing remaining of one, fly-ridden where it lay stinking on the boardwalk. Muddy paw prints covered the wooden planks. The bear had eaten well, but two salmon had escaped the clutches of death. At least for now.

For days the name "sockeye" rang in my ears. Full of majesty, it also seemed full of dark irony. Trip itinerary: swim thousands of miles from ocean to natal stream to mate, only to be intercepted by a predator and crushed in its maws. Or by the same token: reach middle age in good health minus any dependency on tobacco or alcohol—two primary causes of pancreatic cancer—only to find yourself in a predator's sights. A sock in the eye if there ever was one.

While the death of salmon could be explained (bio)logically, in part because a fish's life cycle lies so remotely outside my experience, explanations for the looming death of my uncle were harder to come by. One fishes for pike and halibut and trout, as I did during my visit, without my uncle beside me, and one fishes for answers, too, without catching even one. Clearly salmon are resigned to the inevitability of their fate more than I was to theirs, or my uncle's. Whether to live another day or become a meal, whether to complete the chain of life or prematurely complete the food chain, their submissiveness when I held them in my hand suggested it was all the same to them.

"It's not a matter of *if* but *when*," my uncle said over coffee one morning. Not in submission but merely stating the facts.

The day I was to fly back to Tennessee, I rose at four in the morning to join my brother-in-law and his cousin and their buddies on the opening day of duck season in the role of observer. While bushwhacking in heavy waders through a willow thicket on the way to a swamp, myself last in line, we came to a slough of glacial runoff. Dawn crept over the horizon providing barely enough light to see by.

Crossing foot-deep water the color of chalk was the easy part. It was the muddy margins of each tiny tributary I had never encountered before. "Step where there are ripples in the mud, not where it's smooth," I was told only once it was too late. I would also learn about deaths associated with glacial mud and one man who breathed through the detached barrel of his shotgun when the tide rose before succumbing to hypothermia.

Within seconds I was hip deep in mud as thick as wet cement. There was nothing to grab onto and no safe place for anyone to stand to pull me out, though one person tried before he too began to sink and quickly extricated himself. A year to the day before, my brother-in-law and his companions had discovered the body of a missing man floating in the tidal flats. Now here I was on the verge of ruining another opening day for them. Ruining far more than that in fact.

Lifting either leg more than a few inches proved impossible, and with each bodily movement, I only sank deeper. The others watched helplessly as embarrassment more than panic filled me. So this is how it ends, I thought:

in quicksand, which isn't quick at all, and under the gaze of those who no doubt were wishing I hadn't come.

The only solution was to lie face down in the muck and prop myself up with my forearms while flexing my legs backward. For the longest time I did this, eventually extracting first one leg and then the other, until at last I was able to belly-crawl across the mud's surface and onto solid ground.

Hours later I was sitting on a plane, putting thousands of miles between myself and the location of my own modest brush with death. I had a wish in mind. It was of a hand, or many hands, mine among them, lifting my uncle out of harm's way, out of shallow water that was running out, and setting him in deeper sustaining water, even though I'd learned that morning that this could never be. Sometimes the cup is not removed and there is nothing anyone can do to help. Sometimes there is no other option than to try to pass through the breach on one's own.

I know a number of people who would likely admit they believe the world as they know it stands a better than average chance of ending in their lifetime. The potential causes are as manifold as the sources of their fears: economic collapse, terrorist attack, nuclear annihilation, fascism, world domination by religious fundamentalists, world domination by militant secularists, the Rapture, capitalism, socialism, Democratic takeover of the government, Republican takeover of the government, climate change, viruses, volcanic eruption, artificial intelligence, human overpopulation, declining fertility rates, alien invasion, or modernity itself.

What is the solution for such anxieties? Is it to go to the woods and lie on a bed of pine needles and exhale, even while very real dangers threaten the world, and give praise for what yet remains beautiful? Pay attention to doomsayers, for time may prove them right. But pay attention even more to beauty, including beauty that has grown ugly. Going to the wilderness, where as many wars as peace plans have been hatched, is no panacea. It is more than a salve, however, and it's where my mind often turns toward the mysteries of existence: the accretion of time, the gift of life, and the contours of the infinite.

On a cold winter day several months after returning from Alaska, I went for a jog up the road after work. My uncle, though his health was deteriorating and his prospects were growing dim, was still alive. The long shadows, coupled with the inevitability of my uncle's fate, cast a pall over an already colorless afternoon.

Not quite halfway to the end of the road, I spotted a pair of otters moving in the shallows of the riverbed. They didn't flee at the sight of me, and I understood why when I saw what they were doing. The male was riding on top of the female, gripping her sides with his paws as she struggled to crawl over the stones. Together they flopped over one large rock after another while engaged in coital agony.

It was a cold day for making babies. Snow dusted the ground, and next to the river the air felt even colder. The male shivered violently each time the female stopped to rest, his fur rippling across his back. When she began moving again, he banged hard against the rocks she maneuvered between. Several times he bit the scruff of her neck, yanking her fur with his teeth and causing her to cry out. At one point she tunneled under a fallen limb trying to pry him off, without success. Otter lovemaking is rough stuff.

I noticed movement on the far side of the river. A third otter loping along the bank slipped into the water and let the current carry him to within several feet of the mating pair. He seemed to change his mind and dove back into the water before once more approaching the interlocked pair, getting too close this time. The mating male, the bigger of the two, leaped off the female and collided with the interloper. Male otter bodies thrashed, water sprayed, and cries filled the air. The female, spotting an opportunity, made her exit. The larger male took off after her when the mayhem subsided, while the smaller male stayed behind and traced with his nose the route the female had taken among the rocks before he too departed.

Returning to the spot the following day, I studied the riverbed where the mating act and battle over the female otter had occurred. What I decided to do next would have felt like an intrusion on the otters' privacy the previous day, even once the episode I'd witnessed had finished. Not knowing what I was looking for, I knelt and searched the ground for hair and blood and sniffed the damp earth. Maybe it was only in my imagination, but I thought I detected something other than the scent of the river. It was the smell of Creation, the life-giving force, a sign of new beginnings even amid violence and death, with the promise of babies to come in spring.

Out of the Woods

LIVING AND WORKING at a nature center year after year, I've begun to think, must in some ways resemble the monastic life, what little I know about it. While robes and solemn vows don't figure into the lifestyle, something akin to renunciation does. *Going without* comes with the territory as it relates to access to many modern conveniences and having a social circle wider than one's coworkers. Living in a community as small as ours obliges selflessness and patience on each person's part because not getting along really isn't an option. It's easy to feel at a remove from the outside world all the while, even with a slice of it coming to us in a college van or school bus every week, and despite the arrival of Wi-Fi on campus, or perhaps because of it, news events often seem to belong to a parallel universe.

Our setting inside the national park naturally plays a significant role in making one feel set apart, surrounded as we are by a geographical Sabbath offering sanctuary to residents and pilgrims alike, many of whom come seeking relief from the unrest of their lives along with a more merciful and creaturely rhythm. Perhaps the one kind of vow I've found necessary concerns the cultivation of an unflagging curiosity and sense of wonder about the place I inhabit. Not only for the sake of my students, owing to their keen ability to sniff out a lack of enthusiasm should I ever exhibit it, but because the longer I stay, the clearer it becomes how much I have yet to understand.

Another reason life in the woods feels monkish at times involves the challenge of finding someone with whom I might share it on a more intimate basis. The math is never in my favor. Despite the parade of fresh faces each week—any bachelor's dream—most women I meet are married or twice my age or, if single, hail from far away. It's conceivable that a mutual attraction might develop with a coworker, however shallow the pool of possibilities, as indeed it has among several colleagues who formed couples and eventually married. But as with any workplace romance, such a course of action is fraught with risk should things not work out, not least because many of my associates live next door.

Living the single life in the middle of nowhere, relatively speaking, does come with several advantages. Because there's no one to impress, I can pay minimal attention to my grooming habits and physical appearance. Saving money is easy with so few places to spend it and no one to lavish it on. I can light out for the woods any time I like without regard to someone worrying over when I'll return. And I can think aloud any countrified expression I wish—for instance, "Yonder pine tree looks as lonesome as I feel"—without fretting over whether a pretty girl will peg me for a hayseed.

Mix geographical isolation with a longing for companionship, however, and it inevitably leads to bouts of wistfulness and melancholia. Some years ago, my then-housemate Kostya and our coworker Carter went hiking and fell into conversation about the lack of romance in their lives. The mutual counseling session took an odd turn when they paused to admire a patch of bright green moss hugging the earth at chest level. First one man and then the other plunged his hands into the supple mounds of moss-flesh. "Imagine if this were a woman," one remarked to the other as both closed their eyes and caressed the cushions of moss, which indeed numbers among the more pleasant members of the plant kingdom to palpate. When they opened their eyes, they found a group of hikers staring at them and quickly recovered their senses.

"*Dicranum* I believe," said Carter.

"Yes, of course. A very fine specimen," said Kostya.

Peers living in cities, where the odds of meeting someone are better, have it easy by comparison. But if you live in the woods you have to look very hard indeed, say through binoculars from a mountaintop while gazing at town lights twinkling below, wondering how much better your prospects might be down there. And so it eventually dawns on you that to meet someone, anyone at all, you will have to leave the woods and go to where the people are.

Out of the Woods

During the time I lived outside the mountains and attended graduate school, I met a woman from Texas. Her red hair, shorn within an inch of her scalp because she'd recently donated the rest of it to Locks of Love, was what first caught my eye. We were attending a cookout hosted by the meat-loving director of our graduate program, who, when she explained that she was a vegetarian, said, "Well, we have chicken too."

We made introductions but little more.

"Hi, my name's Élan," she said.

"Élan?"

"Hippy parents," she said by way of explanation.

Our first real conversation took place at a pub students patronized every Thursday, where we debated one topic after another. Opinionated and outspoken, she also was open-minded and laughed easily, and I liked her sass. On an early date during which we attended a reading by David Sedaris in a packed performance hall, her laughter rolled over the heads of the people seated in front of us, louder than anyone else's. Even while slouching into my seat to avoid stares, I decided this was someone I liked being around, and by fits and starts, we started spending more time together.

Three months after we began dating, I finished my studies and moved back to the Smokies. A long-distance relationship was in the offing since Élan still had another year to go before graduating. We made it work by visiting one another once a month, meeting halfway, or taking turns driving six hours to where the other person lived. When she accepted a teaching position after completing her degree, another year apart loomed before us, harder than the first. Breaking up was floated as a possibility.

At the end of the academic year, however, she moved to Tennessee. Now a distance of only twenty miles separated us. An instructor in poetry and English composition no longer, she made ends meet by tutoring middle school students and driving twisting backroads through surrounding counties while making follow-up calls as an encyclopedia saleswoman. Never having lived out in the country, she puzzled over the purpose of the little red flag on her mailbox and couldn't figure out why the mail carrier never picked up her outgoing mail.

Bears terrified her and invaded her dreams. Reading about them in hopes of allaying her fears only made matters worse, for they soon monopolized her thoughts during daylight hours as well. On our weekend hikes together,

I imagined her wondering how many seconds she'd have to regret her decision to uproot her life by moving closer to me should a bear charge. None did, including a pair we spotted sauntering along the crest of a ridge—her first wild bear sighting. The mother and cub minded their business and we minded ours, and Élan found afterward that her worries had vanished.

My reputation as a mountain man preceded me to Boston where we visited her extended family over the holidays. Her grandparents, aunts, uncles, and cousins knew me by the nickname given to me by her charismatic great-uncle, a summer camp administrator and beloved English teacher in his day. "BOONE!" he bellowed from his wheelchair when I walked in the door.

We spent an afternoon by a favorite backcountry creek of mine a year following her relocation to the Smokies. While dangling our feet in the water, we entertained aloud the weightiest question we'd yet asked each other: were we still just dating, or were we heading toward something more permanent as a couple? Tiptoeing around the subject without actually naming it, our mutual responses arrived with the same ease as did the current swirling around our ankles. Marriage indeed seemed to be in the cards.

In spring we flew to Alaska where I saw my uncle one final time. It turned out to be the last occasion when I would see my aunt as well. Two years later she would die while doing the job she loved, succumbing to cardiac arrest moments before she was to lead a group of children on a nature walk.

My uncle told us he'd decided to forgo receiving any more chemotherapy, confessing that he would rather die than undergo another excruciating round of treatment. Quality rather than quantity of life was what he valued most. His pain medication was wreaking havoc on his digestive system and he conversed with us while lying supine on the couch, unable to sit up without growing dizzy. The phone interrupted us each time the new director at the nature center in the Chugach Mountains—a woman who had helped my aunt and uncle rescue it several years earlier when the state cut its funding—called asking for advice. Much business needed attending to before time ran out.

The nature center put us up for a night in employee housing consisting of a ten-by-ten-foot shack. Our plan the next day was to backpack to a yurt my uncle had christened Rapids Camp, which, like the yurt I'd stayed in a year earlier, was located on a hidden spot he'd relinquished to public use to raise much-needed revenue for the nature center through rental fees. The orphaned grizzly, now two years old, was still active in the area. I stepped outside the shack to pee early the following morning, and there it was, foraging at the edge of the woods. I crept back inside and nudged Élan awake. Too sleepy to consider that this was not a black bear but a grizzly, she stuck her head out the door for a better view. Even with its hindquarters pointed toward us it looked formidable, though less like an agent of death just now than an oversized ball of fur.

A six-mile journey ushered us to Rapids Camp, where I chopped firewood and lit the woodstove to fight off the chill. We put our feet up and read until suppertime, though I found concentrating difficult. My thoughts kept circling back to the plan I'd concocted for presenting Élan with a ring the following day. I'd considered hiding it inside a guitar and surprising her when it plopped out of the sound hole after playing a song for her that I hadn't gotten around to choosing. But lugging along an instrument seemed foolish as much as it was impractical. My revised plan hinged on reaching the Dew Mound, a bulge of land visible in the distance, which promised stunning views of the surrounding glacier-formed valley. According to my map, a trail went over it and down the other side. The summit was where I would pop the question.

I checked my pack in the morning to make sure the jewelry box was still there, wrapped snug inside a shirt. One of my oldest friends, alongside whom I'd once terrorized other children and adults as we raced through our preschool's classrooms and hallways as Batman and Robin, had mailed it to me several weeks earlier. Now a jeweler and high school art teacher, Jeff had made bands for several mutual friends when they had gotten engaged. If all went according to plan, he would melt down the engagement ring and craft a final version mixed with other recycled metals.

We ate breakfast and packed lunches before heading out for what Élan could only assume was an ordinary hike. Upon reaching the turnoff for the Dew Mound after several miles, a pond appeared that wasn't on my map. I began to doubt that we were where I thought we were. Geography was complicating matters by refusing to conform to my plan.

Élan wanted to eat an early lunch next to the pond. I studied my map as we ate our sandwiches, a useful diversion from my growing anxiety. A Barrow's goldeneye skimmed over the surface of the water. Wildflowers I recognized from my field guide were blooming at the pond's edge: fairy slippers, Selkirk's violet, windflower, and kinnikinnick. While rehearsing in my mind the lines I would soon utter aloud, assuming I could first locate the Dew Mound, I noticed Élan stoop and put something in her mouth. She plucked another leaf from the same plant and chewed it. One look at the plant, which was growing next to the pond, suddenly filled me with dread.

"Did you just put that in your mouth?" I asked her, even though I'd watched her do precisely that.

"It looked like parsley," she said.

That was what worried me. While thumbing through my field guide that morning, I'd come across the page describing the deadliest member of the parsley family—poison water hemlock—which grew in this very type of habitat. Though I'd left the field guide in the yurt and wasn't certain this was the same species, I'd once met a naturalist whose close friend had died after misidentifying and consuming the same plant Socrates famously ingested rather than renounce his principles. Not wanting to take any chances, I explained to Élan why spitting out what she'd put in her mouth *this very instant* was a really good idea.

"I didn't swallow any of it," she said.

"But you chewed it, right?"

Nodding, she asked about the symptoms in case she'd been poisoned.

"I don't know for sure, but a rapid heartbeat is probably one."

"Well, my heart is beating *really* fast," she said.

So was mine. I'd introduced her on past hikes to wild edibles, which she always sampled eagerly. Now it appeared that following the same practice in a foreign environment might be her permanent undoing. Miles from the nearest road, she was possibly going to die an agonizing death right in front of me: seizures, organ failure, the works. My training as an emergency medical responder had not prepared me for such a moment as this.

"When will we know for sure?" she asked.

"I don't know. Fifteen minutes? Twenty?"

It was a beautiful day, not a cloud in the sky. Tears rolled down her cheeks. I told her to sit as still as possible. There wasn't enough time to run for help. Powerless to do anything else, I wrapped my arms around her in a bear hug.

I'd led people into the wilderness safely more times than I could count. But now I wondered what business I had doing anything of the sort if I couldn't protect the woman I loved from a simple error in judgment. What was I going to do and how would I live with myself should the worst happen? Every plant I'd lay eyes on from now on would only remind me of my failure to keep her from harm. It then occurred to me in a moment of clarity that the only chance I might ever get to propose to her was right now. Forget the ring and just say the words, I thought. If I didn't, I might never get to express my heart's deepest desire. The one thing I could do was give her one last fleeting moment of joy.

My mind racing, I also considered that if these were to be our final moments together, perhaps it was better not to ruin them by squeezing in two of life's biggest moments. One was plenty. Then my thoughts turned sideways and I considered a more drastic course of action: perhaps I, too, should take a bite of the plant. The Shakespearean proportions of the situation were beginning to feel a little overwhelming.

At work in all of this was a case of nerves of a kind that hadn't plagued me since my days as a performing musician. Between Élan and me, I was the one with a reputation for confidence and risk-taking, largely thanks to a job that had conditioned me to accept uncertainty as a fact of life. It was only a partial picture of reality, however, because she was the one who had taken a greater risk by uprooting her life so we could stay together as a couple. It was she who had shown more pluck while we'd courted one another and had realized early on that we made a good match. And it was she who had stepped well outside her comfort zone by hiking in black bear and now grizzly country, all the while entrusting me with her safety. Just now I was the one leading the charge with overzealous worry and expecting events to play out according to my terms, which it was fast becoming clear wasn't going to happen.

One death would indeed occur, my uncle's three months later, the news arriving with a shock despite plenty of advance notice of the inevitable. As for the two of us hugging by the pond, twenty minutes went by, then thirty. The cloud of impending doom passed over and we got back on our feet, breathing mutual sighs of relief. We found the Dew Mound but kept going upon reaching the top. Too much adrenaline was still pumping through my veins to want to stick with my original plan. We reached the Eagle River, fed miles upstream by glacier melt, and hung our feet over the banks just like we had by the stream in the Smokies. Taking a deep breath, I retrieved the ring from my pack and, at last, asked the question.

That evening, Élan described the euphoria she'd felt upon realizing that she not only wasn't going to die but was going to marry. I'd saved a leaf of the culprit plant, coauthor of that day's drama, and looked it up when we returned to the yurt. Not a type of parsley at all, it was instead alpine spiraea, a member of the rose family.

My aunt and uncle were the first people with whom we shared our news. "Welcome to the family!" said my overjoyed aunt.

The following week on our flight home, the pilot announced he was re-routing the plane around a developing storm cell, the largest he'd ever seen. Visible through the port windows over Kansas was a mushroom cloud dozens of miles wide and carrying three times the strength of an atomic bomb. It looked every bit as menacing as described by the pilot, like a floating sky-island preparing to drop mayhem on innocents below. Another potential disaster averted, I kept thinking, still a little nervous over the prospect of hitching my life to another's whose safety I couldn't guarantee any more than I could my own. While stranded in Atlanta for the night after missing our connection, I thought of the dank, cramped eastern deciduous forest filled with its own forms of hazards, and how much I missed it.

We were married on a sultry August day on the Tremont campus in a field Will Walker had sown with corn a century earlier. A hard rain fell hours before the ceremony, soaking the ground and causing steam to rise when the sun appeared once more. A bagpiper played in the woods, greeting guests as they arrived. Jonah, age nine, played ring bearer while friends performed hymns and original tunes we'd composed together on stringed instruments. Jeff's design on the rings we placed on one another's fingers portrayed the layers of the Appalachian Mountains, ridge upon ridge. We exchanged the vows we'd written for each other, walking hand in hand afterward through our gathering of family and friends, and caught our breaths in the woods, just the two of us, before making our way up the hill to join the evening's long celebration.

Homemade dishes brought by guests were placed on a long row of tables and served with barbeque and cornbread. Bottles of George Dickel sat next to a mason jar full of locally sourced moonshine cherries marked "spring water" in case any park rangers stopped by. What might have alarmed them more was the gift presented by Seth and Rachel: an enormous copper ball and tubing that were part of an illicit moonshine still.

Toasts, contra dancing, and swimming after dark in the river were followed by more late-night dancing. We fell into bed exhausted around three in the morning, and it seemed as if by a miracle that I now had a best friend and bride living with me in the mountains.

Secret Spot

THE GROUND TURNS LEVEL once I reach the ridgeline, where I can finally catch my breath. Half the day will be over by the time I'll get to where I am going and back home again, which is why I don't come this way very often. Already I'm thinking, as I do on every visit, that I should have picked someplace closer. But it's too late for that now, and besides, I didn't choose the place I call my secret spot so much as it chose me.

A gaping hole in the ground made when winds toppled a tree and wrenched out its roots marks my point of departure from the trail once I reach it. Stepping over fallen branches, I bushwhack down a slope poised at an ankle-breaking pitch and push through underbrush choked with eye-poking limbs, slipping more than once on woody debris dampened by this morning's rains. The rough terrain decreases the likelihood of anyone ever chancing upon this place, though it's no matter if someone does. I'm all for sharing, so long as it's not at the same time.

It isn't far to the ancient grove below, and upon reaching it, the first thing I do is wedge my hips between two elephantine roots buttressing a giant American beech tree. When I tilt back my head and peer up the face of the trunk, it's as if I am sitting in a bucket seat with a seat-back ten stories high.

A lot can happen in a short time in the life of a deciduous forest. I was reminded of this on a recent hike elsewhere in the woods, where storms had brought down a pair of tulip trees and sunlight poured through a hole in the canopy. A trail crew had already halved and pushed aside the fallen trunks, leaving me to wonder what sort of changes were going on in my secret spot. Not many, I can see now, other than a fresh crop of wildflowers springing up since my last visit.

The discovery of places whose whereabouts I've kept secret began for me in childhood. The first was in the woods behind my house, where there was a rock shaped like a throne, albeit one not terribly comfortable to sit on for long. A second one resides on state game lands several miles away where a boulder resembling a human face keeps watch over the forest. This is one secret spot I share with friends I've known since high school; frequented by no one but us, so far as we could ever tell, it is where we have hatched plans, made mischief, and camped on summer nights. Briars and grapevines have since reclaimed the place, though still visible after all these years is our stone fire circle, which perhaps other teenagers will stumble upon one day. Still another spot is perched on a ridge above the Oasis where it's possible to walk along the trunks of fallen pines for the length of a city block without touching the ground. Taken all together, my secret spots form an archipelago of discrete personal geography—places I've claimed as my own to disappear in for a time.

The one I'm visiting today I first laid eyes on during a hike with students. I'd noticed the crowns of several large trees downhill of the trail, and returning later to investigate, I discovered the beech, its lowermost branches reaching higher than many neighboring trees and its crown so wide a house could fit within its shade. That it was the largest of its kind I'd ever seen was reason enough to keep coming back. Even Élan doesn't know its whereabouts.

I've brought measuring tools with me and get busy wrapping a tape measure around the trunk at breast height to determine its circumference: ten feet, eight-and-a-half inches. After measuring a distance of sixty feet away from the trunk, I hold up a low-budget version of a hypsometer-clinometer constructed out of a soda straw, a string weighted with a steel nut, and a numbered graph taped to a piece of cardboard. Once I figure out the angle and tangent, I make a calculation and learn the tree's approximate height: 121-and-one-half feet.

Timelessness abides in this out-of-the-way corner of the forest. Never touched by crosscut saws during the logging boom, it is a small yet thriving remnant of old growth. However, a more accurate term is "all-age" since "old" implies the presence of only grandparent trees, whereas young and middle-aged trees are plentiful too. "Late-successional" also works, though "late" implies time is running out when time is all a forest such as this one has ever had. Looks are deceiving and the oldest trees aren't necessarily the biggest ones. A black gum tree still thriving in the Smokies after six centuries isn't much larger than many shade trees lining the streets of small towns. In the Obed Wild and Scenic River area located seventy-five miles northwest of the park, some diminutive cedar trees clinging to cliff faces are over a thousand years old.

Notwithstanding the more than 100,000 acres of surviving old-growth forests in the Smokies, the enduring belief about a virgin North American landscape largely devoid of people, which stems from romantic European notions of nature, doesn't hold up well under scrutiny. Indigenous people left their mark on the land in various ways, including by burning vast acres of rich bottomland habitat for game and crops. It was in their absence, once diseases introduced by Europeans wiped out countless communities, that many previously inhabited sites grew wild and took on the deceptive appearance of "pure" places White people first exploited and then mythologized as a wilderness paradise.

All the same, I find the allure of ancient forests, whatever their history, hard to resist. While visiting Natchez Trace State Park in West Tennessee, I asked a forester if any "original" forest—yet another term for old growth—was left.

"Why would you want that?" he said with irritation. "The public likes big old trees, but there isn't any point in saving them. The forest needs us to manage it."

As a consolation, he showed me an oak tree decapitated partway up its dead trunk, which had been the oldest living tree in the park at one time. What I didn't think to ask him at the time, having been put in my place as a nonexpert, was how it is possible to determine the true health of a forest community if all of its old and middle-aged members were missing. Tear down the last acre of original forest, and how is anyone to know what self-willed nature, which seems to have managed just fine on its own for millennia, looks like in all its fullness? It seemed clear even to my nonexpert eyes that a forest served a purpose other than for human use based on the simple fact that they have existed for longer than humans have exploited them.

My secret spot resides at the border of my known universe in this part of the Smokies. I've never explored the area beyond it and have no plans of doing so today. I count five kinds of mushrooms while making a cursory inventory of the forest floor, including a brightly colored button-sized species I've never seen before. I find wild yam, moonseed, and huckleberry, and because it is summer, there's ripe fruit to pick and eat. In the spot where a large trunk lies on the ground, red maple seedlings rush to fill the void, their comically oversized leaves childlike, like they're begging for sunlight—the youngest voices crying the loudest to be fed beneath the dense overstory. Yellowjackets zipping in and out of a hole in the earth alert me to the presence of their nest before I blunder too close. Retreating back to the beech tree, I notice a hole at the base of its trunk—a cozy lair for mice or wood rats or the Little People, guardians of the forest in Cherokee lore. Cool air spills out of it as if from the entrance to a cave.

Nestled once more between the armrest roots of the beech, I catch myself waiting for something to happen. Nothing does until I realize the stillness around me is illusory. Everything's doing something after all. Trees are busy sucking up groundwater and, by some miracle, turning sunlight into sugar. A nearby springhead is busy authoring a brook ounce by ounce. Even last year's leaves are busy in the way they're contributing to the dense carpet of humus covering the forest floor. It's all busyness, just on a different scale.

Secret spots of a sort play a part in classes I teach in Cades Cove, the site of a once-thriving farming community where students investigate nineteenth-century farm life. All that many public visitors experience as they drive the eleven-mile loop road skirting the meadows is what they can see through their windshields, and while the meadows provide an Appalachian-style safari with glimpses of deer, turkeys, and the occasional black bear, it's a far cry from stepping foot in them. Some meadows are as large as fifty or more soccer fields clumped together, and when we get out in the middle of one, I instruct students to spread out and hunker down in a location of their choice. When doing this at the height of the growing season, it's possible to keep out of sight of one's neighbor sitting only a dozen feet away.

The assignment I give everyone in advance is to do nothing. In a sea of grass reaching higher than their heads, lie back and be still, watch the clouds, nap, draw or write in their journal if they choose, but nothing more.

Doing nothing is hard work. Boredom, once endemic to childhood yet now more or less an endangered species—the kind of boredom that now often spurs kids to reach for electronics, which in turn can make the actual, wonder-filled world seem boring—must seem to my students like a form of punishment at first, stuck as they are out in nature. Good old boring nature, out in a joyless meadow where there's nothing to do except obey my instructions and suffer through the dumb boring assignment. And so the students fidget and grow anxious and count the torturous minutes. But behold! A grasshopper balancing on a blade of grass makes an entrance. And spiderwebs dangling on thornbushes come into focus. And the sky so blue and the sun so hot, and the mind stiller than before (plenty of cobwebs still there to sweep away) as if a veil that's obscured the world until now had been lifted, revealing not just the wildness all around but untamed time itself, with nothing to fill it but the attention one gives it. By the time our moment of solitude and stillness ends, it's as if we have carried out a countercultural act by fasting, ever so briefly, from the stampede of modern living. More often than not, students tell me they wish it had lasted longer and crave more such "boring" moments in their lives. For the time being, at least, they've each claimed several square feet of public land to call their own.

 Stillness is what I'm after today myself after walking all this distance, if even just a taste of it. Bills to pay, groceries to purchase, and unfinished chores seep into my thoughts, and I'm reminded that slowing down the body is easier than slowing down the mind. The longer I wait, however, the closer the interior habitat situated between my ears comes to resembling decolonized space. My breaths slow as the wind shuffles leaves overhead and clouds roll along. Infinitesimal droplets of water vapor float in front of my face by the dozens, backlit by sunlight sneaking through gaps in the canopy. As I suck in air and watch the mist rush toward my mouth, it's as if I am inhaling liquid diamonds.

Will Walker, the erstwhile patriarch of the river valley where I live and work, claimed beloved spots in his day, a few of which I suspect he made a point of visiting alone. I know of a place once populated by ancient trees for which he felt deep affection, even to the point of securing a promise by the lumber company president never to log them. The promise was kept for more than a decade after Walker's death, though once the company president himself died, the grove was promptly leveled. An enormous tulip tree discovered by loggers was given the nickname Will's Walking Stick, a fitting compliment for a man large in stature and reputation who cared for three wives at once and fathered enough children to field as many baseball teams. Where it once stood not even a stump remains today, its fibers having moldered into oblivion long ago. Though I'm uncertain of its precise location when it was alive, I picture the second-growth forest taking shape there today producing trees similar in size one day, forming neither an original forest nor a very old one in the vast scheme of things, yet once more becoming a place where someone might go and disappear for a while.

 One afternoon while exploring the area once inhabited by Will's Walking Stick, I encountered a man who was following the same stretch of unmaintained trail I was. Heavyset and in his late sixties, he was the first soul I'd seen all day. In his hands he gripped a stick too short for keeping balance.

He crept forward, pointing one end outward and holding the other end snug in the crook of his elbow while thrusting the stick ahead of him. Then he pulled up and waited a moment before going through the same motions all over again. He hadn't yet noticed me, and despite the decades between us, I understood immediately what he was doing: playing war. I realized then the rare if unsettling opportunity I'd been afforded by inadvertently intruding on a grown man's privacy and watching him act out a boyhood fantasy.

Not wanting to startle the man yet needing to get around him, I scuffed the soles of my boots on the ground to make noise. Without turning, he straightened his back and dropped his arms to his sides, the stick no longer a toy gun but just a stick now. We didn't speak as I passed by. I gave a little wave, pushing ahead, and pictured him marking my back through an imaginary gunsight as payback for having intruded on his secret spot.

Privacy begins with a state of mind, which I suppose makes my childhood bedroom the starting point of my search for secret spots. Though its location was hardly secret, it was nevertheless a hideaway where my thoughts escaped interruption and boredom blossomed, adopting new guises. My notions of privacy expanded outdoors when my parents assigned me the chore of raking leaves each autumn. When our neighbor's husband died and she sold us the back half acre of her property, which my parents bought to prevent developers from building an access road and erecting houses behind ours, my workload doubled. Not minding this turn of events because a bigger yard meant more space to roam, I discovered the usefulness of creating giant piles of leaves and taking a running leap into one, and then heaping leaves over my body until I was hidden from view. I dozed off one day while covered in a pile of leaves and realized when I woke that no one would have any idea how to find me if they came looking. For the moment, at least, I'd disappeared.

To disappear is a luxury in an era in which our choices, desires, and activities are endlessly surveilled and documented. Perhaps, though, it ought to be considered a necessity and moral obligation, if when we put ourselves out of reach of algorithms and empire, we are preserving part of what it means to be human. Living where I do, I am perhaps one person least in need of a secret spot. But perhaps it is because of this stark contrast with every other place I've lived, or ever will live, that I want to hold fast to something hard to come by for many people, so many of whom have been led to believe that the only life worth living is one that keeps up appearances on social media. When I move away someday and won't have a place as secluded as this one within reach, I'll find one wherever I can. I'll seek one out in a briar patch or castaway corner of a neighborhood where others don't dare to tread. Or I'll settle for one hidden in plain view, such as a pile of leaves. Like some students of mine who find it hard to love the places where they live because love doesn't live there, I'll look for something to love about it all the same.

Growing stiff from sitting, I make my way to the spring and kneel to drink. Though I've never found evidence of the wild hogs that like to root and wallow in low-lying damp places like this one, signs of other invasive organisms are numerous. Located partway up the wooded slope is the stump of an American chestnut, which continues its slow rot decades after a non-native fungus wiped out the species throughout its range. Crowded around it are the skeletons of dozens of hemlock saplings that were thriving when I first discovered this place. Once proprietors of deep shade, back when I had to squint upon entering their cover, the hemlocks are shades themselves now, having succumbed to the hemlock wooly adelgid, an aphid-like insect that hitched a ride to North America on foreign lumber. Dante, in the famous first canto of his *Inferno*, speaks of a *selva obscura*, a dark wood, to describe the human condition. If he were alive today, I wonder if he would choose the same metaphor. In the centuries that have passed since his time, more than three-quarters of the world's forests have been razed, and where forests have begun their slow return, in the Appalachians and elsewhere, many are characterized by fragmentation and the loss of biodiversity. At one time I regarded my secret spot as a constant amid change since so few changes of significant or lasting impact ever seemed to take place here. But that is no longer the case, and I dread some other pest or global warming altering its character beyond recognition.

A barred owl calls as I make my way back up the steep hillside and locate the path. Before retracing my steps homeward, I look in both directions and cover my tracks with leaves and branches so they won't be visible to anyone who should pass this way. A symbolic act, as if to throw the posse off my trail, I do this each time I come, always with a little glee since it is something a paranoid person might do. Unlike someone who is paranoid, however, I don't obsess over anyone finding my secret spot or worry about the corporations and government agencies and hackers gathering data about the most intimate details of my life. I don't worry, ultimately, because there is still one place they will never gain entry and claim as theirs: the most secret spot of all, which lies within.

PART IV
Succession

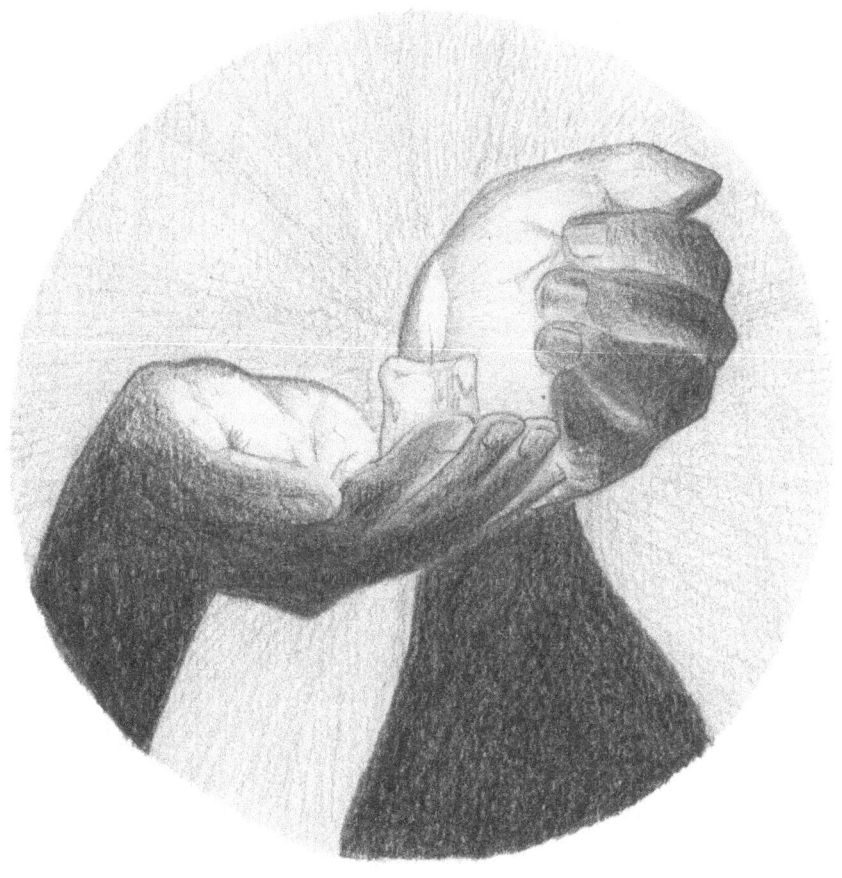

To Be Alone

THE SUMMER SEASON LOOMS like a runaway train. The time of year when tourists swarm to some of the most beloved real estate in the nation is also when duty will call on me to once more don the mantle of summer camp director, a job I relish for the most part despite the toll it exacts on my sleep. Before campers and fellow staff turn the campus into a beehive of activity, I plan to escape over the Memorial Day weekend and journey into the park's backcountry, and, once there, do nothing, or almost nothing: eat, sleep, lounge, explore, fish, read, daydream—repeat. And perhaps also follow the advice of George Herbert:

> By all means use some time to be alone.
> Salute thyself. See what thy soul doth wear.
> Dare to look in thy chest, for 'tis thine own,
> And tumble up and down what thou find'st there.

Where to go? At a glance at my map, I know my destination. Hazel Creek is a watershed bordered to the south by a reservoir and to the north by the Smokies' state-line ridge, two geographical barriers which bolster my hopes that it is indeed a place endowed with solitude. I've also long wanted to explore the part of the mountains Horace Kephart called the "back of beyond" when he resided there a century ago. See what all the fuss is about.

The weekend arrives and it's time to shove off. I wrangle my pack into the back seat and climb in beside Élan, who will join me for the first night. Besides supporting this need of mine to spend time by myself, she doesn't mind in the least the thought of having our place all to herself for several days.

We reach the trailhead in under two hours. A welcome monotony unfolds over the ten relatively flat miles we cover while following the shoreline of the reservoir, a rarity in the mountains that requires little of us other than to keep moving our feet. Once we reach the campsite, we hang a tarp and boil water for a supper of dried beans and rice. Across Hazel Creek's bejeweled waters sits a house from pre-park days, along with a fenced enclosure within which roam a pair of horses, faithful servants of the National Park Service. Nearby resides a boat launch for a ferry that delivers backpackers to the area who do not wish to take the long way here as we did. Lazy bums, I think, though a boat ride doesn't sound like such a bad idea in a pinch.

While settling by the fire after supper, I catch myself selfishly hoping campers in neighboring sites will depart on the ferry tomorrow rather than following in my direction. It's been my dream to avoid contact with other humans and not speak with another soul for several days, better that way to immerse myself in whatever Hazel has to offer and refill my well before pouring it out again over the coming summer.

We repack our belongings in the morning, kiss goodbye, and head in opposite directions, Élan back to the trailhead and myself further up Hazel Creek. Last week I emailed my friend and former colleague Greg, who now lives in Minnesota, to tell him where I was going, and he wrote in reply: *I'll be there in spirit when you hook the bushes with your backcast, when you stop to survey the perfection of the clear cold water running between mossy boulders, when you hook and play a fish to hand, and when you thankfully eat the white flesh of its insect-fortified body.* Never having visited Hazel himself, he reminded me of the bagpipes that author Harry Middleton claimed to have once heard here. *I'll listen for them*, I wrote back. I hear no such thing over the course of the first several miles, grateful that my spell of solitude has finally begun.

It lasts for all of one hour.

A pair of fishermen pass by, and giving a wave while keeping mum, I march on. Another pair appears and then another, the buddy system alive and well. I can't very easily ignore them all and chat briefly with two older gentlemen when they address me. Okay, *now* I'll keep silent, I tell myself once we bid farewell. Already Hazel Creek has presented a different reality than the one I'd pictured, its seeming distance from civilization abridged by the ferry. It also doesn't help that I've come at a prime time of year for trout fishing.

My hopes for finding unalloyed solitude are dashed for good when I arrive at the campsite at the mouth of Bone Valley, where I have a reservation. A dozen men are milling about a makeshift village erected out of patio-sized tents around which sit lawn chairs, coolers, coffeepots, a large stove, and other glamping accoutrements. Parked nearby are half a dozen pushcarts of the same variety several of the fishermen I encountered earlier were wheeling behind them. In stark contrast to the scant provisions I'm carrying on my back, their luxury camp has the makings of a small civilization. My sole consolation comes from knowing that if this were a contest in rugged outdoorsmanship, the only person taking home a ribbon would be me.

Though I'm tempted to go rogue by establishing an illegal campsite deeper in the woods, I search for a spot within the prescribed area as far away from my neighbors as possible. I settle for a tiny clearing wedged between the river and a rhododendron thicket situated almost out of sight of the tent village. The heavens open up before I have a chance to set down my pack. Mud puddles collect at my feet while I wait out the storm, and once it passes over, I make camp. Here I will sleep. There I will eat. Under this tree, I will read and smoke cigars and make merry. Near the fire circle sits an unopened can of chicken and dumplings left behind by one of the fishermen with an expiration date that checks out. Deciding it will make for a convenient lunch, I remove the tab and tuck in.

Hazel, fattened by the cloudburst, is fast on the rise and roaring louder by the minute. The noise becomes so deafening I can't hear myself think. Time to go exploring.

A side path leading off the main trail catches my eye and I follow it. A uniform mat of oak leaves covering the ground tells me this is the way less taken. Within minutes I am high above the river. Where the path comes to a dead end, I find a clearing peppered with headstones. This being North Carolina and a world away from Tennessee back when people lived and died here, I search in vain for familiar surnames. Numerous graves belong to veterans and unnamed infants. The inscription on the oldest headstone I can find reads:

John T. Newman
CO A 19 REGT
Confederate States Army
1826 1862

The futility of supposing world events never found purchase in the lives of people who dwelled in this remote corner of the mountains dawns on me when I spot a headstone belonging to a veteran of World War I. The most devastating agent of change to communities that once thrived here, however, was industrial logging. "When I first came to the Smokies the whole region was one of superb forest primeval," wrote Horace Kephart in 1925, referring to Hazel Creek. "Not long ago, I went to that same place again. It was wrecked, ruined, desecrated, turned into a thousand rubbish heaps, utterly vile and mean."

Whatever Kephart meant by "back of beyond," a phrase he used to describe Hazel in his seminal work *Our Southern Highlanders,* it could have applied only to his early days residing in the area. Arriving in 1904 after leaving his wife, children, and librarianship behind in St. Louis following a nervous breakdown, he found the fresh air and solitude he sought, only to witness the Ritter Lumber Company log the watershed from top to bottom in the decades that followed. It would become the primary reason he campaigned for the establishment of the national park, which came to completion after his death. I'm grateful to see his dire description of the place no longer fits, for despite having lost its former glory, the forest is well on its way to recovery.

While weaving among the headstones I come across one bearing the name of Greenberry Brooks. It's hard not to feel some affection for him, given his colorful name and short lifespan of just twenty-four years. Is there still a place in the world for someone named Greenberry? Somewhere there must be. A makeshift bench constructed out of two-by-fours beckons me to sit, so I do and stare at the open sky brightening the clearing, drinking in the exotic sight before descending back into tree shadow and the cacophony of a rain-swollen Hazel Creek.

I spend the rest of the afternoon collecting firewood, filtering water, hanging rain-soaked items to dry, and carrying out other domestic chores. Once I've finished, all that's left to do is admire my happy little camp and tighten the ropes on my tarp, which, since it isn't buggy or cold, will beat the confinement of a tent for comfort come bedtime.

As evening falls yellow mayflies begin hatching and swarming the air. I piece together my fly rod, step into my waders, and skirt through the woods a hundred yards downstream before entering the water. The current is swift and I cast with difficulty while struggling to keep my balance. I work my way up a side channel where the river weaves around a rock island overgrown with ferns and cast again. A rainbow trout takes my fly. I remove the hook from its mouth and let it go, the first of many, I hope.

After supper I build a fire, watching the damp wood sputter and smoke for the longest time until it finally catches. Darkness falls and my neighbors light a campfire too—or bonfire rather. Its flames soon reach higher than their tents, the spectacle it creates serving as a beacon for everything I'd hoped to avoid. Whoops and hollers from the men fill the air for more than an hour, then around eleven o'clock, the pyrotechnics begin. Bottle rockets whistle into the air and explosions more piercing than firecrackers erupt every few minutes, brightening the night. Each burst of noise makes me jump. By the time the explosions cease and calm returns to the woods, it's too late, my nerves are set on edge and my neck muscles tense in anticipation of another startling boom. So much for experiencing anything even approximating solitude tonight.

I devise a plan to confront my neighbors in the morning and relocate my camp higher in the woods, perhaps near Greenberry Brooks. But as I drift off to sleep with Hazel's bluster in my ears, I know I'll do neither one.

Location, location, location. Clearly, I picked the wrong one. Or the right one at the wrong time of year. Or the right one with the wrong neighbors.

By morning, however, my prospects seem to have improved. The villagers are off fishing, leaving the campsite peaceful and still. I boil water for coffee and oatmeal and sit for a spell, letting my mind wander. When I rise to check on my wet clothes, I wonder why I've bothered since cotton, once wet, never dries in the Smokies.

The fishing is poor as rains return and muddy the river. What I need are submergible wet flies, but all I've brought are dry fly patterns that float on the surface and that fish can't see in cocoa-brown water. I spot a pair of bead-head nymphs snagged by another fisherman on an overhanging branch—a lucky find—trying first one and then the other, though without success.

I take a break, needing to empty my bladder, an operation that involves wading over to the riverbank and heaving myself clumsily onto shore since there aren't any rocks to step on, then removing my fishing vest and undoing numerous clasps and buckles on my waders. While going through the same motions in reverse order, I spot a handsome clump of pincushion moss hugging the bank. The sight of it prompts me to look for signs of otters, whose acidic fecal matter is known to scorch whatever plant matter it is deposited on. I instead spot fresh paw prints left by a bear along a muddy path. Earlier I'd stolen glances over my shoulder, thinking something or someone was watching me, and scolded myself when nothing was there. Now I see that I had good reason after all, and realize too that my senses are acclimatizing to this place.

Over lunch back at my campsite, I retrieve a paperback copy of George MacDonald from my belongings and begin reading:

> Now there is something awful about every wood, especially in the moonlight; and perhaps a fir-wood is more awful than other woods. For one thing, it lets a little more light through, rendering the darkness a little more visible, as it were; and then the trees go stretching away up towards the moon, and look as if they cared nothing about the creatures below them—not like the broad trees with soft wide leaves that, in the darkness even, look sheltering.

Looking up from the page, I consider that a century before MacDonald's birth in Scotland, the Highland Clearances all but wiped out what remained of the great Caledonian forest and replaced crofters with sheep, prompting many of his fellow Scots to migrate to the New World. Whatever might have been the origins of his misgivings about evergreens, which likely came about during his time living in England since most of the forests in his home country were long gone, I suspect the forefather of fantasy fiction would have delighted in the diurnal shade of the broadleaf forest towering over me.

Trading book for fly rod, I head back to the river. The section running by the campsite is wide and straight and the current swift and powerful. Though glassy pools are plentiful elsewhere on Hazel, where I'm standing the water makes a continuous mad dash toward the reservoir miles downstream. Small waves rise and dip in uninterrupted motion, turning hypnotic if I stare too long. The water will eventually recede and riffles appear once more, providing clues to where trout are lurking so long as the rain holds off. For the time being, however, my efforts are futile, even now that the river is less murky. I cast my line as far upstream as possible yet within seconds my fly comes broadside and races past me.

Alternating between fishing and reading over the next several hours, I return to my tarp at one point to find a snake coiled beneath George MacDonald. Given my verdant surroundings, it isn't a complete surprise to discover wildlife making use of my camp, and I should know better than to let down my guard since back home, I once almost blew my nose into a tissue on which I found a scorpion clinging when I raised it to my face. A harmless red-bellied, it opens its cloaca and musks on my palm when I relocate it to a bed of pine needles, our mutually unpleasant encounter virtually guaranteeing we will not meet again. To remove the disgusting stench, I scoop handfuls of pebbles from the river bottom and rub my hands together to exfoliate my skin. It almost does the trick.

No longer in the mood for books or pursuing fish, I decide to go exploring up Bone Valley, named for the grisly aftermath of a late-winter snowstorm in the 1870s when a herd of cattle froze to death there. Today it harbors one of the few dead-end trails in the park, with just one way in and out. An aura of mystique about the place has grown in my imagination over time, and now that I'm going there, I allow myself to hope it may offer the solitude I'm looking for.

Almost right away I begin doubting it can deliver. In place of a woodland path, a veritable highway pushes through the forest marked by fresh tire tracks and gravel, indicating the recent presence of heavy earthmovers. Though I was vaguely aware the park service maintains access to remote cemeteries visited by descendants of those buried in them on Decoration Days each summer, only now does it occur to me this is one such place.

Cemeteries are one of the reasons this area has been the subject of controversy almost since the park's founding. A closely related reason was the proposed construction of a road promised by the federal government in the 1940s. Its purpose was to serve as partial compensation for families who were evicted from the Little Tennessee River Valley when it was dammed to supply energy for Oak Ridge for the development of the atomic bombs dropped on Japan during World War II. Construction was paused in the 1960s when it exposed a highly acidic type of bedrock detrimental to stream health. During the same decade, which saw the passage of the Wilderness Act, the National Environmental Policy Act, and the Endangered Species Act, sacrificing wildlife habitat was deemed a price too high to pay, and the road sat unfinished for decades with no plans on the part of the federal government to complete it. That is until a movement comprised of local citizens and elected officials clamoring for the construction of the entirety of the road reignited the controversy.

I once attended a public meeting hosted by the park service to allow citizens to voice their opinions regarding the completion of the road. I sympathized with descendants of those slighted by the government as they took turns speaking in support of the road, which they argued would provide better access to their family cemeteries. I thought of my grandmother, who had died a few years earlier, and the challenge of visiting her gravesite if she were to have been buried in a place made inaccessible by a large body of water. A further challenge would be if I was elderly and had to rely on the goodwill of the bureaucratic body responsible for causing the hardship in the first place. For many who spoke, the root of the issue was a broken promise and another chapter in the history of neglect over the concerns of rural Americans. The only way to restore trust, it seemed, was for the government to keep its word. That much I could understand. But I also thought about the intrinsic worth of untrammeled wilderness and the backpacking trips I'd led in one of the areas slated for potential road construction where I had witnessed teenagers jolted out of their comfort zones come alive in wild trafficless beauty.

Though I didn't relish the idea of speaking before a hostile crowd, after listening to several proroad people accuse those of us in the audience who wanted to protect a place none of us had stepped foot in, I stood and joined the line of people waiting for their turn to speak. When my turn at the microphone came, I admitted I did not possess ties of kinship to the area through bloodlines reaching back several generations. All the same, I had come to know it through direct experience and believed it ought to be left alone and kept wild. In an attempt to find a compromise solution, I proposed that rather than paving a road through the heart of one of the largest remaining unbroken forests in the eastern United States, the government ought to drain the reservoir and lay blacktop for the road on the empty lake bottom. Chuckles rose from the audience upon hearing my suggestion. At least they were listening.

Speaking my mind didn't win me any friends. An older gentleman accosted me in the lobby after the meeting, saying, "I hope you never step foot there again. You don't deserve to see that place. You don't go anywhere near it, you hear?"

Out of respect, I declined to point out to him that the proposed route for the road would do little to increase access to many of the area's twenty-seven cemeteries. And that the wilderness and its inherent benefits to people—ecological, economic, and spiritual—would become seriously impaired were a new road to slice through it. And that the entire area had for a long time been public lands, granting me welcome and the legal right to spend time there any time I wished. Already I was forming in my mind a plan to return there someday.

A puddle of tiger swallowtails, a dozen strong, gathers nutrients from dried mud on the road leading into Bone Valley. Elsewhere on my journey, a bee lands on my leg while I sip from my water bottle. I let her stay, watching her surface mine my skin for minerals and then brush her away before she finds an excuse to drill deeper.

    I remove my shoes at the first of several stream crossings and walk gingerly atop sharp gravel. No sooner do I reach the other side than a man and woman appear. There's no point in being rude, so for the first time in twenty-four hours I make use of my vocal cords. The woman does all the talking, and less than a minute into our conversation, I discover her sister is an acquaintance of mine. Gone, too, now is anonymity, and it crosses my mind to carry a sign next time I visit Hazel that says, NOT TALKING—NOTHING PERSONAL.

    More people appear, two members of last night's raucous party this time. They talk excitedly while dipping their fishing lines in the creek, then grow quiet when they notice me. I greet them with a smile, but each one says nothing, standing as stiff as lumber while sizing me up. They keep staring at me, and now I begin to surmise that something of a one-way masculinity contest is going on. I do not make very good competition by most standards, bedecked as I am in an old pair of bright blue swim trunks duct-taped at the seam and an even brighter blue rain jacket, which must give me the appearance of a giant blueberry with legs. The one thing I have going in my favor is that I'm traveling alone, something only "real men" supposedly do.

    I run into them again after visiting the cemetery and a settler's cabin situated at the trail's terminus. Once more they grow tense and regard me with suspicion. I'm the proverbial weird guy in the woods, their eyes tell me, my solitary independence a threat for some reason. I am one of you, I want to tell them, for I too love hijinks in the night and chaos around a campfire and all the comforts of home. Only I love peace and solitude and the narrow way far more. It's inconceivable they will invite me to tonight's bonfire, which is certain to take place, and of course, they make no such gesture. A good thing, too, since I might feel obligated to be neighborly and join their pack, abandoning the path I've chosen, which is that of a lone coyote content to keep to myself. When we part ways, we're strangers to one another even more than before.

    Evening comes. An hour after dark the fireworks start up again, pounding my eardrums at regular intervals and testing my patience. Each time I think this explosion—okay, no, *this* one—will be the last, it's only a tease and another one comes. A war-torn Hazel is tonight's soundtrack and there is no leaving the theater.

    Sitting by my campfire, I sip *uisge beatha*—Gaelic for "water of life"—and toast the Scots for inventing delightful words to describe their even more delightful barrel-aged elixirs. Besides gladdening the heart, whiskey serves a practical purpose by dulling my senses and tamping down the fantasy playing out in my mind that would have me marching over to my neighbor's camp, a stout piece of firewood clutched in my fist, to challenge one or more of them to a duel before laying waste to their pushcarts one by one as recompense for ruining another night's peace. I stay put, of course, and settle for playing the long game, trying not to resent their heavy-handedness and for enlarging their presence in the wilderness far more than is necessary.

Unable to concentrate on my book, I contemplate the fine craftsmanship of the cabin I visited in Bone Valley, still holding strong after a century with its corners fitted together hand-in-glove and which ought to be the envy of every modern homebuilder. I ponder the flooded acre of woods I passed by on the way there, an unusual sight in the mountains, and whether beavers were the cause. If so, it is an encouraging sign of the area's appetite for rewilding following their disappearance during the logging boom.

Wilderness also is on my mind, which I suppose is only natural considering I'm immersed in it. Despite its benefits, wilderness remains a controversial subject here and in many parts of the world. Opponents point to the devastation caused during the logging era and past agricultural use, which stripped it of its formerly pristine condition, as evidence that the Smokies is not wilderness, even though it is managed as such. Others have argued that wilderness is little more than a product of Western middle-class values and racism because its designation displaced native tribes in many cases, despite Indigenous people themselves continuing to speak on behalf of what their ancestors lived in harmony with for centuries. The landmark Wilderness Act defines such places as those "untrammeled by man" and secured the protection of millions of acres in the American West when it was signed into law in 1964. The Eastern Wilderness Act was born a decade later when it seemed clear that damaged yet recovering lands east of the Mississippi also deserved protection.

Legal definitions aside, a broad understanding of wilderness comes from acknowledging it as the original source of regenerative agriculture and observing how the natural world behaves when left alone as a self-willed space. Part of the wisdom undergirding the establishment of federally protected wilderness areas is the limits it sets on human will and appetite. Among other things, such constraints allow for the flourishing of what ecologists dryly label "ecosystem services," including food and water production, climate regulation, and the support of natural cycles relating to nutrients and oxygen. It's not by accident that many wilderness areas exist in mountainous regions that protect headwaters depended upon by people living downstream. Domesticated landscapes put to human use under wise stewardship are no less vital to human communities for obvious reasons. But by leaving landscapes intact, wilderness areas allow for wildness to achieve its own ends so that organisms can live as they always have in the places where they evolved.

In the 1920s lumber company attorney James B. Wright fought for the Smokies to become a national forest, which would have permitted timber production to continue, unlike in national parks wherein logging is prohibited. It was instead the vision of fellow Appalachian Club member David Chapman that triumphed and turned it into a national park, setting the stage for the return of its wilderness character. Several decades later the idea for the original Wilderness Act was conceived within view of the Smokies when a group of activists visiting the area pulled over along the highway and hatched a vision that in time would become federal law. As for the road controversy that was jumpstarted nearly half a century later, it was eventually resolved when a cash settlement was made to the county government in lieu of construction. Great Smoky Mountains National Park has never been granted federal wilderness status, but with one of the last remaining obstacles finally removed, chances are better that it will someday be included in the National Wilderness Preservation System.

As the hours pass, the intervals lengthen between explosions, allowing a measure of calm to creep back into the night. I think of home and the pair of phoebes who constructed a nest above the porch light this spring. Each evening at dusk one lingers on the porch railing, flicking its tail until full dark comes within a hair's breadth, and only then returns to its clutch of eggs for the night. I'm doing something of the same just now by delaying the conclusion of a day that has felt full yet too brief. When the bombardment ceases altogether, I wring out a few more moments of consciousness and read my book in blessed peace. Once my fire turns into a pool of dying embers, I crawl beneath my tarp and sink into deep uninterrupted sleep.

So cramped are the valley walls and so thick the foliage overhead that it's impossible to tell in the morning if more rain is on the way. I follow with my eyes the path sunlight makes through gaps in the canopy down to the forest floor, where it warms moist pockets of earth, stirring up something secretive among the leaf decay. The sight of it makes for good entertainment at the start of my final day on Hazel Creek.

Morning blurs into the afternoon. I fish, read, scribble in my notebook, stare at the river. I guess the hour of day and dig my watch out of my pack to see how close I am. There's no need, of course, no other place I should be right now but here, nothing else I ought to be doing, this being forest time after all.

I head out in search of a hole I haven't yet fished and spot a deep pool below a small waterfall where sunlight plays on the crystalline surface of the water. Same as ever, it's a thrill merely to step into the current. It feels like I'm getting away with something, a terrestrial vertebrate interloping in the aquatic realm. I snag my fly on rhododendron bushes several times and catch nothing, a mild disappointment. A tantalizing brightness in the woods on the far bank tempts me to go investigate. Stowing my rod, I clamber through the underbrush and find an overgrown clearing populated by walnut trees, a sure sign of past human habitation. Crowded around a rivulet pouring out of a crease in the mountainside are daylilies and Southern blue flags, ornamentals someone planted in former days. Nearby sits a stone wall and the foundation of a long-gone house. The seclusion of the place is striking, and it occurs to me that I'm standing in a spot no one has likely laid eyes on for a long time.

Shadows lengthen and hunger pangs tell me it's getting on toward suppertime. Back at camp I carry my cooking pot to the river for a refill. I spot two of my neighbors standing waist-deep in the current a hundred yards upstream, their naked bodies shockingly pale. It isn't clear whether they're bathing or just skinny-dipping, until a bar of soap drops from one of the men's hands and plops into the water. I make sure to boil my water for an extra-long time over the stove.

After supper I grab my rod and return to Hazel once more, picking a spot around a bend downstream where chances of catching sight of naked people are slim. On my third cast, I feel a tug on my line and set the hook. Once I've landed it, I am faced with the decision of whether to keep or release the rainbow trout. Out of a desire to make a piece of Hazel a part of me, I choose the former. Main course or dessert, I can't decide which, I dip the fillet in cornmeal and pan-fry it over the stove before savoring the delicious flesh.

I light a fire when night descends and get off my feet. All's quiet tonight in the absence of shouting voices and explosions shattering the peace. Out of ammunition, my neighbors are perhaps as content as I am to stare into flames with nothing else much in mind. A cavern of heat glows between the coals and the larger pieces of wood I feed into the fire. I light a cigar and swallow a mouthful of the water of life, welcoming the cool burn in the back of my throat. I watch the fire's flames lick the air against a backdrop of blackness as shadows play on tree trunks and sparks dance among spirals of smoke rising in a wild anarchic choreography. Shimmering somewhere above the dense tree canopy, concealed from view, must be the Big Dipper. For a second I think I notice movement out in the darkness, curious eyes belonging to some animal looking in on me, and wonder if it's only in my head.

Hours later, my woodpile reduced to a dozen small twigs, I rise and face the darkness. Firelight throws my shadow against a wall of trees bordering one side of my campsite, and suddenly I am glimpsing a gargantuan version of myself. For the moment I am a creature as tall as the forest canopy, a giant on the earth, waving my arms for the sheer pleasure of it. Salute thyself, advised George Herbert, and I have obeyed.

As the fire dwindles, so does my outsized self, shrinking measure by measure back to right proportions until the flames disappear altogether and my shadow along with them. Only once I dig deep into my sleeping bag and stare into the dark for a moment before closing my eyes does it occur to me that I haven't spoken with another person all day.

In the morning I eat a quick breakfast and break camp. My neighbors show no signs of stirring and will likely forget I was ever here once I'm gone. In revenge for disturbing my peace of mind with their mayhem two nights in a row, another fantasy plays out in my mind as I picture myself raiding their village and severing the ropes holding up their tents with my knife while they're still asleep and then watching chaos ensue as they attempt to extricate themselves while I slip away into the forest. Mildly disappointed that some scenes are better left to the imagination, I make my departure in peace.

Though an ascent of three thousand feet and a journey of fifteen miles awaits, I make time for several detours. The first is along an unmarked path terminating at another cemetery, where I spot one gravesite located apart from the others. The inscription on the headstone states simply "A Black Man," marking the spot where a person denied the dignity of a name in his final resting place lies buried. Seeing it spurs me to question the purpose behind the solitude I've been seeking all this time. Solitude seems like a luxury all of a sudden as well as something darker. It is one thing to have a community to which to return, as I do, but it is another to have been denied full membership in one in life and kept separate from it even in death, discrimination and likely worse having turned solitude for this unnamed person into social exclusion on both sides of the grave.

Farther up the main trail, I turn onto another side path and follow it for half a mile, thinking I will spot Kephart's ghost or at least evidence of the copper mine located near where he once lived, though I glimpse neither. The going grows steep when the real work of climbing the mountain begins, so much so that I have to stop several times to catch my breath and let my heart slow. Spring is slouching into summer beneath the fast-closing tree canopy in the guise of wilting jack-in-the-pulpits and decaying white trilliums. However, once I've climbed another thousand feet where the air is cooler, I re-enter spring in all its glory and find painted trilliums and fringed phacelia in full bloom. A pair of ruffed grouse launch noisily from the underbrush at my approach, hurtling through tree cover where leaf-out has yet to occur.

I do not see another soul all day and am alone at last. This is what it takes, it dawns on me. Finding genuine solitude requires climbing one of the steepest and most remote trails in the Smokies, where help will be a long time coming should I suffer a fall or some other kind of accident. Not that help is something I feel entitled to receiving out here—a helicopter swooping in or a search crew carrying me out on a litter—assuming I could contact someone in the first place, which I can't since I chose not to bring a phone or satellite messenger or any other such device with me. I'm reminded of the discussions I have led with college students when someone—always a male—who has grown impatient with talk about nature's beauty and grandeur will point out instances of its indifference and naked brutality. They're not wrong, of course. Part of the allure of wilderness travel is knowing there's no guarantee of rescue and accepting the possibility of coming face-to-face with one's mortality. A sobering fact is that I have no one to rely on but myself just now, having only my instincts and wits to assist me in crawling back to civilization should it come to that. But for precisely the same reasons, acknowledging this is also liberating and deeply satisfying.

An arresting quiet hangs in the air when I reach the flank of Blockhouse Mountain. It persists for several miles more, even when I reach the Appalachian Trail and cross over the spine of the main ridge dividing North Carolina and Tennessee. While descending Bote Mountain I hold my breath and listen, hoping it will last—and then, just like that, it's gone. I hear only voices at first, and then people begin to appear in groups of twos, fours, fives, and eights, more visitors than I've seen in the backcountry in nearly a year, all of them huffing toward Spence Field and its spectacular views, which they'll have earned the hard way. Where did all these people come from, I wonder, before recalling that today is Memorial Day.

One irony is that despite its moniker as the "people's park," a nickname Great Smoky Mountains National Park earned early in its history because it was partly paid for by private citizens, its peopleless spaces rank among its greatest assets. Another is that while wilderness preservation depends in part on people experiencing wilderness firsthand, the number of people using the backcountry has increased dramatically in recent decades, thus altering its character by turning it into a rather busy place. Finding solitude will only get harder in a crowded world populated by seven billion people and counting, and more specifically in Appalachian wilderness, which resides within a day's drive of a hundred million Americans, requiring the wilderness traveler to learn how to share space with others—something much of the rest of the world has already figured out. Just as deserving of attention as wilderness, however, and yet which often goes ignored by conservationists, are places people inhabit as well as those deemed unimportant owing to their less pristine and "ordinary" character, so many of which are sacrificed to exploitation. A goal equally as worthy as wilderness preservation would be to enable access to wild nature in every neighborhood, recognizing it as a basic human right and a building block of healthy communities while prioritizing those neighborhoods where people have historically been denied it. A forest deep in the mountains makes for a pretty good place in which to ruminate over such things.

My immediate concern, however, is finishing my journey injury free, since 90 percent of all accidents occur within a mile of home, as the saying goes, and my left ankle, weakened by past sprains, shows signs of wanting to give out. Banishing from my mind as best I can a picture of myself limping around in an ankle wrap in my impending role as summer camp director, I take better care of noticing where to best place my feet between roots and rocks.

Not quite certain I'm fit for human company or that my well has been refilled, I realize I have no choice in the matter when the sound of auto traffic cuts through the quiet. The hot sun beats down and the dusty air clings to my skin as the noise grows closer and closer. Alternating patches of sunlight and shade blind me in a strobelike fashion, forcing me to refocus my vision each time to avoid tripping and falling on my face. Even more dizzying is the moment when I reach the trailhead where all the cars are—the parked ones and the numerous others zooming past in both directions—providing confirmation, as if there was any doubt, that the summer tourist season has begun.

Deer Stand

ONE SPRING, figuring I needed a new challenge, I gave gardening a try. The thought of working with my hands and coaxing something living from the ground sounded appealing. So was putting food on the table through my own efforts. On a subconscious level also lurked what I came to understand was an unconsummated longing to participate more fully in the life of the place where I lived and thus earn my keep, so to speak, as a member in good standing.

I learned in no time that I was not a gardener, or at least not a very good one. I planted cabbage, peppers, and squash in a small plot in the backyard and watered them daily, but aphids soon decimated the leaves on the few poking up aboveground. The peppers clung on for a couple of weeks until worms gorged themselves on all but two that I harvested before they fully ripened, fearing my efforts might otherwise come to nothing. For the rest of the growing season, my sad little garden looked like a romper room for pests.

Concluding that I was cursed with a black thumb, though maybe I was just too lazy for dirt work, I contemplated other means of obtaining food directly from the earth to supplement my diet. I ruled out fishing as a reliable source, knowing my limited skills at catching them would leave me empty-handed much of the time. Berries were plentiful depending on the time of year, but mushrooms were inconsistent and widely scattered, and both would require covering quite a bit of ground while trying to gather a sufficient amount of either one, so I ruled them out as well. Over the holidays I met up with a friend who sent me home with venison steaks from a deer he'd shot. I stared at the simmering flesh on my fork while sitting down to dinner one evening, marveling over the simplicity of it, and wondered why I'd never given myself permission to consider this possibility before. Maybe I could learn to hunt.

Which is how, several years later, I once more find myself waking before dawn in my childhood home in December to try my hand at procuring meat to put in the freezer. Reluctant to leave the bed's cozy warmth, I rise and dress while trying not to wake Élan. I slip out the door and point my car toward a friend's property twenty minutes away, passing cornfields and cow pastures. Driving too fast because I'm running late, I ease off the gas when unplowed snow sends my tires into a brief slide.

After arriving at the hilltop tree farm and pulling up the long driveway, I march back down it on foot, rifle slung over my shoulder. I cross the road and start down a row of evergreens without the aid of a light, which works fine until I reach the end of the row where the woods begin. With my headlamp illuminated now, I locate the oak tree with the ladder braced against the trunk and climb. Feeling for each rung in bulky clothing is a clumsy business, and once I reach the top I turn and face the abyss, scooting back onto the metal seat as I pull down the safety bar that's supposed to keep me from plummeting thirty feet to the ground should I lose my wits or nod off. It's like sitting on a ski lift that doesn't go anywhere.

A glance at my watch tells me I've made it on time after all: thirty minutes till first light. The crisp air fills my lungs and feels good on my face, at least for now.

The waiting begins.

More than half a dozen deer stands are scattered around the property, each one lending daylight views of rolling hills in the distance and a patchwork of cornfields and hardwoods. Once owned by a coal company and later converted into a Christmas tree farm, the land now belongs to the parents of Joel, a friend I've known since high school, who have left it largely untouched. Somewhere there are three abandoned mine shafts I've never located; they saw their heyday a century ago when the Whiskey Run company town flowed with coal and liquor. These days deer haunt every acre. One year Joel's father, Mike, counted 140 deer grazing on a single hill. I'll count myself lucky today if I see just one. One, though, is all I want.

First light comes quiet and still. I keep as motionless as possible, a pair of binoculars at the ready. Meat, not a rack, is what I'm after, and since males are over-hunted, I will need to make certain any deer I spot is antlerless before pulling the trigger. I've hunted on opening day when the crackle of gunfire greets first light for miles around, a moment when as many as a million hunters across the state are doing the same thing, and a reminder that I'm taking part in something larger than myself. The noise helps other hunters by getting the deer to move, which increases the chance of seeing something and doing one's part in becoming a direct link in the food chain. But because today is not opening day, dawn is met by silence.

Deer stands, I've decided, are misnamed. A deer *sit* is more like it since that's mostly what I do. Sit and wait, sit and think while struggling to keep my mind from straying from the task before me. Hunters talk about the opportunities for viewing wildlife hunting affords, which is true enough. I have observed foxes and a mother black bear and her cub while sitting in deer stands and watched a yearling fawn pass below me, each one oblivious to my presence. Nuthatches and downy woodpeckers dare to come close while working tree trunks in search of insects. And a squirrel is always on the move somewhere, weaving through a maze of twigs and branches that are seemingly infinite in their variety. But most of all there is the waiting—waiting and trying to become at ease with contemplative stillness and observation, neither of which is my strong suit. It's the kind of waiting that will need to turn predatory in an instant should an opportunity arise. Despite my limited experience—I've been successful just once—it unnerves me to know how capable I am of quickly making the switch.

An hour passes and then another. As promised, Mike comes by in his ATV, a ploy to stir up the deer wherever they have bedded down, returning my wave as he motors past. Nothing comes of it. When my muscles grow stiff from sitting, I stand and stretch. Another hour goes by, and when no amount of stretching warms my frozen fingers and toes, I descend the ladder and head down a row of Christmas trees in hopes of springing a doe. Indiana County, which claims for itself the mantle of Christmas Tree Capital of the World, once produced on one of its many family-owned farms a tree that adorned the White House. Few here would make worthy candidates for such an honor, most of them so overgrown it's impossible to see between their bulging midriffs. If a deer was standing a dozen feet away, I'd have no way of knowing. Upon reaching the end of the row, I start up another, thinking that, if viewed from above, I might resemble a mouse clad in neon orange sniffing its way through a maze in search of treasure.

The outline of Indiana County bears a resemblance to Orion the Hunter, a constellation that reminded me of home each time I glimpsed the winter night sky once I moved away. But whatever link there is between mythology, geography, and my present undertaking grants me no advantage so far today. Twice deer dart in front of me and vanish into the brush. It's a magic trick they perform, the stamping of their hooves almost soundless in the snow, and with each disappearing act, I look on in wonder. Skilled hunters are adept at taking deer on the run from a standing position, but a more conservative approach seems more ethical given my slow reaction time. Better to wait until one stands still, should I be so lucky, to avoid injuring it.

A year ago I nearly bagged a doe out in the open after startling three deer and tracking them for nearly a mile through the snow. I spotted them again while following the highwall of an abandoned strip mine and belly-crawled to a ledge where I got off a shot. I missed and the deer fled. My chances would have been better in the company of fellow hunters making a push, which I've done a few times with Mike's family members, each of us spaced several tree rows apart in an attempt to drive the deer from their hiding places. It's just me today, of course, and my efforts to scare up the deer are beginning to feel more futile by the minute.

When I reach the end of the last row, I traverse a meadow and duck back into the woods. The deer are everywhere and nowhere and seem to know my movements even before I make them. There's pleasure enough in getting warm by moving my legs, and I cover ground from one corner of the property to another over the next hour, walking for what feels like miles in search of fresh prints, scat, any sign at all. I cross back over the road and come to more rows of Christmas trees. Snow begins to fall. A depression in the duff at my feet suggests a small deer once bedded down in this spot. I stretch out next to it beneath the low-hanging limbs of a spruce tree. Snowflakes alight on my nose as I drift off.

I wake before noon and brush snow off my clothes. Not well practiced in this business of tolerating cold and hunger, I make a strategic retreat and return home for lunch and a real nap.

It is a source of wonder whenever I hunt to realize I am hunting at all, as if it were a foreign language I've only just begun to comprehend. The fathers of friends speak with eagerness about hunting whenever the subject comes up in conversation, and because I still have much to learn I listen closely to whatever they have to say. Desire counts far more than success in their eyes, and I am surprised by how little effort it took to be welcomed into their tribe.

My father hunted in his youth yet never raised the idea with me when I was young. I'm sure I would have declined if he had since I could not have fathomed pointing a gun at a living creature and pulling the trigger, which I did just once. On a whim when I was twelve years old, I aimed my BB gun at a chipmunk in our backyard and watched it spin in circles when I hit it, the poor creature neither dying nor quite able to go on living. Horrified by what I'd done and unable or unwilling to bring an end to its suffering, I stowed the gun in my closet and did not touch it again for a long time.

As a boy growing up in western Pennsylvania, I was surrounded by deer hunters at every turn. So many folks hunt deer each fall that the Monday after Thanksgiving is a de facto statewide holiday when many schools remain closed. Childhood playmates and extended family members were hunters, and our neighbor's son-in-law once hung a deer he'd shot in the branches of a maple tree outside my bedroom window. Curious enough to creep next door and peer into the empty ribcage and inspect the organs lying on the ground in a puddle of blood, I was sure that I never wanted to be the cause of something so horrific in my life.

I knew several girls who were as enthusiastic about hunting as were a larger number of boys, which helped to insulate it against macho associations in my mind. Hunting instead seemed to have more to do with class. Schoolmates of mine who hunted weren't the sons and daughters of doctors, coal company executives, and university professors. Most were kids living out in the country, whom the rest of us referred to as rednecks behind their backs. Hunting was a birthright for them, much like country club membership was for the offspring of our county's wealthiest residents. Rednecks got their meat from the woods, while the rest of us got ours from the store. Whenever a neighbor or family friend arrived at our door with a gift of fresh venison, I found it unnerving to eat the flesh of a creature I otherwise took pleasure in watching descend from the woods many evenings to browse in our backyard. My sister would sniff her food and put down her fork if she thought she detected the smell of deer meat, despite our parents' reassurances that it was beef. Venison tasted earthy and too close to home. Bullets and slaughter were the reasons it was on our table. We didn't have to know such intimate details about the deaths of the chickens and cows whose flesh we ate and found ignorance far more preferable.

Several hurdles lay in my path by the time, as a failed gardener, I began to rethink my attitude toward hunting. Hunting was prohibited in the national park, game lands were few and far between in East Tennessee, and I didn't know any private landowners, which meant that I'd have to learn how to hunt during visits up north for the foreseeable future. I also didn't own any firearms and knew I would have to come to grips with using lethal force against defenseless creatures. I would have to alter my thinking in other ways as well. Numerous students of mine were hunters, and I'd long been intrigued by their old-fashioned orientation toward the natural world and skill in helping to feed their families with their own hands. Rather than treating untamed nature as a pretty object on display, they possessed firsthand knowledge of using it to satisfy creaturely needs in a way that didn't amount to exploitation.

My former housemate Steve had once helped me work through my reluctance in using nature for my own ends. I had long felt a twinge of remorse after killing a fish I'd caught, and upon returning from my sister's wedding in Alaska, I confessed my regret about reeling in a king salmon that had been minding its own business until I came along and then watching it die, knowing it would still be alive had I gone shopping at a grocery store instead.

"But then something else would have had to die instead. Unless you prefer to starve," he said. "Besides, how is it better to pay someone to do your killing for you? Harvesting your own meat is the most ancient and natural method there is." True to Steve's character, the bumper sticker on his truck read *Save the Neanderthals*.

Blood had been on my hands all along, of course. Even adopting a vegan diet wouldn't change the fact that I was an accomplice in the demise of other creatures merely by taking up space as a living and breathing creature myself. In whichever spot I made my home, droves of wildlife could no longer make theirs. Wherever I operated my automobile, asphalt had obliterated their habitat. Even the vegetables I ate came by necessity from spaces that had displaced generations of wild animals. While commensal species such as rodents and deer flourished as a result of the vast network of human development I depended upon as a modern person, less adaptive species—that is, *most* species—were out of luck. Hunting seemed one way to no longer deny the sacramental reality of human life, which others, rednecks included, had figured out long before me: death is a part of life, and it is impossible to avoid playing some role in it. The consolation prize was having a say in deciding *what* role.

A defense of hunting might call attention to the fact that it leaves wildlife habitat largely intact and, in many cases, helps to preserve and restore it through self-taxation when hunters purchase licenses. Or point out that since the establishment of hunting laws in the early twentieth century, no game animal in North America has joined the ranks of extinct species. Or appeal to a predatory instinct sealed in our DNA that evokes a desire to carry on what our ancestors began doing thousands of years ago. Or argue that in an atomized society such as ours, we have lost sight of the common good in our veneration of hyper-individualism and have extended this same logic to the nonhuman world, often with disastrous consequences. Or question the assumption that killing an animal because it has a face and a mother is worse than killing living things that have neither.

But rational arguments weren't the reason I became a hunter, and, meanwhile, I was aware that becoming one wouldn't sit well with modern sensibilities, especially among individuals who viewed hunting as a barbaric anachronism and a backward step in a supposedly morally evolved era. One day it might even get me labeled a "murderer." A part of me, I knew, wouldn't ever be comfortable killing an animal myself. Some level of discomfort would always be part of the deal.

The main reason I started hunting was that it was the response both the forest and human culture kept offering in answer to my desire to become a more conscientious participant in nature's economy. Submitting to the idea of it long before I first sat in a deer stand meant seeing more clearly my creaturely dependence on the nonhuman world. It also presented the chance to secure a measure of independence from the industrial food economy by not outsourcing every mouthful of food I ate to a distant, impersonal, and efficiency-obsessed source. More and more, it seemed that not only *could* I hunt but that I *ought* to, a decision obligating certain responsibilities that were a burden only in the most liberating sense. Were my circumstances different, I might have raised chickens or propagated native plants, or become an heirloom fruit tree grower, rooftop gardener, or beekeeper. Given my limitations of time and place, however, hunting seemed the most promising choice. What's more, Élan, herself a part-time vegetarian, approved.

The first steps I took were to enroll in a hunter's safety course and obtain a license. I next bought a rifle, neon-orange coat, and gutting knife. No wonder many economically disadvantaged people living in rural areas hunted, I thought, while making my purchases, surprised by how relatively inexpensive each item was, save for the rifle, though as a lifetime investment, it would pay dividends for years to come depending on my luck. I kept expecting something to tell me I was heading down the wrong path while making my preparations. Nothing did, and when I sat in a deer stand for the first time, harvesting a deer neither that year nor the next, it was satisfying nonetheless, as if this was what I was meant to do in this place at this time of year.

When the moment finally arrived for me to pull the trigger, no longer a boy wielding a BB gun but a grown man aiming a high-powered rifle at a deer that seemed to stare right through me with its big brown eyes, questions appeared in my mind in the form of vows. Was I certain I wanted to take this innocent creature's life? I was. Would I bear the weight of knowing an act of violence was required to take it? I would. Did I pledge to honor this creature's life by not wasting its flesh? I did. It was a moment that brought an end to whatever strain of Romantic idealism I still clung to and initiated further acceptance of the hidden depths of human existence. I pictured a day when I might not be able to abide by such promises and would become like older hunters who are content to sit in a deer stand, weaponless, simply to enjoy watching wildlife. But for now, that was a distant fork on a path I'd only just embarked upon.

Rested and fed, I'm back at it several hours before sunset, this time taking watch from a box stand situated near the edge of a meadow. Perched four feet off the ground, it lends views of the ubiquitous Christmas trees, a gas well, and the community water tower. Best of it all, it allows me the luxury of standing while keeping out of sight. Peering through a gap partially covered with a strip of muslin, I notice little movement. Just the yellow tufts of grass poking through the snow that wave each time the wind blows. The waiting commences once again.

Ben was a former colleague of mine who also had a Neanderthal streak. With his barrel chest, beard, and flowing locks, he looked like a model for the cover of a paperback romance novel. Dressing for class some days in nothing but a loincloth, he would dash barefooted out of the woods into the company of shocked students and teachers. While communicating by means of grunts and hand gestures, he would coax them into helping him light a fire using a hand drill, then disappear back into the woods leaving everyone to guess when Earth Man, as he called himself, would show up again. Ben happened upon a fawn browsing in the forest while exploring one afternoon. The startled deer looked up but didn't run, uncertain what to make of the human standing so close by, likely the first it had ever seen. Ben got down on all fours and began copying the deer's eating motions. When he came closer, the fawn stayed put. He inched forward, wondering how near the deer would allow him to get. The pair was only a few feet apart when the mother appeared and snorted in alarm. The fawn, as Ben told it, registered a look of confusion. There was a threat somewhere according to its mother. But where? Surely it was not this four-legged creature sharing in the fruits of the forest floor. Another snort by the mother sent her fawn running and brought to an end a moment in which the divide separating two worlds had dissolved.

Though the blind gives me an edge, deer here and throughout the eastern United States have the advantage of living in the absence of large predators on an ever-fragmenting landscape that enlarges the type of habitat they prefer. This in turn has led to soaring white-tail populations. The result has been degraded habitat including a decline in many woodland plant species, as well as crop damage and scores of human deaths from automobile collisions with deer. As the number of hunters nationwide declines, it's likely that so too will biodiversity and forest health partly for this reason.

To hunt or not to hunt is to play a role both in the life cycle of an ecosystem and a management plan set forth by a state government or other entity, albeit with different results. In other words, taking no action means taking action nonetheless and letting the chips fall where they may, including perhaps by harvesting a deer with one's automobile. I experienced this very thing while riding with Joel on a country road at night. A deer flashed in front of us and kept running when we hit it—there was no time to brake—likely to die a slow, agonizing death. Left behind were a crumpled hood and two shaken riders.

My attempts at becoming a successful predator in the food economy of the eastern deciduous forest almost always end in failure, which isn't surprising considering that my quarry is athletes skilled in evasion and survival. The trick with hunting, as with fishing, is chalking up failure as a kind of modest success. I take consolation in having shown up and being at the ready whenever another year ends in disappointment. The one time I was successful, any thought of having conquered nature was the furthest thing from my mind. After rising before dawn two days in a row and attending a football game the previous night with Joel and Mike, which kept me up till two in the morning, all I felt was a rush of gratitude—and relief over finally getting to catch up on sleep.

The minutes pile up as I keep staring out at the meadow. Though caffeinated and alert, I find my mind keeps wandering. A flock of tundra swans cut through the sky, necks torpedo straight, beaks plowing the air like the bows of ships. I return my gaze to the waving yellow grass and snow and Christmas trees. Still no movement. And then two deer bound out of the trees.

They pause in the middle of the meadow, and I am all eyes and ears. My .30-.06 has a maximum range of three hundred yards. The pair is standing one-third that distance from me. I'm certain that any second something will alert them to my presence—my scent, the muslin cloth which I push out of the way, or the muzzle of the gun I poke through the opening and point in their direction—and they will bolt.

They trot a few feet further, then stop to sniff the air. They're facing the wrong way, hind-ends toward me, which makes taking a shot unwise. Then the one in front, the larger of the two, turns so her flank is broadside. I locate her neck, a thing of strength and beauty, in the crosshairs of my scope, and squeeze.

Ears ringing, I climb out of the stand. Though she's lying still in the place where she fell, I wait several minutes before approaching. It's a sobering moment and no time for rejoicing. I have shattered bone, shed blood. Ended a life.

It's clear when I finally walk over to her that my shot was clean and killed her instantaneously—or almost. Tracks show where she bounded ten feet away before dropping to the ground. Air escapes her lungs when I press a hand to her ribcage. Another set of prints in the snow shows where her companion made a beeline for the trees at the sound of my rifle.

I put on rubber gloves and open the blade of my gutting knife and quickly get to work. Field dressing an animal is a simple if messy procedure. The organs and viscera must be removed within roughly a half hour or I'll risk spoiling the meat. The other time I was successful I had Mike's help dressing and transporting the animal to my car so I could deliver it to the butcher. Today I'm all alone.

Within the hour Mike will return from running errands in town and lend me a hand moving the doe the final distance from field to driveway where we will lift her into the trunk of my car. I will drive to Cunningham Meats located several miles away and ask for permission to watch while they strip off the hide, which I will take home and tan and use for a rug. I will transport the meat to Tennessee in the used hybrid automobile that Élan and I purchased just days ago and she has driven just once, which will result in her dubbing me an "NPR redneck." I will make room in the freezer for forty-five pounds of meat that will take me a year to consume.

But for now, it's just me and the doe, and she is heavy. With no rope or any other means of moving her, I hook my arms under her forelegs and neck. Her fur rubs against my face as I hug her to my chest and begin dragging her through the snow in an intimate embrace, trying to hold up my end in one of the oldest and hardest dances I know of on earth.

Off Trail

ON A RETURN FLIGHT from Pittsburgh after attending a friend's wedding, I was reminded of one of the chief pleasures of air travel: getting to study the surface of the earth from a vantage point of 35,000 feet. As the plane began its descent toward the Knoxville airport and the Smokies came into view, I feasted my eyes on the ground below like a hawk surveying its territory. Trails were impossible to make out at that altitude, though I guessed one ran along this ridge and another through that valley. I'd hiked many of the eight hundred miles of trails in the national park by this time, plus dozens more on unmaintained footpaths, old wagon roads, and abandoned railways. But suddenly I doubted just how well I really knew the place. I knew Gregory Ridge Trail, having hiked it countless times, but how well did I know Gregory Ridge? A trail by one definition is an elongated clearing one spends hours staring at to avoid stumbling and breaking one's teeth. Glancing up to take in one's surroundings is often the exception rather than the rule. As for the rest of the forest through which Gregory Ridge Trail weaved like a lone thread sewn into a vast tapestry, it had never occurred to me to step foot there, and it struck me that all this time I'd been acquainting myself with just threads.

I'd depended on guidebooks a good deal since the start of my apprenticeship in one of the most rugged landscapes east of the Mississippi River and even authored a slender volume to enhance the experience of students and other park visitors. Yet guidebooks can warp the mind a little, and when I noticed how my reliance on them prevented me from making discoveries beyond the prescribed boundaries of established knowledge, I began to distrust their influence. Also disconcerting was the godlike view of Google Earth and its sense of mastery over the globe: nothing to see here that hasn't been seen before. Thinking back on my view from the airplane that day, I realized how often I'd stuck to the rules and stayed between the lines, following in other people's footsteps because it was easier than finding my own way through the woods.

As with other spheres of human affairs, the rules of hiking say never leave the path, which is sound advice for beginners including children on a solo walk. Plan your trip and tell someone where you're going, we're told. But what rules and guidebooks can't do is help us unlearn rules when they become too constricting or instruct us to disregard their counsel when doing so might be what we need to get nearer to the heart of a place. A different kind of guide becomes necessary to help steer a person away from being steered so they can discover the world for themselves. So I began to contemplate a remedy drawn from my own unlearning for other seekers to take under advisement if they wanted to—things I normally couldn't say as a responsible outdoor educator but wished I could: in short, an antiguide.

The first piece of advice an antiguide has to offer is to ditch the highways and byways of human foot traffic. Embarking onto trackless ground, though a sobering thought, places one in good company. How else to find one's way without a guide or path, as many others throughout history have done? Doing so can feel overwhelming to the uninitiated and as if one is facing an existential threat capable of absorbing one's whole being. This is indeed a possibility in the densely forested Appalachians where some people have wandered off never to return. For the initiated, including colleagues of mine and other hardy souls who have an appetite for off-trail adventure—plus a few student groups who have accompanied me on short bushwhacks—the main difference was not letting knowledge of this fact stop them. As for whether it is worth taking such a risk, I'm inclined to agree with Helen Keller, for whom life itself was one long bushwhack: "Life is either a daring adventure or nothing at all."

Parting ways with the beaten path often feels at first like a form of self-punishment. Another name for this means of travel is bushwhacking, a misleading term because I've found it involves far less whacking at bushes than it does getting whacked by them. Bodily contact with all manner of living and nonliving objects is guaranteed, and yet no search for the heart of anything comes without a personal cost. Given enough time and patience, it's possible to avoid many obstacles and accept unavoidable collisions with one's dignity mostly intact. In the meantime, it's best to ignore Descartes's instructions to walk in a straight line in a forest without changing course, a predilection borne of Enlightenment thinking that would impose theory over reality and order over unruly nature. Reality is the point, after all, and because of that, unruliness too.

Speaking of reality, if an antiguide accomplishes little else at this juncture, it at least shows us what is possible by inviting us into those places from which we often exclude ourselves—places visited by few other living souls yet which make up a significant percentage of our neighborhoods, parks, and planet.

One temptation will be retreating to the safety of trails and other developed areas. So will carrying a phone. In keeping with the spirit of an antiguide, however, and because personal communication devices are not the parachutes many people believe them to be, a phone is better left behind. One at least ought to avoid imitating the off-trail hiker who phoned for help after stumbling upon an intersection on an old roadbed as night was falling. A dispatcher connected him with a park ranger who knew the area well. The ranger, whose shift began early the next morning, was at home in bed.

Hiker: Hello there. I seem to be lost and need you to tell me which way to go.

Ranger: Describe your surroundings for me if you can, sir.

Hiker: I see trees.

Ranger: That's a start. Anything else?

Hiker: No, just lots of trees.

Ranger: You're in the forest.

Hiker: Well, yeah.

Ranger: And you got there on your own two feet?

Hiker: Of course, I did.

Ranger: Sir, let me ask you something. If you didn't have a phone right now, what would you be doing?

Hiker: Well, I guess I wouldn't be talking with you, for one thing.

Ranger: Right. Now please tell me exactly how I can help you.

Hiker: Like I said, I need you to tell me which way to go.

Ranger: But all you've told me you can see is trees. That's not very helpful, sir.

Hiker: You're a ranger, I thought you knew this place. If you can't help me, please put me through to an expert.

Ranger: I am afraid to say I'm the best we've got.

Hiker: You've got to be kidding.

Ranger: Not in the least. And sir, if you really want to know what I think, it's that you should put your phone away and start walking. Downhill is your best bet.

Hiker: So you're not going to help me?

Ranger: I am helping you. I told you to put your phone away.

Hiker: But how is that going to help?

Ranger: Sir, I'm going to level with you now. Unless you put your phone away and start using your common sense, well, I'll be blunt—I'm not sure we want you to find your way out.

Hiker: What do you mean you don't want me to find my way out?

Ranger: What I mean is that you haven't made a convincing case that you're fit to reenter human society, which for a very, *very* long time has survived and even thrived without depending on such devices and still does in many parts of the world unless you, too, learn how to function as a self-reliant and fully formed human being without one.

Hiker: I'm starting to see your point. I've been walking all this time and all I can see are more trees. Trees everywhere I look!

Ranger: Welcome to the eastern deciduous forest, sir.

While I was not privy to this conversation firsthand and can only imagine what was said, or ought to have been said, this actual incident had a happy ending. The already sleep-deprived ranger instructed the distressed hiker to call him upon finding his way out of the woods, which the hiker did, safely, at two o'clock in the morning.

The hiker was lucky to have gotten a signal in a rugged region where cell service in many places is nonexistent. And yet while even the most up-to-date technology has its perks, it has at least as many drawbacks. One is its potential for inducing an overdependency on it, along with an inability to resist believing it will take care of us as we increasingly lose our ability to take care of ourselves. Our devices fool us into thinking they are indispensable and we can't get by without them when we can and often should.

Using a GPS device for navigation likewise means forgoing an unvarnished off-trail experience through reliance on space-age technology when a simple map and compass will do. Tiny screens contract the world to near meaninglessness by focusing a person's attention on their present location, which reinforces the falsehood that they reside at the center of the universe. Now that their senses and creaturely instincts are no longer necessary and their skills of observation obsolete, neither is paying close attention to their surroundings. One need only obey the machine. Getting through the wilderness becomes the task rather than reading the landscape and adapting to its rhythms. Pixels will show the way, at least until the batteries run dry. An experienced hiker from Ohio discovered this firsthand when he took a GPS unit into the Smokies backcountry yet managed to lose his bearings for four days barely a mile from his car.

One afternoon I explored a part of the woods I'd never visited, equipped with only a map and compass. My plan was to find a secluded creek located a safe distance from any trails and follow it downstream to where it joined the Little River. Several hours after beginning my journey, I arrived at the precise spot I'd had in mind and crouched at the edge of the woods, feeling proud of my navigational prowess. I watched the road for traffic, which should have been heavy at that time of day, but after ten minutes a jeep driven by a coworker was the only vehicle that passed by—the first sign that something was amiss, though I failed to notice. When I crossed the road and peered down at the moving water, I did a double take. The river was flowing in the wrong direction. Not from right to left but from left to right. Checking and rechecking my map, I was certain I'd found the right place, yet while I had been traipsing around the forest, nature seemed to have rearranged the furniture.

Some time passed before I was able to wrap my mind around the fact that what was wrong was neither the river nor my map but me; that all afternoon I'd been following a different stream entirely and was now standing a mere hundred yards from my starting point, staring not at the Little River but one of its tributaries—the Middle Prong, which I lived beside. It took me the rest of the day to revise my memory and loosen the geographical knot that had formed there, which was strangely liberating as much as it was humbling. The next time I ventured off trail in that area, I knew I would do so with a greater awareness of not only my surroundings but also my propensity for misreading maps whenever I was impatient to get where I thought I was going.

Point of fact: take along a map and compass and it's possible to not know where you are even when you get there. For this reason and more, an antiguide recommends leaving behind these items as well. Though going without them carries the potential of getting lost, chances are decent you will get lost regardless.

Step a mere fifty paces away from a trail and a whole other world will unfold before your eyes. As hikers oblivious of your presence march past, the temptation to spy on them or spook them by howling like a coyote might be too strong to resist. Be forewarned, however, that it is in a forest's nature to lure wanderers deeper into it. Fifty paces become one hundred, and suddenly it isn't clear which way leads back. Should fear creep in at any point, which it will, take heart, for other creatures experience this sensation daily yet do not let it overcome them. It is worth recalling that Hansel and Gretel made it home safe in the end, guided solely by their wits.

For the person who gets lost, an antiguide suggests regarding it as an opportunity. Staying put and calling for help is not a bad idea. But because humans are known to follow rules least often when they need them most, lost persons instead often attempt to retrace their steps until they find their starting point or become even more lost. Another option is to do what my mother and aunt did when my sister and I were young: keep going. While wandering up the smallish mountain behind our house, it came to pass that neither adult had any idea where they were or how to find their way home, so we trod on. Clouds inked to black and thunder smacked the air. Rain pelted us until we were as wet as eels. The poor children! Yet we were no worse off than the adults and only a little scared. We came to a farmhouse and knocked on the door, but no one was home. The rain kept falling and we kept going, following a road past more farms until we reached Mary Ann Hill Road and then ours, named for Ben Franklin—himself a wanderer of a certain stripe—and finally arrived back home where dry clothes, hot food, and my worried grandmother awaited us.

Getting lost is one of the oldest human tendencies on the planet. The first person known to do so got lost in a garden after eating fruit not intended for human consumption. "Where are you?" asks the Creator. A good question, and Adam never does come up with a satisfying answer. Clearly, to be human is to be lost.

An antiguide audaciously declares that everyone should get lost outdoors at least once in their lifetime, should they be so lucky. A rite of passage useful for acquiring humility and self-reliance, perhaps it ought to be considered a human right. This is not to make light of hypothermia, injury, or dozens of other potential dangers, or those tragic cases when a person sets out never to be heard from again. Or those times when other people's lives are put at risk on a search-and-rescue operation due to a person's grave error in judgment. I once took part in a search for a missing young man during which five of my team's seven members were forced to turn back because of injury and fatigue. The victim spent eleven days roaming around the woods without food or potable water before walking out under his own power, chigger bitten and twenty-five pounds lighter. Bushwhacking even in less remote areas means accepting some level of danger as well as the possibility that one's bones may turn up some years hence. Yet there are worse things. One is never facing the unknown, never taking any chances at all.

Guidebooks say to let someone know where you're going and when you plan to return. But an antiguide emancipates the wanderer from this burden by encouraging them to light out with no clear destination in mind. My boss Ken and I share a mutual understanding on this point. An off-trail enthusiast himself, he will ask where I'm headed on my day off.

"Up on the mountain maybe. Or down in the valley," I'll say. "Not sure."

"Oh, *there*."

Consider adopting the *act first, apologize later* strategy even at the risk of causing friends and loved ones obsessed like the rest of us with certainty to wring their hands in dismay. Should they question your sense of judgment, question theirs by having raised no objections to your driving in traffic, which kills dozens of people every day, or by having tacitly suggested that it is safer for you to stay indoors surrounded by dangerous household chemicals while fattening yourself on the sofa and staring at addictive and disembodying screens known to soften the mind and atrophy the soul.

An antiguide's final piece of advice is to wander alone whenever possible and save the pleasures of human company for another day. Bringing even a single companion means inviting society when it is this very thing from which one needs a holiday, however brief. Women especially are advised never to walk in the woods by themselves, but several colleagues of mine prefer doing so. Mary is often told by strangers she runs into that she shouldn't hike alone—strangers who never seem to consider that the Dangerous Person in the woods might be them or Mary herself. Elizabeth likewise often prefers her own company, having once solo hiked the Appalachian Trail during a time of year when thru-hikers were fewer in number, and spends weekends exploring rugged terrain seldom visited by others, whatever the cost to her wardrobe and flesh. Needless to say, she seldom comes into contact with other people while off trail, which if stranger-danger is a concern turns out to be one of the safest spaces anywhere.

People may discourage hiking off trail for a different reason: there doesn't seem to be any point to it. Wandering around the woods while risking life and limb instead of doing something useful doesn't compute with expectations of modern living, driven as it is by maximum productivity and efficiency. It's a waste of time according to any reasonable cost-benefit analysis, assuming such standards of measurement can be trusted to make such a determination. But can they be?

An evaluation expert and statistician who once visited campus boasted that he could measure anything. "Anything at all," he boldly claimed, committed reductionist that he was, his confidence in the rational mind's ability to pin down everything by assigning it a numeric value seemingly limitless. I wish I'd asked him how he would quantify soulfulness, beauty, or a single human life. The purpose of his visit had been to assist us in demonstrating the impact of outdoor education to school administrators and funders for whom measurable results often eclipse other considerations. But a Cartesian toolbox ultimately isn't up to the task of assessing the worth of a person spending time catching crawdads or gazing at the night sky, all the while becoming more fully human. Such a way of thinking diminishes the world to a closed system that leaves out consideration of whatever eludes calculation. It fools one into believing one has gotten to the bottom of things.

If wandering off trail provides anything useful, perhaps it is this: it reminds us that when we think we have gotten to the bottom of things, what we've found is a door, and behind it even more doors, or cells, shall we say; then another door beyond those where there are molecules; and where two or more molecules are gathered there resides an atom, which is made up of electrons that the unaided human eye has never seen but from what we can gather spin around and around like the earth on its axis. All of it perfectly quantifiable until we go through the next door, where we suspect there are quarks, which we can't quantify without changing the very thing we're observing, having now reached an anteroom called Theory and Probability. This room, which is impossible to get beyond, sometimes goes by another name: Mystery. Experts who claim we are on the cusp of a Theory of Everything might turn out to be right, at least until time reveals what it has again and again about the truth of our capacity for knowledge, which is that there are always more rooms to discover, including some we will never enter.

What we've been investigating all this time while following the advice of the antiguide is the mystery of the self and its place in the universe. Inseparable from one another, they're what getting lost in a forest or city can give us a glimpse of. The disorienting feelings we experience upon leaving the beaten path upsets the order of things and rattles our cage. We're no longer in control and must find our way there and back again. We get shown our self-in-place, even as nature rearranges the furniture on us, and we make discoveries no one else can make on our behalf. Allowing the mind to wander takes little more than unoccupied mental space, which is no small thing. But for the whole person to wander, body and soul, takes a world.

Following trails made by others is a necessary starting point for all of this. "You first must be on the path before you can turn and walk into the wild," writes Gary Snyder. One reason we might veer away from the path is

Off Trail

upon recognizing we're on the wrong one or one that has led us astray. Such paths, from Descartes's assertion that bodies are machines to factory-model education to industrial civilization's destruction of the earth, to name just a few, are what I've come to think an outdoor education in part serves to question. When the way, though marked so well, becomes lost, it is time to make new paths, search out ancient ones, and find those that have become overgrown and forgotten. Return to origins and first things. Recover lost connections between body and soul, the past and the present, humans and the rest of Creation. Go bushwhacking.

Some days it occurs to me how neglectful I've been in carrying out household chores and keeping in touch with family and friends, and a creeping sense of guilt spurs me to get up and do something about it. Today, though, is not one of those days. After spending the weekend tracking wildlife with a dozen adults during a workshop on mammal ecology, I'm content to laze at home without moving a muscle while waiting for Élan to return from her new job in Knoxville. Outside my door awaits a half million splendid acres of forested mountains, but here in my living room lies a protected habitat and management area of my own, which for now is enough.

The sun could be shining, or it might not. With the window blinds shut tight, it's impossible to tell, and I have zero sense of urgency to find out. From the comfort of my recliner, I reach for the bagpipe chanter I recently acquired. The chanter is the part of the bagpipes that bears a resemblance to the type of recorder students learn to play in grade school, with one main difference: halfway down the shaft, hidden from view, is a double reed. The oboe my father once played in symphony orchestras is also a double-reed instrument, and it dawns on me that I am following a family tradition of sorts by learning how to play the bagpipes. Notions fill my head of someday entertaining people with the eye-popping sound of an instrument that knows just one volume, though when I blow through the chanter, the noise that comes out resembles that of a dying goose. Multiple attempts at finding the right embouchure deliver the same results. I once played the saxophone and clarinet, but, then as now, instant success is elusive.

No match for the bagpipe chanter today, and feeling cooped up after several listless hours, I haul empty water jugs to my car and drive deeper into the valley to a mountain spring. It's while I am filling the containers that I spot an old road grade from pre-park days carved into an embankment and wonder where it leads and why I never noticed it until now. With only one way to find out, I start walking.

A wide hollow sprawls before me at the top of the embankment. When the old road peters out I join a dry streambed, telling myself I won't go far. The streambed quickly becomes choked with vegetation, so I opt for climbing the bank into open woods, and soon I'm following the spine of a finger ridge. Deciding it's too steep for a lazy person on his day off, I drop back into the hollow and surprise a mother bear with cubs who flee at the sight of me. Not wanting to waste the opportunity to study fresh bear tracks, I search among the pebbles in a shallow springhead where the trio was drinking. Though tempted to drink from it myself, I resist the urge, not wishing to tempt fate in case the bears fouled the water.

The old road mysteriously reappears, and I follow it once more until it narrows to a faint footpath and fades altogether. I push on, not yet ready to turn back, now climbing exposed bedrock that makes for a convenient staircase in a flowing streambed which soon turns into a trickle. Dizzy from climbing, I glance up and spot the summit. Though it can't be more than ten minutes away, I stay put, figuring a walk that began without a destination doesn't need one now.

Naptime. When I stretch out on the ground, the cold buried within seeps through my coat, though not enough to chill me after all this unintended exercise. I close my eyes and feel the heap of earth I've ascended pushing against my back. I recall the time I went wandering behind a gas station at age five while on a family vacation. A few precious moments spent exploring felt right after sitting in the car for hours on end, and the intrigue of what I might discover back there was impossible to ignore. A guard dog I unwittingly surprised left bite marks on my back and sent me screaming back to safety, an experience which luckily ruined for me neither dogs nor the pleasure of sneaking off.

The faraway heckling of a woodpecker draws me out of sleep. It takes a moment to remember where I am and just how I got here, wherever here is exactly. I'm somewhere I never dreamed of going before today, and now that I'm here my next thought is to tell Élan, who must be home by now and wondering where I am. Going home is always the sweetest part.

Staying in Character: A Travelogue

BACK IN THE DAYS when I moved away to start a short-lived career as a bicycle courier and performing musician, I first set out on a cross-country road trip. After trading in my car with its dying transmission for a blue sedan I nicknamed Berry after early White settler Will Walker's trusty ox, I headed west on a monthlong journey, staying with friends and camping along the way. Most stops were no longer than a day in length and cumulatively began to feel like a string of geographical one-night stands—a sweltering night in the Badlands, a pub crawl in Boulder, short hikes in Arches and Yellowstone. Each dalliance left me wanting more.

Though it wasn't my first outing in the American West, I found the dry, oven-hot air and scarcity of trees baffling. I wasn't pining for the verdant green of eastern forests, or not yet. I simply couldn't fathom why anyone would want to live out here, including Edward Abbey, who grew up a few miles away from where I did before spending his adulthood in desert country and writing with deep affection about his adopted home in more than a dozen books. But then how could I, as only a passer-through insulated from my surroundings much of the time in a contraption he once called an "upholstered horseless hearse."

I took my time in Glacier, crashing in the staff quarters of college friends who worked on the park's trail crew before shouldering my pack in the morning and heading toward the shores of Lake Ellen Wilson. Mountain goats and wary marmots greeted me in open spaces along the Continental Divide. "Hey bear, coming through," I hollered when passing through thick woods, as one does in grizzly country. One had recently been spotted in the area, and another had killed a solo traveler in the park several weeks earlier.

Growing bored with reciting the same thing over and over, I resorted to uttering aloud whatever entered my mind.

"Economics is a subject I wish I understood better. But then I hear so do economists."

And then: "Einstein was a genius who was known to leave his house without wearing pants. Tried that myself once but it didn't make me any smarter."

And: "I'll be here all day, bears. Please don't eat the entertainment." The backcountry open mic amateur comedy hour was now in full swing.

I turned to song lyrics next, substituting gibberish whenever memory failed. As time passed, I began to notice the strange effect verbalizing my thoughts was having on me. In any other setting, an inner critic would have kept me from unloosing the contents of my mind into the world, but in this place whatever barrier separated my mind from what lay outside it seemed to no longer exist. It was as if the firings inside my cerebral cortex had pushed beyond the walls containing them and begun inhabiting a larger space. As I moved through unfamiliar woods filled with birdsong and piercing sunlight, I wondered: *my mind—the forest—one and the same?*

I liked this sensation, this blurring of lines between subject and object, me and my surroundings. It smacked of something primitive and premodern though it was hardly relegated to a bygone era. It was available even now, offering a taste of a way of being in the world so unlike the thousands of seat-cushioned road miles I'd put behind me. Maybe I was delusional and was just annoying the birds while filling the space around me with my verbose presence. It was useful staying alive if a grizzly bear was around the corner, however, and meanwhile, the only shred of evidence I left behind were boot prints, which, along with my mind's meanderings, would soon be absorbed into the thick of things.

Among the many benefits of travel is how it recalibrates my perception of home. Imprinted on my senses and always in the back of my mind, home becomes the yardstick by which I regard unfamiliar places, each of which prompts me to reconsider home itself. Travel means taking stock of the wider world and finding what evidence I can for sources of joy, despair, or hope. A cocktail of emotions that begins with wonder and might leave an aftertaste of petty judgment (*wouldn't want to live here*) carries a through line of noticing, including observing myself in the act of noticing. What's grabbing my attention? Often it is people and the mark they've left on the landscape for better or worse. Just as often, it is forests or the absence of them.

For our honeymoon, Élan and I wanted a destination neither of us had visited before, ideally in a climate that would offer relief from the sticky summer heat. Somewhere exotic yet where we understood the language, knowing that putting on a do-it-ourselves wedding would leave us exhausted. Scotland, the birthplace of many of Élan's ancestors, rose to the top of our list. I already had a soft spot for Robert Burns's poetry and his countrymen's fine elixirs. We saved money and earned extra doing side jobs, and a week following our ceremony, we boarded a red-eye flight to Edinburgh.

Scotland bears a resemblance to North Carolina in size and shape, with a few necessary adjustments. Stand the Tar Heel State on end so the mountains reside in the north, replace neighboring states on either side with an ocean, and you've got "The Best Small Country in the World," as claimed by a delightfully arrogant banner welcoming us in the airport. At a booth, we asked for directions to a currency exchange kiosk in the city from a young woman, admiring her thick brogue and way of elongating "church" into two distinct syllables. We picked up our car with its steering wheel on the wrong side and drove northward, white knuckling our way around traffic circles, and rented a cabin outside Cairngorms National Park.

Visits to castles, distilleries, and other touristy destinations filled the week. Everywhere we went I looked for evidence of the forced evictions that occurred centuries earlier during the Highland Clearances when tenants were driven off the land by wealthy landowners, and those able to survive the journey fled to the Lowlands or the coast and eventually to North America. The clan system was systematically dismantled in this manner, as a landscape populated by humans since prehistoric times became the largely unpeopled domain of a new agricultural regime benefiting the upper classes: sheep grazing. For every shell of a stone building that we spotted protruding from the heather, each one possibly a signpost of past human heartbreak, dozens more remained hidden from view. I couldn't help thinking of Will Walker, whose ancestors had immigrated to the southern Appalachians from the British Isles in the eighteenth century, and how one act of dislocation of a people coincided with another on a different continent, occurring the same year as Walker's birth: the Trail of Tears.

Human displacement wasn't the only catastrophe to have visited the Scottish Highlands in previous centuries. A treeless landscape spilled before us nearly everywhere we looked. Only remnants remained of pine and birch forests that once covered the hills and sustained a diverse tapestry of life following the last ice age. Left behind was something akin to a canvas wiped clean of all but a few paint strokes of the portrait it once contained. Missing altogether were tribes of wildlife—lynx, brown bear, wild boar, beaver, polecat, and wolf—that inhabited the land before humans drove them to extinction.

Like droves of other visitors, I became enchanted with Scotland the moment I stepped foot there. Yet for all its photogenic qualities, the Highlands presented a picture of ecological impoverishment, or what Fraser Darling, father of Highland ecology, called a "wet desert." The heather-covered hills themselves, which have been romanticized in verse and song, are to a high degree a manmade creation, the result of deforestation and centuries of burning and grazing. Wildlife such as badgers, birds, and two species of native deer, along with two more that are nonnative, still populate the country, but mainly there are sheep. Sheep everywhere. Damn sheep and the land mines they deposit on seemingly every square foot of earth they trod. In the absence of natural predators, sheep and deer prevent rewilding from taking place by keeping young trees from reaching maturity and allowing forests to return. The land, while inviting to the human eye, is troubled.

We retired each evening to a pub to absorb that day's events and review the flora and fauna we'd seen. I added chough and ring ouzel and rowan, the holy tree of Scotland to the list. Left off was what in former times might have made the most remarkable sight of all yet was long gone: the old forest itself. In its place, we'd seen little more than its ghost.

It is a subfreezing day in late January, and I am driving to West Virginia for once instead of merely passing through it. I come this way several times a year when visiting family and friends further north, but this occasion is different. I've departed a day early, and with my spare time, I plan to investigate the southwest corner of the state and see firsthand whatever evidence I can find of the controversial method of coal extraction known as mountaintop removal. I also hope to locate a mountain that until recently was under threat of having its top dynamited into oblivion.

Off the interstate, a road guides me to my first stop in tiny Bramwell, where century-old mansions once owned by coal company executives line the main street. A brochure inside an interpretive center tells me the town was the richest in the nation for its size in the decades before the Great Depression. It is the last visible sign of wealth I will see all day.

Farther along Route 52, in Keystone, railcars loaded with coal sit idle on tracks, and a tipple frames the sky like an antiquated amusement ride. The surrounding mountainsides are situated so near to one another and at such precipitous angles that the only buildable space is a narrow strip of land adjacent to the river. Though a food bank and several businesses look open, far outnumbering them are ramshackle storefronts and other abandoned buildings, including once-elegant homes with broken windows, empty shells of houses of worship, and a hollowed-out school.

A federal prison greets me upon entering Welch, where wards of the state clad in orange jumpsuits roam an asphalt lot ringed by razor wire. While sitting at a stoplight, I wait for one of the men to make eye contact with me, but none do. The prison grounds practically jut out into the street, occupying the only level surface that's available. The message it sends is clear enough: no more space to build, but there's room inside for anyone who breaks the law.

I share a distant connection with Welch through a great-great-uncle who once owned a small coal mine here. Harry Shuttleworth, one of twelve children born to parents who emigrated from the British Isles and whose father started working in the mines at age nine, first dug coal alongside his five brothers in Dagus Mines, Pennsylvania. According to family lore, once his two older brothers left home it became his privilege each Saturday—bath night—to wash first, scrubbing the thick layer of coal dust off his skin before his younger brothers took their turns bathing in the blackened water. A photograph taken around 1915 captured him posing in his white catcher's uniform with the company baseball team. He and a friend eventually scratched together enough cash to purchase a mine near Welch.

As my grandmother tells it, Harry's sympathies remained with his workers even as a mine operator, as he did not approve of the schemes of large companies that were trying to break the miners' union. *I owe my soul to the company store* did not apply in the case of his employees, who claimed he never cussed and was the best boss they ever had. He sold the mine after two years, likely outcompeted by larger operators, and returned home. He died at age ninety-one when I was ten years old. Though I never met him, I was introduced at a family reunion to his youngest brother, who by then was confined to a wheelchair and suffered from black lung, a disease afflicting miners exposed to coal dust over a long period of time.

The next pair of towns, Iaeger and Justice, come and go. I pass by a church with a telling name given its bleak surroundings: the Ark of Safety. Columns of ice clinging to blocks of sandstone outcrop create the illusion of a place frozen in time, and yet history in this region has been anything but static. Communities with economies based on a single primary source of income carry a collective memory filled with dreams, boom and bust cycles, hope, and despair I'm not privy to. As an outsider visiting for just the day, ignorant of the lives people lead here and seeing the region at its gloomiest in the dead of winter, it's easy for me to judge. I remind myself that people call this place beloved, call it home.

I turn south onto a twisting road upon entering Mingo County and pass a sign that warns "Blasting Zone." Around the next bend, I understand why. The hillside, presumably once covered by a hardwood forest, is gone. In place of trees, topsoil, and even stumps, there is only bedrock, as if the mountain's flesh has been stripped away to expose bare bone. An active worksite with trucks backing up and workmen milling around, it is not an ideal place to investigate further, so I press on.

I follow the Elkhorn River through Red Jacket and eventually reach the town of Matewan, where the Tug Fork divides West Virginia and Kentucky. A historical marker states that events related to the legendary Hatfield-McCoy feud took place nearby. Matewan has long fascinated me. John Sayles used it as the title for his 1987 film, a moving portrayal of the early twentieth-century movement to organize miners across racial lines and the repression they suffered at the hands of the Baldwin-Felts Detective Agency when it forced workers and their families out of company houses during a strike. At the film's climax, a shootout occurs between security agents and police chief Sid Hatfield, who had sided with the miners. Though not depicted in the movie, Hatfield would be gunned down several months later on the courthouse steps in Welch by Baldwin-Felts agents.

Owing to my family's ties to coal mining and a worker's strike that I witnessed in my hometown as a boy, the film captivated me when I first watched it in my twenties. It captured a moment in American history when citizens took action in choosing their fate rather than serving as mere cogs in the wheels of industry. Up close and in real life, it looked equally messy. The school bus I rode each day passed by a tire plant where workers angry about proposed wage freezes and lost benefits protested the hiring of nonunion replacement workers by chanting and holding signs announcing, "Scabs Go Home." The father of my friend Matt lost his job when the strike ended without success. Another man lost his life while trying to set a homemade bomb to knock out the plant's electrical power.

The usefulness of unions is a subject of debate in my family. One of my uncles argues that the steelworkers' union contributed to the mill closing in the town where he and my father grew up and where my grandfather worked as a foreman. According to my uncle, relentless demands made by the union's leaders forced the company to make so many concessions it could no longer compete. On the other hand, historians blame the economic recession in the 1970s for the demise of American steel companies. My father meanwhile reminds me of the role the state teachers' union played when he was a university music professor by helping our family climb into the middle class and send me to college a generation following his working-class upbringing.

Walking the length of the tiny downtown, I pass by the regional office of the United Mine Workers of America and an inn catering to ATV enthusiasts. I come to a concrete floodwall etched with scenes illustrating the region's colorful and violent history: miners wielding pickaxes and other tools used for digging coal, the Hatfield-McCoy feud, and the Battle of Matewan. Though I am not limited on foot by a windshield's abbreviated view of the world, what I've come seeking isn't here in Matewan.

Back in my car, I brake for a family of goats crossing the road on the outskirts of town. I pass by an austere retirement home and a squat building resembling a military bunker, which I realize is the high school. Outside town, the road winds once more between parallel ridges. It all feels so foreign yet oddly familiar and cramped, very cramped, and I think *the sky*. I've seen so little of it today.

What time is it? Always that question. The gray winter light is deceptive, though not as much as my defective dashboard clock, which reads 2:98 p.m. So is the landscape itself. When I crane my neck to catch a glimpse of the ridgetops, something about them doesn't seem right, as if they're trying to mask something happening on the other side. Mountaintop removal is a method of mining by which a peak is logged and then blasted apart to expose the coal lying beneath the surface; dynamited earth is then carried away and dumped, often in streams. Land areas totaling the size of Delaware have been permanently altered in this manner. What strikes me now is that a person might live in a house wedged into any one of the valleys I've passed through for their entire lives without ever knowing firsthand what was occurring on the other side of the mountain. As with cosmetic strips lumber companies use to conceal clearcut forests from passing motorists, coal companies largely hide evidence of their activities from public view. There's no way to confirm my suspicions without trespassing and scaling one of the steep wooded slopes. But I know now that I should no longer assume green spots in my road atlas represent undeveloped forests. Soon I begin doubting every mountain I see.

With only a few hours of daylight remaining before I'll need to push on to Charleston to find lodging for the night, I make a stop in Logan. Inside a Burger King, I ask the teenager behind the cash register for directions to Blair Mountain. A slight conspiratorial look in his eyes suggests he possibly understands my reasons for asking, though I haven't given any, and he tells me how to find it. The remote mountain, situated twenty minutes to the east, is the site of the largest armed rebellion on American soil since the Civil War. A year following the Battle of Matewan in 1920, more than ten thousand union miners exchanged gunfire with company representatives and county and state police, their outrage sparked by the murder of Sid Hatfield and the acquittal of his killers. Irish-born Mary "Mother" Jones, a champion of the union cause, warned miners against marching into Logan and Mingo Counties. Her worst fears were realized throughout the five-day battle during which as many as one hundred miners and thirty company men perished. Amid the skirmish, in what was described as one of the most egregious acts ever carried out by the United States government against its citizens, the Army was ordered to drop bombs on the miners. One unexploded bomb later provided evidence of the government's extreme measures and helped lead to the acquittal of union leader Bill Blizzard. Though union membership declined in the years that followed, victory ultimately belonged to organized labor. The ensuing attention brought about by the miners' predicament eventually led to the establishment of labor laws enshrined in Roosevelt's New Deal, which helped secure a brighter future for workers and their families—my own included—in the decades that followed.

Where the road crests at a gap separating the north and south ridges of Blair Mountain, I pull over and park. I lace up my boots and begin trudging up the north ridge on a single-track dirt road. Two pickup trucks roar by on the main road behind me, their drivers paying me no mind.

I reach the top after five minutes and survey a hardwood forest of a similar character to what I've seen elsewhere today. Deep snow dimpled by coyote tracks covers the ground, obscuring from view everything I'd hoped to see—which is what exactly? Bullet shell casings? Craters marking where bombs landed? An advocate for the protection of the mountain whom I'd contacted about the site and who knows the area well, asked that I leave behind any artifacts I might find. No worries on that front. I haven't come for souvenirs and whatever evidence exists of the Battle of Blair Mountain lies buried under a foot of snow.

Blair Mountain was listed for a time on the National Register of Historic Places, which is the first step toward granting any such site protection in the national park system. In a rare and controversial act, however, pressure from coal companies led to its delisting. Coal-related jobs are dwindling throughout Appalachia because mountaintop removal requires fewer workers compared to traditional mining methods and because of the boom in hydraulic fracturing for natural gas, otherwise known as fracking. Coal remains king in many parts of the region nonetheless, and the power coal companies wield is immense. For example, in southwest Virginia, companies possess the right to mine coal beneath your house and fill the void with any waste product of their choosing. This is the other Appalachia, called America's National Sacrifice Area by some, and which is rarely glimpsed by the public because it resides far from the tourist meccas of the Great Smoky Mountains, Linville Gorge, and Roan Mountain. The places we don't know about and don't want to know about because the truth about them indicts us all: cheap coal provides cheap energy.

Legal action by a coalition of environmental and historic preservation groups eventually helped to restore Blair Mountain to the National Register. It might yet become an official monument to the men who fought and died for a movement that brought a measure of justice and dignity to the lives of working-class people. If the mountain remains intact, it will prove an exception to the rule among countless other mountains stripped of their peaks, their forests, and their history for short-term profits.

While retracing my steps back down the dirt road I glimpse a peculiar-looking mountain perhaps half a dozen miles in the distance. On its summit appears to be a snow-covered meadow, which strikes me as odd—a meadow on top of a mountain and with no farming structures in sight—until I realize it isn't a meadow at all but a scalped peak. So that's it, I realize. The evidence I came looking for and as near as I'm bound to get to it and see for myself the consequences of mountaintop removal. I snap photos, all of which turn out blurry in the fading light. I climb back in my car, feeling a strange mixture of dissatisfaction and mild accomplishment.

I coast down the far side of the mountain and enter the village of Blair in twenty minutes. When I notice a side road that looks abandoned, I get a wild hair and turn down it. It dead-ends at a spot where my car is hidden from view off the main road, a good thing considering what I'm about to do. Without any clear notions of what I'll say should I get caught trespassing on private land, I hop across a swollen creek. Then I begin scaling the side of a mountain which, if I've guessed right, is the one I photographed moments ago. My boots slide in mud and snow, and thorns catch in my shirt. A smaller creek gushing down the mountain promises clear passage with fewer obstacles, so I head up it. My feet are soaked in seconds. When I startle a deer and it bounds away uphill, I decide to follow its tracks. A welcome guide.

False summits are ubiquitous in mountainous regions. A peak visible from a lower vantage point, once climbed, turns out not to be a peak at all. Yet there's no mistaking the top of this mountain—a false summit of an altogether different sort—once I reach it: a mountaintop that's no longer there. In its place are flat treeless scrubland and a pond where a pond doesn't belong. Judging by the size of saplings growing at the edge of the forest, bulldozers and demolition crews have been gone for several years. Reclamation of such sites falls by law to mining companies, but other than planting a grass monoculture, little effort seems to have been made toward restoring habitat to even a modicum of its former character. Unruly nature has been tidied up and given a manicure, a shaved face in humanity's image. Even the logging era at the turn of the twentieth century didn't cause this level of irreversible deformation.

With the mountain gone and so too a forest whose recovery no one alive today will live long enough to witness, what is left to desire for this place whose riches human appetite has turned into ruin? I think about the Ark of Safety church and the machine flood that swept through here. I think about Blair Mountain, which has escaped such a fate for the time being, the umpteen other gaping voids like this one that once supported a rich diversity of living things, and those awaiting the chopping block. I think about the contaminated groundwater and extraordinarily high cancer rates in communities where scenes like this one have played out, along with the moral failure of those in the coal industry who ditch human obligations to neighbors, future generations, and Creation itself under the cover of "clean coal" and "job security." Understood in mythical terms, a forest is a place of bewilderment as well as enchantment and imagination, but, as with the mountain's peak itself, that's all gone now. And for what? Massive profits in a few pockets and keeping a dying industry alive for several more years.

The irony of the moment strikes me. As an uninvited guest trespassing on private land, I have no legal right to be here passing judgment and mourning for lost forests and mountains, whereas coal companies possess the right to rape the land at will and allow scenes like the one before me to keep happening. I suspect it is a moment I'll bear in mind as climate change takes its toll, perhaps including—in what would be a double blow—in this place.

The snow-covered ground holds what remains of the light as night descends. I stare for a while, unable to prevent the emptiness of this place from creeping inside me, before making my way down what's left of the mountain in the dark.

Staying in Character: A Travelogue

A dozen students taking part in today's living history class amble up the trail. The year is 1926 and I am in character as Silas "Tip" Tipton. When they get close, I step out from behind a tree and ask if they've seen a hog—a made-up hog owned by my made-up character, which has broken out of its imaginary offstage pen.

"Ugly as sin?" I add by way of description. "Answers by the name Barnabas?"

The students, thrilled and terrified of the stranger in overalls addressing them, shake their heads. I tell them hog-butchering time isn't till November but that if I catch Barnabas while my temper is up, bacon just might garnish my breakfast table tomorrow. Bolstering this threat is a black powder long rifle (real but not loaded and broken beyond repair) I'm holding. Never mind that mountain people in the old days allowed hogs to roam freely to fatten themselves on chestnuts and acorns rather than penning them up. Tip prefers to keep a watchful eye on his livestock.

Before meeting me, the students were briefed on the point of this exercise by volunteer extraordinaire Robin Goddard. Portraying a real historical figure, Ann Davis, she informed them that she and her husband visit Yellowstone every year but wish there was a national park closer to home and would like to see the Smokies preserved for just such a purpose. The Davises and other local citizens have formed a commission to explore this possibility. Since the Smokies contain timber holdings, twelve hundred farms, and five thousand lots and summer homes, the task is daunting. Tip and other residents need to be interviewed to find out if the park idea is feasible and how it will affect their lives.

"Everything," I say when a student asks what I do for a living. I ask the students who they think my grocer, butcher, and pharmacist are, and answer with pride, "You're looking at him." Neighbors help mill corn, put up one another's cabins, and bury the dead, but Tip otherwise makes do by farming, hunting, trapping, and keeping bees.

Tip isn't the gruff type. That would be Ken's character Travis; they'll meet him next when he barks at them, "State your business!" Ken once accidentally spat tobacco juice on the shoe of a girl who was standing too close. Remarkably, no one broke out of character, including the girl, and my hat's off to her—staying in character is one of the more challenging aspects of living history. There is no script because it's not a reenactment and a constant temptation is to resort to the familiarity of the present day. Even harder is sustaining an uncomfortable yet necessary suspension of disbelief while entertaining the notion that how people lived in a former era, the adversity they faced, and the sources of wisdom that gave their lives meaning might have something to teach us today.

The students eventually get around to asking if I will consider selling my land for the establishment of a national park. Tip's feelings on this subject are complicated. Were he to sell, he would lose the bonds he's forged with this place over a lifetime. Blindfold and march him miles away, and he would know exactly how to find his way home; but ask him to live somewhere else and he would feel lost the moment he stepped out his front door. Along with lifelong neighbors, he would have to give up self-sufficiency and increasingly become dependent on the middleman. Getting a job at the aluminum plant in town would provide a steady source of income yet also uproot his family life by depriving him of close daily contact with his wife and children. In short, he would enter modern life, for which he has little use. At the same time, however, the steep acreage he owns is getting harder to farm each year as the topsoil erodes little by little. Industrial logging creeps closer to his doorstep every day, and he knows vaster changes in society are bringing an end to his way of life. Either choice, leaving or staying put, will be difficult.

Satisfied with this response because it isn't an outright refusal, my interrogators bid me farewell and good luck in finding Barnabas. At the afternoon's end, they will discuss their findings and reflect on the sacrifices mountain residents made that helped turn the national park idea into a reality. They will learn about citizens whose land was taken by eminent domain when they refused to sell and about children who raised money to purchase land for the park by asking for donations in their neighborhoods. They'll speculate on what might have become of the mountains in the hands of private enterprise had the park movement failed. And they'll reflect on what it was like to work together to help create what was fittingly given the nickname "the people's park."

Once the students depart and I'm alone again, I don't return to the present day just yet. Still in old forest time, I think of actual people Tip would have counted as neighbors in his lifetime. Will Walker and his enormous family, of course, and Sook Turner, a formerly enslaved person rumored to be his fourth wife. Her son George who married a White or possibly mixed-race woman, each solemnifying their union by cutting their fingers and drinking one another's blood to avoid persecution under anti-miscegenation laws. Fred Webb, who spent two summers in Walker Valley, instructing pupils aged three to thirty on weekdays and delivering sermons on Sundays. And Ashley Moore, who became a skilled hunting guide despite losing a leg and who performed his grandfather Will's hunting songs while performing with the Grand Ole Opry. Later on, he served a prison sentence for bootlegging. Having inhabited the same spaces each of these individuals once did for over a decade now, I feel I've come to know them a little. Sometimes I think it would not come as a shock to hear Will's voice booming over the river, as it was said to have done whenever he was in the mood for music, "Heeeeey Ashley, bring your banjo."

The neighborhood has changed drastically since their time living here. The forest empire that Will refused to sell to the lumber company was cut down acre by acre following his death. Though it has recovered in significant ways, its character has been altered to such a degree that he and his neighbors might have difficulty recognizing the place they once called home could they see it today.

My education in this place has taught me hard truths about the southern Appalachian ecosystem and its prospects for the future. Forest invaders have wiped out chestnuts and ravaged hemlock and fir populations while other nonnative pests and diseases have attacked elms, dogwoods, butternuts, American beeches, and ash trees, threatening to deplete the Smokies of its biodiversity one species at a time. The Smokies are downwind of coal-fired power plants scattered throughout the Tennessee River Valley, which for several decades made high-elevation forests more susceptible to air pollution than any other monitored site in North America. Deregulation of power plants beginning in the 1970s resulted in stunted growth from acid deposition among red spruces and made headwater streams uninhabitable for Southern brook trout, until enforcement under the Clean Air Act led to improvements. But particulate matter and ozone damage continue to fall short of public health standards, and visibility from the park's highest peaks remains far less than historical conditions.

Data collected by students and volunteers have confirmed on a local scale what experts have been saying for years about climate change. Migratory birds such as the Louisiana Waterthrush now return to Walker Valley from their wintering grounds two weeks earlier compared to twenty-five years ago, and the first frost is occurring a month later than it did a decade ago. The pattern is similar parkwide among wood frogs, which are emerging from hibernation twenty days sooner than in the 1980s. Shorter winters increase the chances of desynchronization, a process in which pollinating insects hatch before blooms appear and migratory birds return before an adequate food supply is available among insect populations.

The Smokies are warmer, wetter, and windier than historical conditions. With winter shrinking by a day each year, cold temperature-loving brook trout may lose even more of their range. By another estimate, Jordan's redcheeked salamander, which lives nowhere else on earth, may become extinct by mid-century, and as much as 17 percent of the park's mammal species may vanish because of shifts in distribution ranges. While some plants and animals are likely to survive warming temperatures by moving northward, the spruce-fir community, which hugs the highest peaks of the Smokies, has nowhere to go. As a result, both the critically endangered spruce-fir moss spider, one of the smallest tarantulas in the world, and an endangered subspecies of the northern flying squirrel face an uncertain future.

Despite the decline or loss of many species, reintroduction projects have restored elk, otters, peregrine falcons, and the smoky madtom—a rare catfish species—to the Smokies. Brook trout populations are higher than they have been since the turn of the twentieth century thanks to restocking efforts. Elsewhere in the east, fishers and elk once more roam Pennsylvania after a long absence, endangered red wolves again make their home in coastal North Carolina, and indigenous grasses displaced by invasive varieties are making a comeback in Georgia. Increasingly, however, biologists have to play defense in response to the growing number of threats to ecosystem health, including a precipitous decline in bat and bee populations.

Human communities, too, have experienced extraordinary disruptions since Will Walker's time. One can only guess what someone so rooted in place as he might have thought of the notion of leaving home to "go to work" or to what extent the decline of small farms and the rise of fossil fuel-dependent agriculture and globalization would have disturbed his sleep. In light of his refusal to sell out to timber companies, I like to think the creation of the national park would have pleased him in some ways. More confounding for him likely would have been the loss of agrarian values and local knowledge as people moved off the land and grew more distant from "nature," eventually coming to know it—if they know it at all—as tourists.

My journeys to distant places strike me as a sort of time travel when I consider the Smokies and their changing character. Alaska remains an intact and self-willed ecosystem with all its members present despite a pervasive mindset summed up by former governor Walter Hickel, who once declared, "You can't let nature just run wild." While visiting Alaska is like stepping back in time into a largely unimpaired landscape, Scotland offers a possible glimpse of the future. Even with rewilding efforts underway there—birch woods returning and natural peat bogs replacing Sitka spruce plantations—as a whole, it remains a largely tamed and ecologically barren environment.

The Smokies reside somewhere between these two poles. Despite protections afforded by the national park, the mountains are subject to an ever-increasing human influence. The night sky is disappearing in a haze of electrical lights originating in cities as far away as Atlanta. The natural soundscape has become increasingly compromised by engine noise from automobiles and jets. And the viewshed is cluttered by ugly development that's turning the park into a penned-in wilderness. To whatever extent the seemingly endless construction of rental cabins is a matter of supply and demand fueled by a human desire to spend time near rugged beauty, with developers providing people with what they want, supply is dwindling. The main result is a larger human footprint diminishing the very thing people come seeking.

Forests elsewhere in the world are also undergoing change, and the threats they face carry global consequences. Fires, drought, logging, agriculture, livestock grazing, and oil and gas extraction have devastated forests in the Congo Basin, the lowlands of Borneo, the Australian bush, the Amazon, Canada, Siberia, and elsewhere. At the same time, however, the increased amounts of carbon that have been released into the atmosphere as carbon dioxide have enhanced plant growth. Defenders of oil and coal industries point to this as a benefit of climate change, or at least a reason not to be concerned, but looks are deceiving. When forests fall prey to drought, invasive species, and deforestation, they release more carbon than they take up. More carbon in the atmosphere leads to higher temperatures, which disrupts natural cycles and delays recovery, pushing ecosystems closer to a tipping point that's often not discernible until it has occurred.

The eastern deciduous forest biome stretching from southern Canada to Florida may play a critical role in mitigating the effects of climate change. Though fragmented, it has rebounded from its grim condition following the logging era as the industry has adopted more sustainable harvesting practices and former agricultural lands have reforested. It has shown resiliency despite the threats it still faces and is predicted to act as a sponge for carbon as global temperatures rise, making the task of conserving it an important one.

Forests undergo continual change whether we notice it or not. Such changes are more noticeable in times of disruption or cataclysm, such as when hurricanes or straight-line wind events occur, sometimes grabbing headlines. We learn how to see them in the meantime by getting to know them firsthand and paying attention. It is not loss alone that I see in the rearview when thinking back on my encounters with forests in other corners of the world and my own backyard. I have witnessed stability and resilience in equal measure with tragedy on my travels. And yet, like a generation weaned on a steady diet of impending catastrophe, I feel a sense of foreboding when I consider what the not-too-distant future may hold.

What should be the goal of outdoor education in all this? Is it to teach students the names of plants and animals before they blink out? Press young people into service as ecowarriors in hopes they will stem the tide of the Anthropocene? Coax citizens into adopting environmentally friendly lifestyle behaviors such as recycling even as the world burns?

No. Of course, it should be to mold people into ecologically literate citizens with an awareness of their impact on the more-than-human world and a sense of obligation toward it. It is to chart a new path out of a recognition that something must change if we are to escape a collision course with history, whether locally or on a global scale. "Love your mother" and "conservation is conservative" are but two mottoes relied on in some corners to motivate members of particular demographic groups into taking action. In the many forms it takes, environmental education is often treated as a means to an end. Instrumentalist approaches do have their uses: show people a landfill and perhaps they'll stop buying and throwing away so much stuff. But when reduced to a mere tool for changing human behavior, education often ends up reflecting the conditions of the age and the very utilitarian paradigm it purports to dismantle.

The kind of environmental education I try to practice drives at something deeper. Its starting point is the human, treated not as a problem to solve but as something of a waylaid traveler welcomed home. Its ultimate goal isn't reducible to standard units of measurement. It is an end in itself.

Let us call outdoor or environmental education what it truly is without qualifiers suggesting it is secondary to whatever else may be considered essential for human learning: simply *education*, which is the process of cultivating a person's capacity for recognizing truth, goodness, and beauty. Done well, it is similarly a discovery of one's cultural inheritance and unique place in time. Among other things, it renders the realization that one's time will run out someday and others will come along—those who themselves will inherit the gifts of Creation, tradition, and human achievement in equal measure with leveled mountaintops, melting glaciers, faltering institutions, injustice, and a fraying social fabric. In practice, education is a continuous act of receiving and giving, learning and passing on. At its best, it regards conservation as part of the process of regenerating not just "nature" but also human culture. As much as it is about understanding the past that has shaped us and choosing how we will live in the present, it is also about how we will prepare for tomorrow, which occurs in part by preserving and renewing the best in human character today.

One way to recover a more holistic form of education is by acknowledging the role of the body in human learning and that we are more than analytical minds. If human beings were machines, the task would be as simple as treating knowledge as prepackaged information ready for downloading into the brain. As embodied creatures, however, experience is as vital to our formation as any other form of study. Living laboratories found in national parks and schoolyards offer possibilities for other ways of knowing and gaining wisdom and a chance for students to imagine a future other than the ways the industrial economy will make use of them. In such settings, there is something analogous to what Celtic peoples call "thin places," where the distance separating humans and the divine is diminished. Thin places in education are often found outside the traditional classroom, where obstacles to learning can be numerous, as countless teachers I've worked with can attest. The thin spaces of the natural world are where we're reminded of our identities not as consumers and shape-shifters but as ensouled creatures in possession of a sense of belonging to the places we inhabit, whose fate is also ours.

Embodied immersion in such places helps to reunite body and mind, spirit and flesh. The healing and restorative power found there when we connect with them make us more fully human because they ground us in reality. This, in turn, might lead to the recognition that the world exists not to make it conform to human will but for guiding our will into harmony with it.

Any authentic education at some point becomes a bushwhack. There are no paved shortcuts. Home is both the starting point and the final destination. The world, for all its vexing challenges, will have to be loved. The work ahead includes not just rewilding nature, but also restoring humans and a sense of what it means to be one. But it starts with love. The only way I know how to receive the gift of such an understanding is through reverence, gratitude, and awe—and by sharing it with those who have yet to receive it themselves.

Still dressed as Tip Tipton, my mind by now having wandered far afield, I listen to a familiar sound floating across the river and into the trees. The Walkers, their neighbors, and I think also the Indigenous peoples who inhabited these woods for a much longer time span would be pleased to hear it: the exaltation of children at play following a long day spent living and learning in the forest. They'll need that same energy in subdued form a few hours from now. For soon it will be time to enter the dark.

Nightwalking

THE GIRL BEHIND ME grabs my jacket as we head out the door. A dozen middle school students follow her, their classroom teacher in the rear. We go dark and with voices off, a flashlight tucked into my pocket for backup. Moments ago, still surrounded by the comforts of the visible world, we were standing in the bright interior of the dining hall, our reflections gleaming in anarchic color in a long row of windows. Now we're as blind as moles as we creep forward, wary strangers in a suddenly mysterious landscape. Yellow light spills from the lobby and grows fainter with each step we take. Where it fades altogether, we enter blackness.

We trace a service road through campus, where for the time being there's nothing to bump into except one another. Partway across an auto bridge, we peer over the railing into the invisible waters below while taking in the sound of the river sculpting Walker Valley. Further on, we reach the woods and step onto a footpath. The blackness turns even blacker than before. The girl tightens her grip on my jacket as muted squeals of alarm issue from several students. We keep going, deliberate and slow, feeling for tree roots and other obstacles at our feet, each of us a link in a chain.

My companions, perhaps for the first time in their lives, can see for themselves how precious a thing true darkness is, driven by our cities and towns into refuges such as this one. Even here, we would be hard-pressed to find it on clear nights when city lights bleed across the northwest horizon. Tonight, though, the sprawling darkness consumes everything.

Nights free of cloud cover afford stargazing and endless stories about constellations and the Milky Way—or perhaps not endless since I've committed just a few to memory. A student will ask, "Are those real stars?" a question as revealing about the realities of childhood today as those delivered in daylight ("Is that a real cemetery?"). We'll lie on our backs and wait for a shooting star or an orbiting satellite to sally past. Stars in Cherokee lore are cornmeal scattered across the sky—manna from heaven or perhaps manna going to the heavens. According to one version of the story, a giant dog stole food from villagers, who chased it away, and as it fled cornmeal fell from its mouth and hung in the sky. Contrary to notions of feeling alone in an otherwise empty universe and what we moderns often tell ourselves (which is that we no longer need to live by stories), the story implies an intimate relationship between humans and the dome overhead—an intimacy as close as the darkness is to each one of us just now.

Let's say we have to start over. Civilization has run into trouble. As usual, the cause is human fallenness, which we have cast upon the world for all to see, some to deny, and many to despair over. Where to begin? I would pick up where I left off and work for a nature center inside a national park straddling the backbone of the Appalachians. A psychologist might have much to say about someone who feared the world's imminent demise in his youth and entered a profession whose mission is to preserve it as an adult. Originally an act of desperation, outdoor education became something of a career for me as I chose it, again and again, each time other opportunities came along. When I understood how well it suited me it turned into a vocation. Something like the process of forest succession has taken place along the way. While I'm the same person I've always been, time and experience have nevertheless molded me into someone other than the young man who sat down in Ken's office for a job interview years ago when I was asked about my nonexistent "vision" for environmental education.

The first moon landing occurred within months of Tremont's founding. One event, otherworldly in scope, marked the pinnacle of human technological achievement. The other was a local endeavor whose mission was to help people find their place on earth, to learn to take care of it, and to not use it all up. One represents a dream of human aspirations that became a reality, while the other remains an ongoing effort.

The essence of the work has changed little over the years. Go outdoors. Move your body and open your senses. Let curiosity be your guide. Stoke its flames by looking and listening and following your nose. Don't hurry.

Welcome the rain falling on your skin and the winds drying it. Listen to the poetry in the river's steady roll and the wind moving through the forest. Discover how much more you are capable of than you thought and how much less you need to be content.

Participate in the life of a place by immersing yourself in it. Learn its vocabulary and make contact with its inhabitants. Read the landscape. Get down on all fours. Put pen or pencil to paper in the open air. Discover that by peering outside yourself, you are also peering within.

Share living quarters, meals, and campfires with strangers and new friends. Claim belonging in the community where you find yourself. Find your voice and trust the good intentions of others. Look out for one another. Practice being still.

Locate yourself within a chapter belonging to a much longer story in time. Grasp the hard truths of history, including the grave injustices suffered by Cherokees who were forcibly removed from their land yet still thrive as a people. Celebrate the shared wealth that has become public lands and the sacrifices mountain residents made, not by choice in all cases, to create them. Take inspiration from those who came before you. Walk in their footsteps with humility and joy.

Interrogate your desires measured against essential human needs: food, water, shelter, and belonging. Lean on others in moments filled with anxiety and bodily discomfort. Regard suffering as part of life and a tutor you can learn from. Salute one another's ability to blossom amid hardship.

Consider the farmers and laborers who grow the food on your plate, the farms where it is grown, and the plants and animals whose deaths sustain human life. Enter into moments set aside for reverence with gratitude. Feast on the gifts of Creation while fasting from civilization's excesses. Know yourself as an ensouled creature with a hunger for something other than what the zeitgeist has to offer.

Get out of your head and discover a fullness of being unknown to you until now. Be at home in the world. Merge with the river and the forest and the salamander perched in your palm. Return home at week's end with newfound insight. Tend it in your soul as you would a seed planted in a garden and share it with others. When the time is ripe continue the work of renewing the world already underway in yourself.

Outdoor schools, perhaps better than any other cultural institution, are ideally suited to help people discover such gifts. They are likewise positioned to give lost connections with nature a more central role in formal education and lifelong learning. In their daily routines, they foster ways of being aimed at achieving harmony with the natural world. In so doing, they function as laboratories for innovation in education by engaging the whole person in the learning process, which other institutions—business, civic, and otherwise—would do well to model. They invite the understanding that we are not only stewards of the natural world in the abstract but also a part of the places where we live. Nature, according to this fundamentally different orientation, isn't just out there. Nature includes us.

Undeniably the part we humans play in the natural order sets us apart in essential ways. We rely on symbols and wear clothes to adorn our bodies. We worship, make pictures, tell stories, and debate the nature of being. We pass laws and govern ourselves. We further set ourselves apart by making peace and offering forgiveness. If wise, we practice the virtues and learn from elders how to pursue truth, goodness, and beauty with dogged determination. Yet all the while, our bodies are made up of the soil we walk on.

Organizations whose purpose is to restore humankind's connection with the rest of nature through discovery, wonder, and caretaking are remarkable for the fact that they exist at all. Undreamt of because unnecessary before the industrial age and the rise of modern institutions, outdoor schools and other nature centers have played an indispensable, if largely unsung, role in remedying the alienation felt by many people in an era marked by fragmentation and dislocation. Vulnerable to disruption because of their small size, yet adaptable for the same reason, many operate at a minimum expense in a climate of constant funding challenges. North Cascades Institute, located in the Pacific Northwest, for example, relied on tents and tarps in its early years, moving from site to site with relative ease until it found a permanent home. The nature center where I work makes do with aging buildings constructed for entirely different purposes.

Particular to every outdoor school I'm familiar with are practices tied to the history, biodiversity, and cultural traditions of the places where they exist. Winter classes at Wolf Ridge in Minnesota include snowshoeing and ice fishing. Camp McDowell in Alabama operates a farm school where students harvest food that's cooked and served in the dining hall. Ijams, a nonresidential nature center in Knoxville, runs a forest school in which preschoolers spend most of their day learning outdoors in an urban wilderness. Localism is part of the genius of nature centers, and ours "trains the trainers" by preparing classroom educators to conduct hands-on nature study in schoolyards. Activities from species monitoring to landscape-level investigations enhance students' understanding of complex systems while fostering civic ecology and participatory democracy.

The life of a public-school educator gets harder all the time. A growing number of challenges include shorter planning periods, distrust by parents and administrators, and strict requirements and benchmarks predetermining every minute of a teacher's day, all of which can lead to burnout. A caring teacher's classroom all the while provides a refuge for many kids, where they receive the love not showered on them at home. One more demand on a teacher's time is the week they spend with their students at an overnight learning center such as ours, though it very often offers a refuge for students and teachers alike.

Outdoor schools, from their very beginnings, have worked to overcome economic barriers by making outdoor learning experiences available to everyone, including children who have never had them. Many collaborate with low-income communities and communities of color by providing opportunities for students who have limited access to wild places and have historically felt unwelcome in them. Increasingly seen as an essential aspect of human existence and a human right, time spent in nature is healing and builds resilience among those who face economic injustice and the ghosts of slavery and Jim Crow. It's a chance as well for such students to gain hands-on experience on public lands and to embrace the cultural inheritance they too possess. If outdoor schools deserve greater recognition for cultivating human beings through experiences that are transformative and lead to heightened care for the natural world, none that I know of are waiting around for it. There isn't much time to spare, with thousands of students scheduled to arrive each week at hundreds of centers around the country. And not only school-aged youths but also undergraduates, families, working professionals, and retirees who are also in need of immersion in forest time, farm time, canyon time, desert time, marsh time, and more.

It is into another frontier of outdoor learning I embark with members of a Boys and Girls Club chapter one morning alongside my coworker Emily. We arrive at an elementary school located an hour away in an industrial and ethnically diverse neighborhood of Knoxville. Inside we locate our cohort of eight- and nine-year-olds, not a White child among them, who one day will visit the Smokies as part of their class trip. After making introductions we stride down a windowless corridor until we reach the rear exit and step into daylight.

Though it's raining, the kids, giddy with excitement, don't seem to care. Before us lies a sea of grass surrounded by a high fence with a security gate and populated at most by a dozen trees. Not what I'm used to, but it works the same way. We hand out bug boxes and set the students loose. Within moments a frenzy of investigating leads to the discovery of roly polies and centipedes scurrying beneath decaying lumber. A girl finds a dead bird among a small pile of windblown trash in one corner of the schoolyard. Wearing lipstick and a pretty floral dress, she parades it around, balanced on a pair of sticks, before giving it a funeral.

"Now its spirit can find its way back," she says.

Issuing a challenge for everyone to turn a natural object into a musical instrument, I demonstrate the usefulness of blowing air through a blade of grass clasped between one's thumbs, and soon a chorus of duck sounds fills the air. Emily introduces her pet tarantula housed inside a terrarium and asks the students what they notice about its body structure. A nesting mourning dove eyes us warily from a ledge of the school building all the while.

We depart the school grounds the next hour and venture into a neighborhood park. The students race like uncaged stallions and meet up on the far side along the banks of a creek littered with garbage. Trading bug boxes for nets, the students begin catching minnows swimming in algae-ridden pockets of water, paying no mind if they get their feet wet. Brooklyn, in her flowery dress and makeup, has shoes that now look like they've been someplace.

We journey further afield later in the week, heading into the neighborhood on a mile-long walk I've never undertaken before toward gardens I've never visited—new territory too for Elizabeth, who's accompanying me today. A tiny, privately owned yard overflowing with life provides a living textbook for how to make the most of little space. We pause to admire its ripening peach trees, tomato plants, and bean vines climbing a chain-link fence planted by a Central American family whose children attend the school. In an expanse of industrial wasteland adjacent to a scrap metal yard, we identify passionflower, Tennessee's state wildflower. A train grinds past yards away from us as we pump our arms until the engineer delivers a whistle blast.

And so it goes: a tractor-trailer backing up on one block, shaggy White men in filthy clothes on the next block glaring at us from the derelict front yard of what appears to be a meth house. The scent of flour wafts from a baked goods company, and a metallic clanking grows louder as we approach the garden's gates.

Founded by Hungarian-born Ivan Racheff in the 1940s, the gardens occupy a former waste site several acres large. The nearby steelworks, still in operation, run the length of the gardens and then some, an imposing fortress that provides a study in contrasts as well as something of a model for the coexistence between nature and industry. Our host, a woman in her sixties, grants us free rein of the place. We waste no time and play several rounds of I Spy, spotting red and orange and yellow objects, each one a dazzling bloom. Elizabeth initiates a game of Camouflage that lasts all of ten minutes because time moves swiftly at this age.

We reach a play area at the opposite end of the gardens where a tantalizing pile of dirt prompts Keesiya, a girl with long braids, to ask, "Can we dig? Can we smush it?"

"Good idea," I tell her.

Our host reappears in work gloves and begins dragging a tarp loaded with trimmings toward a door in the iron fence. She means to place the trimmings out on the curb, but it's a heavy load, and when I make a motion to help her, several kids volunteer their efforts, including Abdul, whose face has abruptly lost its permafrown and registered a sense of purpose.

A steelworker from next door who somehow spotted us through the dense foliage shows up bearing a gift of a case of Gatorade. With bottles clasped in their hands, the students cross back and forth over a fairy bridge spanning a koi pond. They're everywhere at once, scrambling up and down stone steps, hunting for bugs, prowling about the pond—all of it a crash course in indulging their curiosity, which an untrained eye might mistake for chaos. They'll be well primed once they visit the mountains in a few years, a trip that will be supported in large part by financial aid.

Too soon, the time comes to return to school for lunch. Many kids don't want to leave.

"We'll come back next week," I tell them.

On our trek back to the school, we again pass by the dilapidated house, its lawn overtaken by waist-high weeds and its front entrance covered by a bedsheet. I consider other hazards of an equally sinister kind lurking in the neighborhood's soils, waterways, and air. Given the heavy presence of industry, an intrinsic honesty abides here compared to neighborhoods in possession of enough purchasing power to consign industrial activities and their consequences to places such as this one. I consider as well the neighborhood's wealth when measured by the beauty and caretaking conspicuous on every block and the failure of "impoverished," a word often used to describe this part of Knoxville, to fully describe it.

I think about the time we've spent exploring this landscape, extraordinary for the fact that students here and in other places like it are so rarely given such opportunities. I think about how much more students everywhere would gain were administrators to empower teachers to integrate such experiences into the school day by making regular use of the outdoor learning environment rather than relegating them to once-in-a-lifetime field trips. I think about the habitats whose well-being depends on young people knowing them firsthand and whose own well-being, in turn, depends on them. I think about all the reasons to retreat into cynicism and hopelessness over the state of the world contrasted with the unbridled joy evident in the rapturous faces of the thousands of students I've taken into the woods over the years.

I recall the girl who, at the end of a day very much like today, turned to another student and said, "I've never felt so alive. I *love* nature." And I recall my less-than-inspiring job interview long ago and the question asked of me: "What is your vision for environmental education?"

I think back on all the miles I've walked with children and adults alike, following in the footsteps of the pair of women who taught me at McKeever and trusting that someone will follow in mine someday, and at last, I know the answer.

More of this.

When you're young and awaiting entry into what adults call the "real" world, you perhaps suspect that society isn't going to have much use for you. Something of the reverse for me was also true. Of all the possible walks of life to choose from, it wasn't clear how any would make a difference in the long run. Superhero narratives weren't of much help, having planted notions of saving the world in my imagination, which there was no chance of achieving even if increasingly it was the only thing that seemed to matter. It was considered as normal as trees losing their leaves in fall that those of us on a college track would never return to the place we were from once we left. Missing from our way of thinking at the time, in part because we'd never been encouraged to consider such questions, was asking what we had to offer our community, what we could do here that needed doing.

Questions like these weighed on my mind years later in the mountains, and there was no doubt about the answers. Floors needed mopping, firewood cut, and trails kept clear among a host of other duties society said were beneath me because working solely with my mind rather than also my hands befitted getting ahead for the college educated. Such tasks needed doing nevertheless and were satisfying to carry out for precisely this reason, as well as because people were depending on me to do them. On top of it all, there were classes to teach and eventually much more.

Unpredictability is a fact of life at an outdoor school, which calls for a make-it-up-as-you-go approach more than in any other place I've worked. Weather events, injuries, and equipment breakdowns regularly oblige a change of plans. I've helped feed sixty people and conducted activities by lantern light when storms knocked out power. I've guided a dozen nervous adult hikers across a raging tributary during a flash flood. More than once, I've delivered an hour-long address to a room packed with college students (without preparation) when a guest speaker failed to show up. The lessons that such moments and many others give rise to amount to a kind of life training. For instance, how to shoulder tasks outside my training with grace and accept poor decision-making as a necessary step toward exercising sounder judgment. How to trust in vulnerability when negotiating disagreements. How to overcome feelings of uselessness and watch interns and teenagers manage just fine without my help when an ankle sprain forces me off my feet during a backpacking trip. And how to regard it as a compliment whenever a guest refers to me as a guide or camp counselor, even now that I'm older, since whatever else it means to educate, it certainly includes guiding and counseling.

Perhaps what I've learned above all else in this line of work is realizing that I do not always see. A fundamental tenet of environmental education is the importance of observation, of grasping both the particularities of a place and the systems binding it together. One would think I were an expert at this by now. What the work has shown me, however, often with the help of students and colleagues whose own distinctive ways of seeing broaden mine, is how much I miss. The millipede I fail to notice while lost in thought and the menagerie of sensations the forest has to offer, which I too often take for granted as a year-round resident. The costs I ignorantly pass on to the natural world through the choices I make as a participant in an overconsumptive economic system. Training the skills of observation that I've acquired inward comes with strings attached, for awareness means no longer being able to cling to a comfortable ignorance and recognizing an obligation to do things differently in part by attending to the ceaseless work of paying attention.

It's tempting at times to imagine a more efficient course of action to address our predicament and find an alternative to the painstaking process of education and the soul-searching it requires to come to any meaningful good. Indoctrination. A technological fix. But again, there are no shortcuts.

I think nothing would please environmental educators more than for their mission to be declared unnecessary because harmony between humans and the rest of nature had at last been achieved. I'm tempted to say that until that day arrives my job security is guaranteed. But so long as the mind-body-soul experiences that outdoor schools provide are considered inessential there are no such assurances. After many years doing so, the school district in which I grew up stopped mandating weeklong trips like the one I had in sixth grade at McKeever Environmental Learning Center. More recently, the university that managed the center closed its doors after more than forty years in operation, not from lack of funds or student interest, or human need, but in the name of efficiency.

To whatever degree some quarters of society recognize outdoor education and forest time as indispensable features of human flourishing, national parks and other wild places will continue to provide a critical function not just as refuges and reservoirs of biodiversity but as laboratories of lifelong learning. So, too, should those places that reside closer to home, which hold rich potential for city time, sidewalk time, and schoolyard time. The natural world, wherever it is found, is too often treated as a space requiring expert knowledge before it can be sufficiently utilized to engage students. But if anyone's experience disproves such a misconception surely mine does. Lacking any formal training in natural history and teaching, and fearing I would expose my ignorance each time I opened my mouth, I was happily reminded again and again that I had a reliable co-instructor to lean on at every step: the woods itself. How was it possible that I could so often teach without teaching in the conventional sense, not as an oracle dispensing facts, but by giving students a nudge and stepping out of the way, and allowing them to rely on their inquisitive natures? But it was. I sometimes wonder if the reason I've stuck around for so long was to see if the spark that kindled curiosity in students young and old, through the deceptively simple act of outdoor discovery, would ever go out. It never has.

Nightwalking, without a doubt, has slowed all of us busybodies down. We move together like a clumsy inchworm, bunched together one moment and stretched out the next. Toeing our way forward, we have no choice but to take one small step at a time, lest we fall on our faces.

We reach a level spot and sit and listen. An owl calls in the distance—one of my colleagues, I realize, who's mimicking a barred owl to fool one into answering. The real owls, however, are silent tonight.

I've led high school and college students on night walks, as well as middle-aged adults and retirees who are understandably less eager to traipse around in the dark for fear of a fall. At times I've wondered how many of them came to terms with an altogether different sort of unspoken darkness they perhaps harbored within. If a star-littered sky can induce the kind of awe in which the self gets momentarily forgotten, a visible darkness sometimes embodies a void in which the self is located once more. Though darkness isn't where one wants to stay for very long, it can offer comfort and relief and a refuge to dwell in until the time comes to find one's place in the world again. My consolation on their behalf comes from knowing that at least we're all in this together. As someone whose job it is to push the boundaries of personal comfort in others within the bounds of compassion, few things are as humbling as leading a night walk.

The unease is palpable among the students seated around me. What if someone gets hurt or we can't find our way back? I break the silence by introducing the subject of human sight. We discuss cone cells that help us see color, rod cells concentrated at the outer edge of our retinas which help us see in the dark, and the genius of a far more powerful night vision many of our fellow creatures possess. But seeing in the dark has never been our forte, and perceived helplessness comes with the territory.

Fear of the dark is cousin in certain ways to fearing what the future may bring. Turn on a light, and at least one has the illusion of control over the space one inhabits. Controlling time, on the other hand, isn't possible. On my mind just now are the challenges young people may face in their lifetimes if they and their families aren't facing them already: loneliness, instability, debt, addiction, broken communities, crime, inequality and class immobility, the hollowing out of rural America, shortened life expectancy, the loss of cultural memory, the disintegration of social norms, authoritarianism, spiritual decay, and despair. Theirs is a generation all too aware of the world they've inherited, one in which humankind's success has come at the cost of a diminished future and the further dismantling of the natural world. One also in which wild places and the places we inhabit seem farther apart than ever. What to do just now in the face of so much uncertainty but tell them a story?

Once there was a boy who ventured into the woods as darkness was falling and lost his way. Which direction led home? The boy had no clue. Finding his way back seemed hopeless without a light to guide him. His situation worsened when he made out the shape of a wildcat perched on a limb above him. As it readied to pounce, he fumbled through the forest, trying to make his escape. Bats swooped down and clawed at his head. He ran, and ran into things. Now even more lost than before, he came upon the terrifying shape of what could only be a bear and knew he was a goner for sure. The end had come and he waited for it, frozen with fear.

But the end did not come. As time passed, a remarkable thing happened: his eyes adjusted. The bear, he could see now, was only a mossy boulder. The bats were only the bough of a tree he brushed beneath, and the wildcat was just the knot jutting out of a tree trunk. Home lay mere yards beyond the forest's edge.

All this time, each of us has kept one eye closed while staring with the other into a lighted candle cupped in my hand. When I blow out the flame, we see the woods much as the boy did, dark and sinister. We are as blind as when we first began our walk. Yet when we switch eyes and look around with the one preserving our night vision, the contrast is striking. Shapes emerge against a backdrop of sky. The silhouettes of one another's heads and shoulders appear. The blackest of nights suddenly isn't as black as before.

Real dangers exist in the world, much of it our own making. There are legitimate reasons for fearing for oneself and the world. Fear teaches us to be on the lookout, keep watch, and discern what is real and what isn't—what won't get us and what indeed might. The world which we bend to our will won't bend forever. Long before that day comes, we will have to find our way without letting our imaginations get the best of us, yet with imagination nonetheless. "So the darkness shall be the light," writes T. S. Eliot, an apt description of tonight's journey as well as perhaps a metaphor and foretaste of what is to come. Whatever the future holds, it's not as improbable as it might have seemed to my companions only an hour ago that a night walk has in some ways prepared us for it.

When we rise and begin retracing our steps through the woods the way is far from clear. But we know something now we didn't before: we can see in the dark better than we thought.

Coda: Exit Music

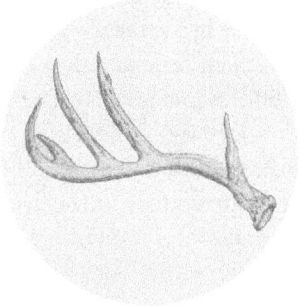

SPRING ARRIVES and I marvel at another year gone by. The sun rises, lingers awhile, and slides behind Fodderstack Mountain. Seasons wheel past and trees grow fat. The shape of days over time come to feel like knotted-up links in a chain, most beyond any hope of disentangling. It's as if I've gathered moss; rather than rolling, I've stayed put. How many generations of house spiders have come and gone under my roof? The college students I hire as interns these days were in kindergarten when I was starting out in this field.

One by one, my fellow educators move away to pursue graduate degrees in education, forestry, environmental law, or careers at other nature centers. After nearly thirty years as executive director, Ken pushed on too, relocating to Yellowstone with his wife Jennifer.

"My oldest neighbor, Travis, is gone," I now tell groups while in character as Tip Tipton. "Headed west to live with the buffaloes and grizzly bears."

Greg became a forester and moved with Rebecca and Jonah to Minnesota, where a daughter was born. When he returned for a visit, we hiked to a part of the forest devastated by pine beetles years ago. He wanted to see firsthand if what he'd once told people concerned about the destruction had come true, and indeed it had: the pines were regenerating. As we speculated over what the forest might look like a century from now, I thought of the Iron Age fort that Élan and I stumbled upon on a windswept heath on the coast of Scotland. All that remained of it was a stack of stones that rising sea levels may one day cover. In Britain and other parts of the world, historical memory is counted not in hundreds but thousands of years. In contrast, the Organic Act, a piece of American ingenuity that established the national parks and inscribed sustainability into law for the first time in human history, is barely a century old. A remarkable achievement for a nation still as young as ours, it's one I choose to regard as a sign of more good things to come, provided each generation upholds the promises kept by those that came before and builds on that heritage. This is by no means guaranteed.

These days I spend as much time at a desk as I do in the woods, often more, since my responsibilities include planning programs and hiring seasonal staff. A reward for a job well done, I suppose, though some days it resembles a form of punishment. Days I dart off to teach a class bring the kind of satisfaction no amount of office time can ever hope to fill. Whatever my workday holds, at the end of it, I walk home through campus—a three-minute journey—to enjoy supper with Élan. Her daily commute to Knoxville, one hour each way, along with the size of our living space (tinier than many tiny homes at three hundred square feet) were the reasons we'd decided to look for a roomier place in town after marrying. That was four years ago, and we're still here. Look at us with our cabin in the woods, we kept telling ourselves. Look at our backyard, the wildest and most splendid we knew we'd ever have. I, for one, was in no hurry to leave.

All the same, I fantasize from time to time about living in a city or on the road, chasing the twenty-first-century American dream of being anywhere in the world I wish to be, anytime I want. But then come those moments when the world seems to spin too fast, even here in the woods, and I recall Edward Abbey's admonition to techno-utopians: "To be everywhere at once is to be nowhere forever," and I know I'm better off staying right where I am.

A friend who works in finance and travels the globe worries I am becoming a mountain man and that soon there may be no turning back. But he needn't fret, for modern life already has sunk its claws into me. Élan and I live in high mountain luxury these days, having a landline and spotty Wi-Fi at home. Full-on cell coverage, should it ever reach us, will complete the invasion of so-called convenience and instant gratification. That day will be particularly distressing for the physician who returns with his children's school each year, though his kids have grown, because it's the only week all year long when his patients and colleagues can't reach him and, he tells me, he can hear himself think.

As spring gets cranking in fits and starts, our attention turns to the forest floor on weekend hikes as we reacquaint ourselves with each bloom, first trailing arbutus, detectable by smell as often as by sight, followed by hepatica, and then, too briefly, bloodroot. Loads more hidden packages come unwrapped once the threat of a hard frost passes, and the carpet of paradise rolls out once more. Resisting the temptation to linger over every species, we'll hasten homeward to beat nightfall and get back without having stepped foot outside the park. To be the spouse of an environmental educator and live in a marginally remote area means surrendering many things I know she misses. But there are rewards, too, and days like these bring the kind of contentment neither of us has known elsewhere.

Back home, we'll turn on the radio and open a bottle of wine while making dinner. I'll tease, "What movie do you want to sleep through tonight?" since it is her habit to slumber through many a weekend night's source of entertainment. Late in the evening, book in my lap, I'll drift off too, waking to the room's stillness and lamplight glow and the sweet sound of nothing. I never tire of such moments, of long days in the woods and lazy evenings.

For all the close bonds I've forged with this place, I'm not so naive as to believe I know it in all its fullness, or that I ever could. I've barely scratched the surface of forest time and only just begun to understand the extent of my ignorance. In one sense, I haven't been living in the woods at all but in a clearing, or, to be precise, living in a cabin, shielded much of the time from everything outside it. The language that forms the basis of my knowledge of the woods, though it brings me closer to it in many ways, distances me as well by acting as a door to a mansion I can pry open, only to just get so far inside. To comprehend the forest at a depth I wish sometimes were possible, I suspect, would demand a kind of knowing that would not resemble human knowledge at all. *Foresta*, from the Latin, means "outside," according to Robert Pogue Harrison, so to a certain extent, I am forever an outsider trying to get in, happy in the meantime to stick close by the surface and be reminded of the necessity of human limits.

A measure of risk accompanies making one's home on public land. From the start, it was never a matter of if I'd leave but when. I'd done that once already, and now almost ten more years have passed, and no matter how many times I tell myself I haven't settled down—an impossibility, anyway, on land I'll never own—it never rings true. While picturing the day I'll rip out the roots I have grown here, I've become anxious about discovering how deep they have gone. How much this place has become part of me, its rhythms and moods saturating my senses, such that when I'm gone from it for a week or longer, I find I can no more take it off than I could my skin. And how the intimacy I've gained with it as one of its inhabitants will begin to ebb once I leave it.

That day is closer now that Élan and I have bought a house. Our realtor friend David showed us a fixer-upper that had been put on the market that morning. Listed as a cabin in the property profile, it wasn't much to look at with its moldy vinyl siding. Traffic whizzed past yards away from the front door, and the gravel driveway was so short our car practically jutted into the road. Yet when we walked through the musty interior and stepped out onto a second-story deck, we found ourselves standing midway up the tree canopy and peering over a floodplain and river—the same one partly formed by the Middle Prong upstream. Besides a neighboring house camouflaged by trees, signs of human habitation were virtually nonexistent.

"This one will be gone by tomorrow," said David, whose patience we'd put to the test each time we passed up the chance to place an offer on other houses. "If you don't buy it, I'm going to."

It was the kick in the pants we needed to make an offer, which to our surprise was promptly accepted. A year followed spent tiling the floor, painting walls, installing a staircase, replacing kitchen countertops, and cleaning mouse droppings out of the basement by the hundreds. In time my work would be cut out for me outdoors as well. I discovered a lone yellow trillium sheltering beneath an understory of privet and other invasive shrubs in the woods next door. It was strange yet pleasing to think that as the soon-to-be latest arrival to this place, I would devote my efforts in the days ahead to driving out these newcomers to make room for more of the forest's original inhabitants.

The mountain in whose shadows the house sits makes it an ideal setting for the likes of me, spoiled as I have become by affixing my gaze on a landscape largely devoid of people and left to its own devices. Though a still point in a busy world, it's also a noisy one. In our version of "quiet" country living, the roar of traffic coming from the highway will invade the house at all hours, and the walls will vibrate each time motorcycles and trucks rumble down our street. This new soundtrack awaiting our lives, while hardly unfamiliar or unexpected, had much to do with my reluctance to leave the park. So did fears of becoming swept up in the currents of modern living and losing something irretrievable, much like my living history character Tip Tipton. Habituated to a calmer rhythm and long insulated from the daily realities most Americans face, I'll have to adjust to a different tempo now that I'll join the fray of commuters each morning. The inevitable accumulation of material possessions accompanying homeownership will likely commence too, no matter how modest our appetite may be for such things. The relative simplicity I enjoyed while living and working on the same plot of ground will become a thing of the past.

I will still have one foot in forest time, returning to the park every workday. I imagine I'll continue to wonder if what passes for normal should really be considered normal, including pollution in all its forms—noise, air, light—even as I contribute to it. If I fall prey to the modern habit of chasing time under the belief that I can "save" it, especially now that my responsibilities have grown in number as a homeowner, I'll need to remind myself to slow down and be at peace with "wasting" it. And I'll keep in view two versions of the world still growing farther apart: the one we continue to carve up and try to control and the one we're slowly learning to live in harmony with.

For all the changes we're about to face, many for the good, including a shorter commute for Élan, a familiar melody will accompany our arrival in our new home: the sound of moving water. Softer than the rollicking Middle Prong, I could hear it better standing on the bank behind the house. Better still if I waded out into the river to listen and stare. Our property boundary extends across the river and up the far bank, which, according to state law, means we own the river bottom. With my feet planted on rocks pushed into place by the current's force, which the next highwater event would no doubt dislodge again, I was getting a closer look at the rest of our "yard" for the first time. I chuckled at the thought of it: owning the riverbed.

Little was going to change in the larger scheme of things. I'd still get to live in something like a cabin in the woods. Still live with the knowledge that while I might inhabit a plot of earth for a time, I'd never really possess it. Still live under the illusion from time to time that I'm escaping the world, even while knowing this isn't remotely true. Still wonder over the ephemeral nature of a single earthly life and the flow of time always on the move like the rocks in the river.

Before moving day arrived, I decided to spend some time in quiet solitude. Months had passed since I'd last visited my secret spot, and because this occasion would mark a sort of benediction on the years I'd spent living in America's most beloved national park, I decided to bring an object to leave as a token of my gratitude. I settled on a deer antler I'd discovered years earlier and adopted into my care. Shed antlers seldom last long in the Smokies since calcium-hungry rodents quickly devour them. Stumbling upon one has been so uncommon in my experience that whenever I have it is like finding a hidden treasure. Fully intact with no visible teeth marks, this one was the largest of any I've found. It has hung all this time from a floor lamp next to the couch, the first object that catches my eye when I come through the door, each of its five tines pointing around the room like fingers. Like other borrowed items unearthed in the moving process, the time has come to give it back.

On a weekday morning, several hours before teaching class, I stuff the antler into my pack and skirt the edge of campus. Voices rise in the woods below as students gather for class, then fade once I start up the trail. Before long, all I can hear is the muffled bluster of the Middle Prong. I catch glimpses of Fodderstack Mountain framed against a backdrop of higher mountains and judge my progress by its diminishing size until it is out of view.

Once I reach the beech tree, I retrieve the antler from my pack and study its off-white surface, smooth to the touch, and the places where it darkens to brown, as if it had been left in an oven too long. I hold it up to my head, resting it against one temple and then the other: a right antler. I pull away handfuls of duff between two buttressing roots of the beech until I've excavated a small cavity and wedge the antler inside as far as it will go, then cover the opening with leaves. Whatever creature discovers and uses it according to its needs won't be human.

My mission accomplished, I keep still and listen to the hush of the forest, delaying for as long as possible the moment when I'll rise and descend the mountain and step into the busyness of the day and what comes after.

Once while sitting in this spot, I was overcome by a feeling that I was being watched. On more occasions than I can count, I have observed animals unaware of my presence, though I suspect the opposite more often was true—an owl or bobcat spying on me without my knowledge. Something moving in the woods told me I was not alone. Its movements were slow and deliberate and interrupted by long silences, which made me wonder if I'd only imagined it until there it was again. It was a beastly, earthy sound like the throaty call of a raven, but it was shorter in duration and came from somewhere on the forest floor. My amphitheaterlike surroundings made it impossible to tell where it was coming from. I wasn't afraid, only unnerved by my inability to discern its identity and whereabouts. I wondered if I was being stalked.

A longer period of silence elapsed, and when I felt certain I was alone I started back down the trail. I'd gone only a short distance when I spotted a fresh paw print in damp soil likely left by a bear. I placed my hand next to it and saw that we were the same size. Removing my boot and sock, I set down my foot and made an impression in the soil beside the bear's. Maybe the message I was sending was: *It was you, wasn't it?* And perhaps also: *My woods too.*

I passed by that way again a few days later while leading a solo hike with students. The forest's gratuitous welcome left me feeling nearly breathless. Like today, the woods were a living cathedral filled with columns of numinous sunlight streaming through a dazzling green dome down into a sanctuary where the silence of the place was interrupted only by the sound of my feet. In the same patch of soil where I'd left my footprint, I noticed a paw print fresher than the one before.

Mine was gone.

ACKNOWLEDGMENTS

A veritable forest of people provided assistance in ways large and small to bring this book to the printed page. Many thanks to Simone Gorrindo, Emily Dings, Michelle Coppedge, and Seth Elliott for graciously reading an early draft, warts and all, and to Katie Hannah, David Brill, and Kim Trevathan for their sharp insights later on. For providing invaluable feedback on particular chapters, I thank Elisabeth Tova Bailey, Margaret Lynn Brown, Annette Saunooke Clapsaddle, Doug Frank, Ted Genoways, Sebastian Matthews, Mac Post, Richard Powers, Scott Russell Sanders, Lee Zacharias, and my fellow Maverick House writers at the Vermont Studio Center.

I'm likewise grateful to the editors of the publications in which excerpts and chapters appeared in different form: *Sierra*, *Gray's Sporting Journal*, *Fourth Genre*, *Smokies Life*, *Hunting and the Ivory Tower*, and *Permanent Vacation*, volume 2. For background on the eastern deciduous forest, I am indebted to Rutherford Platt's *The Great American Forest*. For the support they showed in numerous ways, I thank Rachel Elliott, Frances Figart, the late Harvard Ayers, David James Duncan, Jennifer and Jason Love, Jim Costa, Dana and Bill Pugh, the Westsylvanians, and those I will doubtless later regret for failing to mention by name.

My heartfelt thanks to the multitude of Tremontsters I've had the honor of working alongside over the years, and to the leadership of Catey McClary, Jen Jones, John DiDiego, Amber Parker, and Ken Voorhis, who first took a chance on me. My gratitude likewise extends to the hardworking and dedicated staff of the National Park Service, Smokies Life, Friends of the Smokies, and Discover Life in America.

Thanks to all the staff at the University of Tennessee Press. Thanks also to the Association of Nature Center Administrators, the outdoor schools and nature center community, and to the many students, teachers, principals, and professors I have had the pleasure of spending time in the woods alongside.

Much gratitude to Highlands Biological Station and the Hambidge Center, which provided space for me to write and have come to feel like homes away from home. I am very grateful to fellow Tremontster, outdoor educator, and visual artist Kelly Lecko for her exquisite illustrations. Check out geckoleckoart.com to glimpse more of her creations.

And most of all, more thanks than I can ever hope to express to Élan for your sacrifice, support, and love.

www.ingramcontent.com/pod-product-compliance
Lightning Source LLC
Chambersburg PA
CBHW070615030426
42337CB00020B/3802